STEINMETZ:

Maker of Lightning

Books by Sigmund A. Lavine

"WANDERING MINSTRELS WE"
The Story of Gilbert and Sullivan

STEINMETZ: MAKER OF LIGHTNING

STEINMETZ:

Maker *of* *Lightning*

by

Sigmund A. Lavine

ILLUSTRATED WITH PHOTOGRAPHS

DODD, MEAD & COMPANY

NEW YORK

1963

LIBRARY OF CONGRESS CATALOG CARD NUMBER: 55–5852
Printed in the United States of America

FOR *Gertrude:*

In partial payment of eighteen years of dog hairs on just-vacuumed rugs, frozen daphnia in ice-cube trays and going without a dining-room so I could have "books from floor to ceiling."

⊷ ACKNOWLEDGMENTS ⊱

The list of people who have helped make this book possible is almost as long as one of the trans-continental high-voltage lines visualized by Steinmetz. It begins with the kindly policeman who showed me the shortest way to reach the campus of Union College that stormy day in Schenectady and ends with my ever-patient and helpful editor, Miss Dorothy Bryan. There are so many individuals in between that there is every possibility that I will neglect to mention someone to whom I am indebted.

However, I do wish to thank: C. W. Hammond, director of publicity at Union College and the gracious ladies in the Alumni Office of that institution who ripped their files apart at my request; Mrs. Mary Haverty of the Boston Public Library; the staff of the reference library of the Boston *Herald-Traveler,* who not only allowed me to consult the "clips," but suggested additional sources of information; Leo J. Kramer of Raytheon who, at considerable expenditure of time and effort, tracked down some very elusive data; A. Lawrence MacKenzie, Sunday editor of the Boston *Post,* who drew freely on his excellent memory and journalistic skills to help me in many ways; Doris Bramson Whitehouse; and Miss Claire Yorke of *Nicholaus'* in Schenectady.

A special "thank you" is due to two of my associates in the Boston School System: Mr. Arthur Robertie, who tested my explanations of technical matters in his science classes, and Mr. Felix Losco, who proved he was interested in the book by giving up that most treasured of schoolteachers' joys—"unassigned periods"—to explain complicated electrical theory to the author.

I am also very grateful to Mrs. Stuart Huckins for her cheery co-operation, and I would be extremely unappreciative if I did not express to Mr. Neil Reynolds of the Public Relations Division of General Electric my sincere gratitude for his giving me so much of his time and for unlocking many a door that would otherwise have remained closed.

Sigmund A. Lavine

CONTENTS

ILLUSTRATIONS

STEINMETZ:

Maker of Lightning

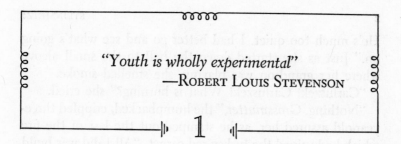

1

THIS is the story of Charles Proteus Steinmetz, a genius in mathematics, a talented chemist and a wizard in electricity. Like Jove, king of the Roman gods, he hurled thunderbolts at will, but his entire career was devoted to lifting heavy burdens from the shoulders of workers in factories and on farms through the magic of electricity. Every time you snap a light switch on, ride in an electric streetcar, shoot up a dozen or more floors in an elevator or employ an electric motor, you are making practical use of Steinmetz' life-long investigation into the creation, control and distribution of electrical energy.

It was quiet in the modest five-room apartment on Tauenzeinstrasse in Breslau, Germany. Too quiet. Of course, from time to time, the noise of trains as they entered or left the nearby station of the Ober Schlesisch line could be heard, but no one who lived in the four-story brick buildings which lined the street paid any attention to such familiar noise.

In the kitchen where she was making raisin cookies, Grandmother Steinmetz muttered to herself as she briskly rubbed flour off her hands, "I wonder what that boy is doing. There hasn't been a sound out of him for over an hour.

He's much too quiet. I had better go and see what's going on." Just as she started down the hall to the small alcove where her grandson was playing, she smelled smoke.

"Carluszek! Carluszek! What is burning?" she cried.

"Nothing, *Grossmutter*," the humpbacked, crippled three-year-old assured her, as he stamped out the last of the fire which had ruined the turkey red carpet. "All I did was build a fort with my blocks. It was dark inside and I knew the soldiers couldn't see, so I lit a candle and put it in the middle of my fort. One of the soldiers must have knocked his gun against it and tipped it over and made that little burn."

"Little burn! I'll little burn you! No, I won't either. I'll wait until your father comes home. He'll take care of you. Playing with fire! What a child! Why did I ever leave Poland and come to Germany to take care of you—all you do is cause me trouble . . ."

"I'm sorry, *Grossmutter*," murmured Karl, as he painfully hobbled toward her, arms spread wide, asking to be hugged and forgiven.

At once the frown vanished from the elderly woman's face. She drew the boy close to her and soothed him. "Now, now, *liebchen*, don't cry. You must have been terribly frightened when the fire started. Here, let me hold you tight, *Jungling. Grossmutter* won't let anything happen to you."

Grandmother Steinmetz never let anything happen to Karl. She felt sorry for the boy who, like so many other male members of the family, had inherited deformities. Ever since the day she had arrived to take the place of the child's mother, who had died of cholera in 1866, when Karl was one year old, she had pampered and spoiled her grandson. His father was just as lenient. Mr. Steinmetz was a kindly sort of man who had married his brother's widow, Caroline, and adopted her two little girls, Marie and Clara. Like his son, the older Karl was a cripple, and so he found it impossible to punish his malformed, motherless boy. As a result, no child in the ancient city of Breslau was so spoiled.

That night when Mr. Steinmetz came home from his office in the yard of the government-owned railroad, where he was in charge of preparing train orders, his mother met him at the door. Taking him by the arm, she led him to the alcove and pointed to the ruined carpet. "Carluszek almost burned down the house today, Karl," she began. "He was doing another one of those 'experiments' which you claim show how inquisitive he is. I was going to punish him, but he looked so miserable I just couldn't. You'll have to talk to him, Karl. You are his father, you have just got to make him understand . . ."

"Now, Mother," interrupted Mr. Steinmetz, "I encourage the boy to use imagination. Let us try not to be too hard on him. Remember, he is still a little fellow. After all, it is only a carpet. We must remember that he'll never be able to make a living except by mental work; therefore, we must not stop him from trying to investigate things for himself. Who knows, some day he may become a great inventor!"

So once again Karl went unpunished. The effect was to make him think he was the most important person in Breslau—not even his grandmother or father dared to correct him! When Karl played in the park with the other children in the neighborhood, he insisted on winning every game. At home, his stepsisters, Clara and Marie, gave in to him as a matter of course, so the youngster expected the same treatment from all his companions as they sailed boats in the park's duck pond or played their childish games. The pond was the old moat of a fort from which General Tauenzein had led his men in a gallant charge during the Napoleonic Wars, to drive the French from Breslau. It was in honor of this event that the street where the Steinmetz family lived was called Tauenzeinstrasse.

On Karl's fourth birthday, his father came home with a

toy locomotive which ran by steam, generated by wood alcohol. It was a logical gift for a railroad man to give his son. The boy was delighted with the engine, which was brightly painted, and used blocks, boxes and furniture to lay out a "right of way" for his new toy. Chairs were broken, tables were marred and cracked as he laid them on their sides to make room for his "railway system." *Grossmutter* and Mr. Steinmetz merely smiled as they observed the damage, because they liked to watch their beloved boy enjoying himself.

The youngster never wearied of playing train. Whenever Clara or Marie wanted a turn with the locomotive, he would snatch it away from them and scream. No one who heard Karl as he hobbled out of the room, loudly yelling, his precious toy clutched close to his chest, would guess that some day, as the most famous engineer in the world, he would advance the theory that everything should be shared and shared alike.

It was about this time that Karl, like all German boys and girls, was sent to kindergarten. There he acted as so many children do on their first day of school: he threw himself on the floor and cried bitterly. No one paid any attention to him, but he continued to sob. Taken home to lunch by his grandmother, he wailed all through the meal, "*Grossmutter*, don't make me go back, don't make me go back!"

Mr. Steinmetz, who came home for lunch every day, was so upset by Karl's tears that he was unable to eat. Nothing he said seemed to comfort the boy and, at last, alarmed at the child's condition, he told him that he did not have to go back to kindergarten. A year later, when Karl was five, his father, realizing that the crippled youngster must learn to use his mind, insisted that he return to school. "Mother," he thundered, "we have been wrong. This spoiling of Carluszek has got to stop. He goes to kindergarten tomorrow whether he likes it or not!"

Strangely enough, Karl did like it. Perhaps he had been

lonely with his playmates away all day at school and wanted
to join them. On the other hand, he was a year older, and
therefore more able to meet the rigid demands of a school
routine. Now there were no tears, but smiles and laughter
when the time came for him to go to class.

When the boy was eight years old he was sent to St. John's
Gymnasium in Breslau. Unlike an American "gym," the
German gymnasium is a classical high school at which students are prepared for the university. Anxious to learn how
his son was progressing with his studies, Mr. Steinmetz made
an appointment and went to see the headmaster of St.
John's.

"We haven't a very good report for you, Mr. Steinmetz,"
said the headmaster. "I don't like to say this, but it seems to
me, and to all of Karl's teachers, that he is not very bright.
We give him special attention, but . . ."

"I am very grateful, sir," interrupted Mr. Steinmetz, "and
if there is anything I can do at home to help, I certainly
will."

"There isn't much anyone can do," continued the educator. "Karl just doesn't seem to be able to learn the simplest
things. Take the multiplication tables, for example. He can't
memorize them. I am afraid that you will have to resign
yourself to the fact that your son is not only physically handicapped, but mentally retarded as well."

Sadly, the worried father returned to the apartment on
Tauenzeinstrasse, confused in mind and heavy at heart. If
Karl couldn't learn the multiplication tables, what chance
was there that he would be able to learn anything? Were
all those dreams of the boy turning out to be an inventor
only foolish ones? Now it looked as if the youngster never
would be able to do work of any kind, yet how could that
be? Mr. Steinmetz was a puzzled and unhappy parent.

Then, almost overnight, the problem child began to show
evidence of understanding everything his teachers discussed

in class. By the time he was ten years old, Karl was considered the brightest pupil at St. John's. At faculty meetings, his instructors tried to find a reason for this transformation. Some of them thought it was because the boy was unable to play as long and as actively as his fellow students, so he devoted more time to his books. All agreed that, no matter what had brought about the change in Karl's scholarship, he wouldn't have the slightest difficulty now in earning honor marks. His program, incidentally, was what junior high school pupils in this country would call a "college course." It consisted of Greek, Latin, French, Polish, Hebrew, philosophy, algebra and geometry; all of them were required subjects. Electives were unheard of at a German gymnasium.

Every moment of the school day was enjoyed by Karl. The compliments he received from his instructors made him extremely happy. Long used to being treated in a kindly fashion by his family, he responded to the approval of his teachers and was stimulated to do outstanding work. The member of the faculty at St. John's who impressed young Steinmetz most was Herr Fechner, or to give him the title granted all schoolteachers in Germany, "Professor" Fechner. A brilliant man, Fechner first instilled in Karl the true scientific point of view—never to accept facts at face value, but to investigate every detail carefully. All his life Steinmetz was to remember this instructor's teaching and to follow it.

The nine years at St. John's passed quickly, and at seventeen Karl was to be graduated. Like other members of his class, he took the long, difficult oral examinations, which lasted for days. When he had finished the last one, he walked home slowly, tired but happy.

"How did the examinations go, Son?" inquired his father that evening.

"I think I did well, Father," replied Karl. "The only thing that I am worried about is whether I passed with honors or not. You see, if I receive honor marks, I will be excused from the graduation exercises—they put a list of those excused on the bulletin board outside the headmaster's office. I hope my name is put there! Otherwise we will have to buy a full dress suit; tailcoat, stiff shirt, white tie, and top hat for me to wear on graduation day. We can't afford the expense, but I'm afraid we have no choice, for I'm sure I didn't earn honors."

"Now, don't you worry about the expense my boy—we'll go and buy that dress suit tomorrow. I'm proud of you, Karl. It isn't every young man who is graduated from St. John's. If only *Grossmutter* were alive to see you get your diploma, how proud she would be!"

The next day Karl and his father bought the dress suit. It fitted as well as could be expected. All head and shoulders, barely four feet tall, no tailor's skill could make young Steinmetz attractive. With the suit hanging in his closet, the worried student paid a visit to St. John's. He had absolutely no hope of being excused from the graduation ceremonies, but thought it wouldn't do any harm to look. Hobbling through the corridor, he stopped in front of the bulletin board. Only one name appeared on the entire list of those who did not have to attend graduation. That name was Karl August Rudolph Steinmetz!

With no classes to attend, Karl found little to occupy him. The apartment on Tauenzeinstrasse had been a lonely place since *Grossmutter* had died, and Clara and Marie had left home to go to work. In order to have something to do, Steinmetz formed the habit of visiting his father's office, where he would sit near a window and watch the trains for hours. When the older man had finished with his work, the two would draw their chairs together and discuss the future.

"What are your plans now, Son?" asked Mr. Steinmetz

one afternoon. "You have got to decide. Remember, you are
seventeen years old and it is time you gave some thought to
earning a living. I am not going to tell you what you should
or should not do. You must make up your mind, yourself.
Frankly, I would like you to become an engineer. Have you
ever thought of a career in that field? I can tell you this,
engineers earn excellent salaries. Who knows, perhaps you
could go to the university, study engineering, become an
inventor and . . ."

"You'd like that, wouldn't you, Father?"

"Indeed I would, but the choice is entirely up to you. Tell
me, how do you feel about it? Does the idea sound interesting?"

"I really don't know, sir," replied Karl. "I just can't decide. Right now, sitting here and watching the trains rush by
seems the most pleasant thing in the world. I'm afraid I
haven't much ambition."

Mr. Steinmetz laughed. "You have ambition enough,
Karl. That's not your trouble. What you need is to get out-
doors and clear your mind. I'll tell you what we will do.
Sunday we will pack a lunch and take a long walk in the
woods. It will do us both good. What do you say?"

Karl agreed at once. There was nothing he liked better
than to wander through the countryside, picking flowers,
looking for colorful rocks and birds' nests. So on Sunday,
father and son followed a woodland path to the top of a tall
hill overlooking Breslau. Tired, they sat down and watched
the sun glint on the Oder as it wound through the city
spread before them. Never did the two feel closer than on
that afternoon. As they munched the sandwiches they had
brought from home, they had a heart-to-heart talk. When
they scrambled to their feet to begin the difficult descent to
the city, they had decided that Karl was to enroll as a student at the University of Breslau.

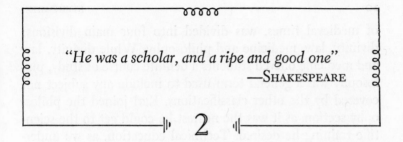

THE River Oder divides Breslau into two towns. The largest is the ancient inner town with narrow streets, crossed by well-landscaped promenades on the site of the ramparts torn down when Waterloo brought an end to Napoleon's dream of conquering Europe. None of the many medieval buildings which attract tourists is more famous than the main hall of the University of Breslau. This was built by the Jesuits on the site of a former imperial castle presented to them by Emperor Leopold I, in 1702, which contains some of the most magnificent frescoes in the world.

Unlike American universities, there are very few other buildings near the main hall. As the institution grew in enrollment and more classrooms were needed, they were acquired wherever they could be found. When the University of Frankfurt an der Oder became part of the University of Breslau in 1811, the necessity for more lecture halls was so great that the school was finally nothing but a collection of studyhalls scattered throughout the city. There was no campus, nor were there any dormitories, or Commons where the students could gather.

When young Karl enrolled as a scholar in the University of Breslau, it was still steeped in the traditions of the Middle Ages. Its curriculum, like the "Faculties" of the colleges of medieval times, was divided into four main divisions: divinity, law, medicine and philosophy. While divinity, law and medicine offered students a definite course of study, philosophy was a general term used to include any subject not covered by the other classifications. Karl joined the philosophy section, as it was the nearest he could get to the scientific training he desired. Technical education, as we understand it, was unheard of—it would be seven years before Thomas Alva Edison's perfection of the incandescent lamp would take the teaching of electricity out of the lecture hall and put it in the laboratory.

On the first day of classes, Karl found his program was to include courses in higher mathematics, astronomy, physics, chemistry and medicine. Quite a list of studies for a seventeen-year-old boy! It wasn't until his fourth year, as part of a course in physics, that he was to have any instruction in the subject he was to master, electrical engineering. Armed with a large notebook, a gift from his father, the young student began to attend lectures.

One evening, shortly after the start of the first semester, Mr. Steinmetz peered over his son's shoulder as the boy sat studying by the light of a kerosene lamp, and noticed the signatures of several professors on the pages of the notebook. "What's this, Karl?" he inquired. "Are you becoming an autograph collector?"

"I should say not!" Karl laughed. "Didn't I tell you how very easy it is to cut classes at the University? In the first place, students are not required to attend classes every day; in fact, we have to be present only at two lectures in an entire course. All a student must do is to have a professor sign his notebook at one of the first three meetings of a course and at one of the last three, and his attendance record is considered perfect."

"Supposing the professor gives an examination and a student isn't there, what happens?"

"There are no examinations except for a student who wants a government post as a schoolteacher in the public schools, or who wants to earn the degree of Doctor of Philosophy," replied Karl. "Incidentally, we don't have any recitations either."

"Son, if you don't have to attend classes, are never called upon to recite and don't have to take examinations unless you want to, why are you always studying?" demanded Mr. Steinmetz.

"Don't forget, Father, it costs five dollars each semester for every course I am taking. I want my money's worth. We don't have so much that I can throw any away. Look here, each of my professors lectures four times a week, and if I pay any attention at all to what he says, I have plenty of material to study. Then, there are the free lectures. I go to as many of them as I can, and I like to review my notes so I will remember what was said. Oh, I've plenty to do."

Karl did do a great deal of studying. While most of his fellow students took as much advantage as they could of the university's lax rules, he never missed a lecture. Nor did he sit quietly while the professors advanced their theories. When puzzled or annoyed by what was said in the classroom, young Steinmetz would start a lively discussion with the speaker. Usually, these talks became so technical that the only ones in the hall who could follow the arguments were Karl and the instructor. The rest of the class sat in stunned silence as the two exchanged views.

Karl's favorite subject was higher mathematics, and both his classmates and professors were astonished by the ease with which he memorized complex formulae. Throughout his life, Steinmetz' phenomenal memory was to astound his associates. While they were forced to spend hours studying a sheet of complicated engineering data, he had only to glance briefly at it in order to learn it by heart. It was gruff Professor Schroeter who first noticed Karl's mathematical genius. An extremely stern and unbending man who demanded outstanding work from his students, this teacher limited his classes to only three pupils. The more difficult he made his lectures, the more Karl enjoyed them, and it wasn't long before Schroeter frequently invited young Steinmetz to his home, where they could continue their heated classroom debates.

Another professor who had great respect for Karl's ability was John Galle, who as assistant chief of the Berlin Observatory had, on September 23, 1846, discovered Neptune, the outermost of the then known planets. One day, as the youth was leaving the lecture hall, Galle called to him: "Steinmetz, I've been watching you all semester, and it seems to me that you write down my words as fast as I am able to speak them. Would you mind telling me how you are able to do it?"

"It is really very simple, Herr Professor," replied Karl. "I have devised a system of abbreviations."

As the years passed, his method of taking notes was to become world famous. A. Lawrence MacKenzie, Sunday editor of *The Boston Post*, recalls interviewing Steinmetz as a "cub" reporter, and asking the electrical genius for an explanation of his personal shorthand. "It was about 1922," recollects Mr. MacKenzie. "I had been sent to interview Steinmetz in Pittsfield, Massachusetts, where he was consulting with other engineers of the General Electric plant on the possibilities of creating artificial lightning in his laboratory. On reaching the hotel where he was staying, I saw him in the lobby. He greeted me heartily and led the way to a pair of comfortable chairs, chatting like a parakeet. I had been told to ask him some questions dealing with physics and chemistry, which I did. His answers came so fast that I had great trouble keeping up with him as I wrote them down. Steinmetz noticed my difficulty, and spoke more slowly. His gentleness and patience as he waited impressed me greatly and made it easy for me to ask him about his own method of shorthand.

"He willingly told me all about it. 'It is not,' he said, 'an invention in shorthand, but a knowledge of the transmission of sound to paper. Either in English or in German I can register phonetics as quickly on paper as they are spoken. This is done by writing on paper just what the words sound like. For example, take the word height—I write down h—i—t. You see, it is really quite simple.'

"It didn't sound simple to me at the time and it still doesn't, but perhaps it *is* simple—if you are a Steinmetz!"

Every night when Karl had finished studying the notes he had made during classes, his father would sit beside him and listen to a complete report of what had happened at the University during the day. Despite the fact that the older man lacked the training and education to understand the greater part of what his son was talking about, Mr. Steinmetz thoroughly enjoyed these discussions. Years later, in a newspaper interview, Karl must have been thinking of the days when he talked over his lessons with his father, as he said, "I owe my father a very great debt, for the one thing he was determined I should have was an education. Probably I also owe him a good deal through inheritance. He was interested in science and invention. He bought and read books on those subjects. He talked to me about them; and my father's books first stimulated my interest and added to my knowledge."

Many a time as the two Steinmetz men looked over the younger's lecture notes, Mr. Steinmetz must have remembered the dour words of the headmaster of St. John's Gymnasium and realized how foolish all his fears had been. Karl was far from stupid. Proud of his son's ability, the happy father decided to reward the boy as best he could. By doing without many things he needed, he was able to save a few dollars out of his small salary. Next he consulted some of

Karl's special friends, who helped him choose a meager collection of scientific apparatus. Then, in the very room where little Carluszek had once burned *Grossmutter's* turkey red carpet during an "experiment," Mr. Steinmetz carefully set up a laboratory. The college student was delighted with his father's surprise, and it would be hard to say which one of them was more pleased. Thereafter, the young scientist spent many happy hours in the alcove, engrossed in engineering problems.

Some weeks later, awakened in the middle of the night by a howling wind, Mr. Steinmetz noticed a stream of light coming down the hall from his son's den. Thinking Karl had carelessly neglected to blow out the lamp before going to bed, he slipped on a robe and slippers, and went padding down the hall. As he entered the alcove he saw his son mixing a thick white paste. Silently, he watched as Karl stuck two copper wires into the mixture. At last, unable to restrain his curiosity, he asked, "What in the world are you doing at this hour, Son?"

"I'm reducing aluminum to its metallic state by electricity, Father."

"Aluminum, what is that? Why, I have never even heard of it!"

"You will, sir, you will. It is bound to be the metal of the future," Karl asserted confidently.

"Never mind the future, go to bed immediately," retorted Mr. Steinmetz, little knowing that his son would some day be responsible for making aluminum play a major part in the electrical industry.

Karl went to bed, but he didn't stop his investigations. One day he suggested to a group of fellow students that they conduct an experiment in terrestrial magnetism on the frozen surface of the Oder.

"What do you say, boys? Professor Schroeter showed me one of the charts which lists the variation in the angle be-

tween true and magnetic north in every part of the world,"
he explained. "As you know, the needle of a compass points
to the magnetic north, which has shifted over the centuries
from the true north. We'll take a compass reading out on
the ice, and then by looking at the Professor's chart, we'll
check to see if we have figured correctly the deviation between true and magnetic north here at Breslau. All we will
need is a magnetic needle mounted on a swivel for equipment. You chaps will only have to watch as the south pole of
the needle swings around and marks magnetic north. I'll do
all the figuring. Are you game?"

An outing on the ice appealed to the group, and plans
were made to meet early Sunday morning, near one of the
many bridges that spanned the Oder. It was a bitterly cold
day but the entire party was present when Steinmetz called
the roll. The students clambered down the bank, fought for
a firm footing on the slippery ice and then set to work. Ears
and noses were nipped as the wind grew stronger. One by
one, Karl's friends left the river and went to a near-by inn
for coffee and the comfort of a log fire. Busy with his calculations, Steinmetz did not discover that he was alone until he had finished a long column of figures. Then he, too,
went to the inn.

"What a crowd of scientists you fellows are!" he chided.
"There I am, the ice freezing my toes, the wind almost cutting me in two, thinking you chaps are carefully checking
the compass, and when I look up, what do I find? Everyone
has vanished!"

"If you want to be a polar scientist, Karl," retorted one
of his chums with a laugh, "that's your affair. The rest of us
will confine our experiments to a warm laboratory. Here,
drink this cup of coffee and toast yourself by the fire."

"Thanks, but I don't want any coffee just yet. First I must
finish my figuring," said Steinmetz as he spread his notebook on a table.

After a few minutes of frantic computing, he turned to his friends with a bewildered look. "I just can't understand what has gone wrong!" he exclaimed. "According to my calculations, the entire experiment has failed!"

"Serves you right for trying to freeze us to death. Come, forget the whole thing and drink your coffee."

"Very well. Tomorrow I'll ask the Professor what we did wrong," agreed Karl, taking the proffered cup. The steam from the hot liquid caused his glasses to fog, and he put the cup down in order to wipe the lenses. As he held the spectacles in his hand, a smile suddenly broke over his face, and he announced, "Here's the trouble, fellows. The steel rims on my glasses affected the compass, causing an error in our reading."

Amid loud laughter, the pages of the notebook which Karl had completely covered with figures were thrown into the fire and the experiment was declared "a scientific failure, but a great social success."

Young Steinmetz was never happier than when he was enjoying the companionship of his fellow students. Even though his classmates laughed at his earnest mien in the lecture hall, and probably envied his ability, they did not consider their friend a "grind," and welcomed him to all their social affairs. If he had not been malformed, he assuredly would have been invited to receive the highest honor German college boys can give one of their number: a membership in a *Verbindungen*, or duelling corps. The qualifications for admittance into these groups are much higher than those required by American fraternities, and the various colored caps of the corps are worn with justifiable pride.

Members of the *Burschenschraft*, a student organization set up at all German universities, would gladly have welcomed Karl to their ranks also, but he could not afford the expense involved. Once a patriotic society, the *Burschenschraft* had been regulated by law, so by the time of Stein-

metz' college days, it was a social club and much too costly
for a poor man's son who found it necessary to tutor in order
to have any pocket money. Incidentally, hoping to appear
dignified when calling at his pupils' houses, Karl wore a long
black tailcoat, which only had the effect of making him
look like a mournful crow!

It was in the Mathematics Society of the University that
Steinmetz found the comradeship he so greatly desired. He
was admitted into probational membership, along with several other "foxes," as first-year men were called. Like the
others, Karl had to obey the orders of a "Fox Major," an
upperclassman who was in charge of hazing. At meetings of
the Society, the "foxes" were obliged to sit on hard benches
in a certain section of the room and do everything they were
told. The group usually met in an inn at about eight o'clock
on a Friday evening, and after a short business meeting, a
scientific paper would be read by one of the members. Then
for an hour, the author of the paper would have to defend
it against the criticism of the rest of the membership, which
included alumni and professors, as well as students. When
this portion of the meeting was over, the chairman would
resign his post in favor of a "Beer President," who took complete charge of the rest of the evening's activities. Steins of
beer were then set before the members, and the second part
of the program began, which consisted of singing songs and
drinking toasts.

Recalling his student days, Steinmetz once said, "Drinking was done under strict rules and regulations. You did not
drink unsocially by yourself, but you drank to 'somebody'
and the drink was only a sip. The idea was to make the beer
last as long as possible. Meanwhile, a 'beer court' had been
set up with three judges and a sheriff. Their duty was to try
'foxes,' who of course had absolutely no rights. However,
each 'fox' who entered the Society adopted an 'old man' who
watched out for him, and if a member amused himself by

hazing this 'fox' too much, the 'old man' would hail the culprit before the 'beer court.' "

The social part of the meeting lasted until midnight, when the older alumni and professors would go home. Most of the younger graduates remained, however; all would call for more beer and demand that the "foxes" entertain them. Steinmetz, unable to sing or dance, would stand upon a chair and deliver a lecture as his part of the festivities. Sometimes he would discuss the ancient myths of Greece; at others he would make up an impossible mathematical equation and prove it. He could shift from one subject to another with great ease, so often, when the "Fox Major" deliberately interrupted him with the brusque command that he "change the subject," Karl would do so without a pause, to the intense delight and admiration of the group.

It was two o'clock in the morning before the meetings broke up, but the carefree students did not have the slightest intention of going home to bed. Arm in arm, they would wander up and down Breslau's narrow, cobbled streets, singing at the tops of their voices. Only when they reached the Ring, or market square, with its fourteenth-century townhall, did they sing softly, for here there was a chance that they might be heard by the watch and taken to jail for disturbing the peace. Once this danger zone was passed, they would raise their voices again and prance gaily through the town until they reached one of the city's many all-night restaurants. One of the students, pockets weighed down with unexpected allowance money, would treat the crowd, knowing that when he ran out of funds, someone would probably treat him.

The favorite café of the Mathematics Society was "Liechtenstein's"—given that name by the collegians because its owner came from that small independent state, once part of the Holy Roman Empire. Perhaps the reason why this tavern was so popular with Steinmetz' associates was the fact that if no member of the group had money enough to pay for refreshments, one of the waiters, or even the owner himself, would advance sufficient cash to pay for the fun!

When they had finished eating, the entire party would set out on a walk into the country to watch the sun rise. Steinmetz, always an ardent lover of nature, greatly enjoyed these hikes. It was often nearly eight o'clock on Saturday morning before the group sauntered back to Breslau. Most of the members of the Mathematics Society then would go home to sleep, but Karl merely dashed cold water on his face, picked up his notebook, and went to class. Even staying out all night was no reason to miss a lecture!

At the close of the first semester, the "foxes" were admitted into full membership in the Mathematics Society and given nicknames. These names were always matched with some physical or mental characteristic of the member, and from the time they were designated, a student was never known among his friends by any other name. He might rise to hold an important government position, become the rector of a university, establish himself as a doctor or wear a judge's robe, but his title of honor was serenely ignored by his fellow members of the Society, who had the inalienable right to call him by his nickname.

On the evening of the name-giving ceremony, the president rapped for order and called the role of the "foxes." As each man answered and stood before him, he bestowed the name that had been chosen by the organization for the new member, and everyone drank a toast in the newcomer's honor. At last it was Karl's turn; he shuffled to the front of the room and nervously awaited his new title.

"Here you are, gentlemen," intoned the president, "look at him and look well. There you see the only man in the entire University of Breslau who can change his thoughts in the middle of a sentence. He is like the old man of the sea who could shift from one form to another in a matter of

seconds. Therefore, hark well, all of you: Karl August Rudolph Steinmetz, I bestow upon you the name of the old
sea-god and dub you Proteus."

Karl was overjoyed. Despite the fact that none of the
members of the Mathematics Society had ever made the
least bit of fun of his appearance, he had been worried for
fear that his nickname might be based on his unattractive
physique. To be called after the old man of the sea, who
knew all the secrets of the world, made him extremely
happy. He proudly answered to the nickname, and when
he came to America, he discarded the August Rudolph and
took Proteus as his middle name.

Quickly and happily the student years passed, and at
twenty-two Karl was ready for the very difficult oral and
written examinations that would give him the highest degree
a university can award—Doctor of Philosophy. His plans for
the future were quite definite; he had decided to become
a professor of mathematics. Professor Schroeter had promised to do everything in his power to help his brilliant student secure a university post. Carefully Karl prepared the
dissertation he would have to read and defend against the
full faculty of the University, in order to be graduated with
a diploma. There were no experiments in the alcove now.
Every bit of time was spent in smoothing out his report
*On Involuntary Self-Reciprocal Correspondence in Space
Which Are Defined by a Three-Dimensional Linear System
of the nth Order.* A most formidable sounding assignment
for a scholar of any age!

Then in June, 1888, his thesis written and accepted, Karl
discovered that he had to cast aside all his plans for the
future. There was to be no professorship in a German university, no going to meetings of the Mathematics Society as
an alumnus, nor any Doctor of Philosophy degree. In fact,
Steinmetz could be sure of only one thing. If he didn't get
out of Breslau immediately, he would be arrested and
thrown into jail!

"Whoever tries for great objects must suffer something" —Plutarch

3

THE secret police of the German Imperial Government had been shadowing Karl for several months. In fact, he had been extremely fortunate not to have been arrested and thrown in jail at any time during his junior and senior years. For, like many other students at the University of Breslau, young Steinmetz had joined the Socialist Party, hoping by its activities to bring about better working conditions for the lower classes and gain increased political freedom for thousands. German students had long advanced the cause of social reform; in 1848, thousands of them, unable to secure in their native land the liberties they desired, migrated to the United States. Large numbers of these well-educated men settled in the Middle West, and when the War Between the States broke out, answered Lincoln's call for volunteers and fought bravely for the Union and the emancipation of the slaves.

There was nothing Otto von Bismarck hated more than democracy. As "The Iron Chancellor," who had unified Germany after the Franco-Prussian War and made Emperor William I the most powerful ruler in Europe, Bismarck considered only the privileges of the upper classes, and ignored completely the needs of the common folk. At first, busy with the affairs of state and thinking they could do no harm, he overlooked the idealistic dreamers in the universities who talked about political and social reform. His attitude changed, however, when they began to support candidates for election to the Reichstag, the representative legislative body of Germany. Firmly determined to put an immediate end to all activity on the part of those interested in bringing democracy to the empire he had so brilliantly created, Bismarck issued an edict forbidding all associations, meetings and publications aimed at criticizing the Imperial Government or any of its officers. This stringent law gave the police power to interfere with, to arrest, or to expel from the country anyone who advocated a more democratic form of government. In carrying out the Chancellor's orders, the Breslau authorities investigated all of the students in the University and found evidence enough to warrant placing Karl's name high on their list of undesirable persons.

Steinmetz had become vitally interested in the proposed reforms of the Socialist movement through his close friendship with Heinrich Lux, an extremely clever fellow-candidate for the degree of Doctor of Philosophy. Heinz, as he was called, was well known to the police as a political agitator long before the imperial decree against reformers had been issued, and he had been kept under constant observation. It was Karl's association with Lux that brought him to the attention of the police. In order to cover up Lux's activities and to confuse the Chancellor's agents, the Socialist group in Breslau went through the motions of disbanding their organization and gathered secretly. They held meetings behind locked and carefully guarded doors, and no one could get in who did not know the secret knock and password, both of which were changed frequently. If the officers did manage to break in, they found nothing wrong. Inside the room would be a group of students attending a tea—for the young reformers kept a teapot and cups handy so they could be picked up quickly in case of a raid. Although Karl took an active part in these clandestine sessions, there is a possibility that he might never have been considered dangerous to the Imperial Government by the authorities if Heinz and some of the others had not been arrested for editing a Socialist newspaper.

Steinmetz brazenly assumed the task of publishing *The People's Voice* when Lux went to jail. By this foolish act, he called attention to himself. Bismarck's agents immediately reported his action to Berlin, and carefully watched his every move. Meanwhile, the authorities, respecting the fact that the imprisoned Lux was a brilliant scholar, allowed him to continue his preparation for the oral and written examinations he had to pass before earning his degree. Strangely enough, the messenger they permitted to bring the necessary books and papers to his cell and carry back the finished work was Karl Steinmetz! Every day Lux would make out a list of the various materials he needed and it was handed to his friend, who was waiting in the warden's office. Years later, safe in America and a world-famous engineer, Steinmetz revealed how this arrangement made it impossible for the government lawyers to convict the leader of the Breslau Socialists on a charge of treason.

"The officials would examine Heinz' list very carefully, but as it never seemed to contain anything harmful, the prosecutor always would permit me to have it. But one day when I read it over to see what I had to bring him, I noticed that a certain symbol of a chemical formula was not correct. It was fortunate that there were no chemists among the jailers, for if there had been, the scheme would have miscarried; for the symbol was that of a solution to be used in invisible ink. Naturally enough, I included a large bottle of it the next day in the materials I delivered to the warden's office.

"From then on my friend used to send me letters which seemed to contain nothing of more than casual interest. But between the lines of the visible writing were his confidential communications in invisible writing. We wrote the same way on the fly-leaves and margins of the books we sent back and forth. And thus we prepared our legal defense, making all our stories tally so perfectly that when Lux and the rest of the group were finally tried in court they were not convicted.

"During all this time I was under suspicion myself. The University was a government institution, and the authorities first ordered the rector—the president as we say here—to bring me before the faculty for investigation. This was done; but the professors tabled the charge. Later they were directed to examine me again; and again they let the matter drop."

Cleared by a friendly faculty of the accusations brought against him by the secret police, Steinmetz would have received his coveted degree and probably the desired professorship at a university if only he had stopped his political activity at this point. However, young and full of reckless zeal, he continued his editorial work on *The People's Voice*, and lost all chance of ever achieving his ambitions when he printed: "We don't know what the Government wants, but we disapprove of it."

With the publication of such a seditious statement he went much too far. Not even the friendship of his professors could save him. The authorities were determined to punish this fervent young fellow and if the University would not take the necessary steps to do so, they would stop him themselves. So by evoking an almost forgotten, ancient law, which stated that a university student could not have a profession or business while enrolled in classes, the secret police prepared to arrest Steinmetz.

The impetuous Karl had no idea of what was in store for him until two days before he was to receive his doctorate, when a member of the Socialist underground, employed at the headquarters of the secret police, warned him that a warrant had been sworn out for his arrest. Then a note signed "One of Your Professors" was silently slipped under Karl's door, suggesting that, in the writer's opinion, it would be wise if he left Germany immediately. Steinmetz was stunned by the information his friends gave him, but he wasted no time in deciding what he was going to do. He was an "idealist," but politics were not nearly so important to him as science, so he determined to flee to Zurich, Switzerland, and continue his engineering studies in safety.

There was only one flaw in this plan. If he left Breslau in order to avoid being thrown into jail, he would never return. This meant he would in all probability never see his father again.

Karl paced the floor all night, his mind in a turmoil. Early in the morning he went to the bedroom and awoke his father. With difficulty the young man kept his voice from breaking, as he explained he was going on a day's excursion into the country, in order to be fresh for the lengthy graduation exercises at the University the next day. Mr. Steinmetz, his eyes heavy with sleep, muttered a few unintelligible sentences, and as he rolled over mumbled, "Have a good time, Son. I'll see you when you come home." Karl, with tears streaming down his face, stumbled out of the room, picked up the bag he had packed and made his way through the shadow-filled streets to the station.

Although he did not see them, Steinmetz was sure that the secret police were following him as he hobbled down the Tauenzeinstrasse. When he entered the station, he went directly to the ticket window and loudly demanded a round-trip, one-day excursion ticket to a small town near the Austrian frontier. Of course he had no intention of using the return portion of the ticket, but he wanted the authorities to think he was planning to come back to Breslau that night. As soon as the gates were opened, he clambered into the train, expecting every moment that a hand would fall on his shoulder and that he would be dragged away to jail. His nervousness increased as other passengers entered the car, but none of them seemed the least bit interested in the humpbacked youth who was reading a textbook. At last the train started and Karl breathed more freely—perhaps he had not been followed because of his ruse of buying a return trip ticket. If so, he was safe.

On arriving at his destination, Steinmetz called at the house of a former university student with whom he had been very friendly, explained the peril of his position, and asked for help. His school chum offered to do anything he could to assist him.

"I'm very grateful," said Karl. "Now here's what I would like you to do. Go to the railway station and buy two return-trip tickets to the nearest town over the Austrian border. I am quite sure that none of Bismarck's agents have followed me, but if they have, I don't think they will be the least bit suspicious if we travel together and have round-trip tickets. They'll think that we know nothing of their plans and are merely going on a spring outing. Once in Austria, I'll take the first train toward Switzerland, and you'll come back alone. They may ask you some very embarrassing questions, but all you'll have to do is to say I decided not to return. The police won't be able to do anything drastic to you, and by the time they realize what has happened, I'll be miles away."

Karl's plan worked perfectly. Once over the frontier, he thanked his friend, boarded a waiting train and went on to Vienna and Prague. He finally reached Zurich—safe, but exhausted in body and mind. A cup of coffee in a restaurant near the railroad station revived his spirits and he was able to consider his next move. His greatest problem was the fact that he had very little money, but he faced the future with confidence, sure that he could get enough tutoring assignments to support himself while he earned a degree at the famous Zurich Polytechnic School.

However, life in Switzerland was not going to be as simple as Karl had hoped. The Polytechnic flatly refused to admit him as a student because of his inability to produce a *heimatschien*, a legal paper which stated that the bearer had been an honest and law-abiding citizen in his native city. Moreover, as a non-resident of Zurich, without the proper papers, he had to pay a weekly fine. His meager funds dwindled, despite the fact that he practically starved himself in an attempt to save money. He began to dread the appearance of the policeman who came regularly to collect the required fee.

Meanwhile, back in Breslau, a sorrowful and lonesome Mr. Steinmetz tried in vain to get a *heimatschien* for his son. The police laughed at the distraught father and made it clear that the only thing they would give Karl Steinmetz was a jail cell! Nor did the rector of the Polytechnic offer the harassed youth any encouragement; a foreigner lacking the necessary papers would never be considered for enrollment as a student while he was in office!

Karl was nearly destitute when he met a newspaper editor for whom he had written a scientific article while a student at Breslau. When the journalist heard of the difficulties young Steinmetz was having, he promised to see what he could do to help. In less than a week, a letter from the rector of the Polytechnic arrived, announcing that Karl had been admitted as a student. As for the required *heimatschien*, the authorities suddenly seemed to have forgotten that Steinmetz was living in Zurich. Joyously he threw himself into an intensive study of mechanical and steam engineering and soon, by writing and tutoring, he was earning just enough money to meet his expenses.

While attending classes Steinmetz became friendly with Oscar Asmussen, a Dane, whose wealthy uncle in California was paying for his education. Karl, always a friendly person, found in the blond giant who towered above him a kindred spirit, and the two became fast friends. Before many weeks had passed, they decided to room together. Their apartment, "on the top floor of the last house at the end of the last street on the edge of town," was officially opened with a party given by Steinmetz for all those who had been kind to him since his arrival in Zurich. Generous to the extreme, he had spent his last cent on refreshments, and for several weeks afterward was forced to live on bread and sausages to make up for his extravagance.

Then, to add to his financial troubles, Karl had the ill fortune to lose several of the pupils he was tutoring in mathematics. Normally, he would have borrowed money from Asmussen, but his roommate's allowance check had been delayed, and the young Dane was also without funds. Just when the pair were desperately wondering how long they were going to be able to pay their rent, Steinmetz received a check for some articles he had written before leaving home, and they were able to settle all their accounts and to buy a fresh supply of sausages.

When Asmussen and Karl had finished their classroom assignments for the next day, they would tell each other about their past experiences. Nothing his roommate said fascinated Steinmetz as much as the stories he told about America. One night, after Oscar had described the opportunities working men in the United States had to establish their own factories, Karl exclaimed: "If things in America are the way you say they are, my friend, it is plain to see that all men have an equal chance for success in that wonderful country! If that were the situation in Germany, I never would have got into trouble with the authorities—opportunity for all was the only reason I joined Lux and the others. Oh, how I wish I could visit this land you describe, but it is impossible. Where would I get the money to pay my passage?" There was no quick answer to that question.

Karl was left alone, however, while Asmussen went to call on a beautiful Swiss girl whom he hoped to marry. One night Oscar came into the room flushed with excitement and told Steinmetz that he had proposed and had been accepted. "I have cabled my uncle and told him the good news," he announced. "He will be delighted, I know." Karl, never so happy as when one of his friends was enjoying good fortune, congratulated his roommate, and after chatting until the early hours of the morning, the two young men finally went to bed. The next day, on their return from classes, there was a blunt cablegram from Asmussen's uncle in California waiting in the mailbox. Its message was brief, but unmistakable: Oscar was to give up all ideas of marriage and return to America at once. To make sure that he would do as he was ordered, his allowance had been stopped and passage money was being cabled.

"What shall I do, Karl?" moaned Asmussen. "I love her madly but I am in no position to marry without the allowance my uncle sends me."

"There is only one thing to do, Oscar. Explain everything to your beloved. Then go back to California, find a job so you won't have to rely upon your uncle, save your money, and when you have enough, send for her. I'll hate to see you leave Zurich, we have been such good friends. If only I could go with you . . ."

"You can, Karl, you can!" Asmussen broke in excitedly. "Look here, if I take the money Uncle will cable for a first-class passage home and buy two steerage tickets instead, we'll both be able to make the trip! What do you say?"

"What do I say! Why, Oscar, I can't say anything. If you only knew . . ."

"You'll come, then? Good! Now, let's not waste any time

talking. The sooner I get to America and start working, the sooner I can be married. We'll take the first boat, Karl—let's begin our packing!"

Clothes were taken out of closets and heaped on the floor, books were piled on tables and chairs and the roommates started to fill their suitcases. Their activity was disturbed by the ringing of the doorbell and Steinmetz hobbled to the door to see who their visitor might be.

A distinguished-looking gentleman politely raised his hat and bowed as the door opened, and inquired, "Is this the residence of Karl Steinmetz, formerly of Breslau, Germany? I am Uppenborn, the publisher. Steinmetz has written some articles for me, and on hearing that he is now living at this address, I have come to offer him a position on my staff."

"I am Steinmetz, sir," replied Karl, "and delighted to meet you. Come in and sit down."

Uppenborn entered the apartment, but there was no place for him to sit. Every chair was piled high with clothing or papers. "What is going on here?" the publisher inquired. "Are you two moving?"

Karl and Oscar explained that they were about to leave for America, and Uppenborn wished them well. He then suggested that Steinmetz act as the American correspondent for his magazine, an offer which was gratefully accepted. After a short conversation, the journalist shook hands with the young men and left. A moment later the doorbell rang again. It was the magazine publisher, who apologized for interrupting them a second time, and said, "If you can find a clean piece of paper in all this disorder and clear off that table so that I can have a place to write, Steinmetz, I'll give you a letter of introduction to Rudolph Eickenmeyer. He is considered one of the leading electrical engineers in the United States. Perhaps he might have a job for you."

Papers, books and clothing were pushed onto the floor, and Uppenborn quickly wrote a note, signed it and handed it to Karl. More good-bys and grateful handshakes, and the thoughtful editor was gone.

"See, Karl," cried Asmussen, "just as soon as you make up your mind to go to America, your prospects change for the better!"

Before Steinmetz could answer him, the whistle of the postman was heard. Oscar went downstairs and came back with a letter for his roommate. Opening it, Karl found a royalty check, in payment for several astronomy articles which he had written some time before, and which had now been put into book form. It was Steinmetz' first published work. He was to write many more distinguished works—but nothing he ever earned by his writing made him as proud as that first check for three dollars and a half. Flushed with the excitement of crossing the ocean, Uppenborn's visit and the check, Karl rushed out and celebrated his newfound prosperity by buying a cigar. At that moment a life-long habit of cigar smoking began.

It took Steinmetz and Asmussen only two days to pack all their belongings and to end their association with the Polytechnic. Then while Karl paid a few last visits to his Zurich associates, Oscar spent a sad evening with his fiancée. He left her with the solemn promise that he would send for her within a year. Now there was nothing to keep the two friends in Switzerland, so they took the next train to France, heading for the port of Le Havre, from which they had made arrangements to set sail for America on the liner *La Champagne*.

While Oscar deeply regretted every mile that passed beneath the clacking train wheels, because it meant that he was getting farther and farther away from his beloved, Karl had no such feelings. The sooner he reached the United States, the golden land of opportunity, the happier he would be. Only one thought dimmed his glowing dreams of achieving success in a land where all men had an equal chance—

now there was absolutely no possibility that he would ever see his father again. Unless, perhaps when Asmussen sent for his bride-to-be, he could send for his father. . . . So, full of hope for the future, Karl Steinmetz, like millions of other Europeans, resolutely turned his back on the Old World. What would the New World hold for a hump-backed cripple who had already traveled so far from his grandmother's turkey red carpet? Would America prove a magic carpet to success?

> *"The great man is the man who does a thing for the first time"* —ALEXANDER SMITH

‖ 4 ‖

KARL and Oscar mounted a steep gangplank and boarded the *La Champagne*. On the deck they were stopped by a stern-faced, gold-braided officer who carefully examined their papers and directed them to the steerage, a section deep in the vessel's hold set aside for those passengers who had paid the least amount of money for fare. The two friends, laden with bulky baggage, stumbled down a series of narrow companionways and then walked along a dimly-lit passage until they reached a large room lined with rows of bunks.

Most of these were piled high with the belongings of passengers who had come aboard the ship earlier. Oscar, towering above the excitedly chattering crowd milling about the room, soon found two unoccupied berths, threw his bundles on one, and then helped Karl stow his possessions on the other. The two friends then pushed their way through their shipmates and climbed back to the main deck to watch the snorting tugs nose the *La Champagne* out of the harbor of Le Havre and into the open sea. Once deep water was reached and the pilot was dropped from the liner, the young men were roughly ordered to return to the lower deck and told that for the rest of the voyage none of the steerage passengers would be allowed to leave the section of the vessel assigned to them.

Karl did not mind this confinement. He was planning to learn to speak English on the voyage and so had no desire to go roaming over the liner. While most of his fellow immigrants sat on the crowded deck, talking or singing in their native French, German or Italian, he spent the time trying to memorize the simple sentences Oscar had written out for him. If they had been complicated mathematical equations, Steinmetz would have had little difficulty with them, but the strange words gave him a great deal of trouble, and he had not learned a great many when, after a stormy crossing lasting eight days, the *La Champagne* sailed into New York harbor on Saturday, June 1, 1889.

Until the port authorities gave permission to land, the steerage passengers had to remain cooped up aboard the liner. Karl, huddled close to the rail, looked with amazement at the skyline of New York and hopefully at the Statue of Liberty. Would he find the opportunities he desired, once ashore? Dreaming of a new life in America, he did not notice the bitter cold rain and went below thoroughly soaked. In the morning, when orders to disembark were issued, his face was badly swollen from an infected sinus. Staggering under the load of his precious books and scientific papers, Karl could hardly see as he lined up with the other aliens in front of the immigration officers for the required interrogation.

At last, after several hours of waiting to be examined, his turn came. The official in charge took one brief look at the puffy-faced, malformed dwarf who walked with a painful limp, and shook his head. His orders were to admit only the strong, who could help develop the farms and factories of the United States. Anyone could see that this cripple could contribute nothing. In fact, it was extremely doubtful that he could even support himself! Little did the immigration officer realize that this humpback was to become one of the greatest scientists of all time and that his genius would make it possible for thousands of men and women to do their daily tasks more easily and efficiently.

"I can't pass him," muttered the official to himself, "nor could any-one else." However, the dwarf's papers had to be filled out completely, regardless of the disposition of his case, so the questioning began.

"Your papers seem to be in order. Now answer these questions. Tell me, do you speak English?"

Karl, shaking with fear, tried desperately to remember the sentences he had studied on the trip across the Atlantic. For once his phenomenal memory failed him, and all he could whisper was, "A few."

In the proper space, the examiner wrote, "No English."

"Very well, then, have you any money?"

Steinmetz was unable to utter a single sound and just stood helpless, shaking his head. Down went the words, "No money." The officer then grasped Karl firmly by the arm and began to lead him toward the detention pen, where immigrants unfit for entrance into the United States were kept until placed aboard a ship returning to Europe. Just as the gate was about to close on the terrified young man and his ambitions, Asmussen came rushing to his rescue.

"Just a minute, Officer, if you please, just a minute!" he cried breathlessly. "This man is a famous German scientist and represents several important European technical journals. Look here, this money belongs to him. I am carrying it for him. Count it—see, there is plenty to support him until he secures employment here. I'll vouch that he will never become a charity case. I assure you, there's nothing for the authorities to worry about."

The immigration inspector looked doubtful, but there was nothing he could do. If this handsome and obviously well-educated young man was willing to assume the responsibility for a grotesque creature, the matter was out of his hands. So he gave Karl an entrance permit and the two friends left Castle Island, walked under the trees of Battery Park, and made their way to Brooklyn, where Oscar had relatives. On the way they saw the Brooklyn Bridge, and Steinmetz, recalling the old stone bridges that spanned the Oder in Breslau, gasped with admiration at the engineering skill which had made it possible to throw this steel structure across the East River.

At the apartment of Asmussen's relatives, a hearty reception greeted the weary travelers. Karl was immediately put to bed and ordered to stay there until his cold was completely cured. Never happy when idle, he spent the time studying his English lessons. By the end of his illness, he was able to carry on a halting conversation in the new language. Now he was ready to go in search of a job. Looking over the letters of introduction that he had brought with him from Europe, Steinmetz decided to apply for a position in the Edison plant. In lecture after lecture, his professors at Zurich had praised the work of Thomas Alva Edison in inventing and developing methods for the generation and exploitation of electric light, heat and power. If only he could work under the guidance of the great electrical genius! Full of hope, Karl tucked a letter of introduction to the chief engineer of the Edison Company into his pocket and set out for the plant.

He had no difficulty in meeting the person to whom the letter was addressed. But that individual merely glanced at the recommendation, threw a sharp look at Steinmetz, rolled the letter into a ball, tossed it into the wastebasket and said curtly, "There's nothing here for you. We've got more engineers now than we can use. Good-by."

Karl smiled and politely thanked him, but he was terribly disappointed. He had so wanted to work with the man who had helped to perfect the incandescent lamp, invented the stock-ticker, mimeograph, and phonograph, and improved the dynamo and electric motor. The worst of the incident was that Karl went out of the Edison plant feeling that he had been refused a position, not because of his lack of ability, but because of his appearance. Am I, he wondered, to starve in America because of my looks? Yet Oscar had often told him that all men had a chance to succeed in the United States. Troubled and worried, he was unable to sleep that night, but in the morning hope returned, and with Uppenborn's letter to Rudolph Eickenmeyer in his pocket, he went to Yonkers, where the firm of Eickenmeyer and Osterheld was located.

Despite the fact that the main business of this organization was the construction of hat-making machinery, Eickenmeyer was considered one of the leading electrical engineers in the United States. He had left his native Germany during the Revolution of 1848, and unable to secure an engineering post, had worked as a day laborer for the New York Central Railroad. By the time Steinmetz reached America, Eickenmeyer had one hundred and fifty inventions to his credit, mostly in the field of electricity, and he had completely mechanized the making of men's felt hats.

Before going to Yonkers, Karl put on his best clothes. This outfit consisted of a pair of baggy pants, a wrinkled coat and a torn cap. Recalling his seedy appearance later, Steinmetz said, "I looked like a singed cat!" On the long trip from Brooklyn, he rehearsed the speech in English which he had memorized. Over and over he practiced it, and he had it letter perfect by the time he reached Eickenmeyer's office.

Whipping the battered cap off his head, Karl made a deep bow and began his speech, "Honorable sir, I have the honor to make application with you as an electrical engineer for a position."

Eickenmeyer started to laugh, then stopped as he looked at the earnest, worried face of the bewildered immigrant, and quietly inquired, *"Sprechen Sie Deutsche?"*

Immediately Steinmetz' face brightened and a torrent of German poured from his lips. Digging into his pocket, he pulled out Uppenborn's letter and offered it to Eickenmeyer. Before looking it over, the hat manufacturer pointed to a chair beside his desk and invited Karl to sit down. When he had finished reading the letter, Eickenmeyer carefully placed it back in its envelope, dropped it into the middle drawer of his desk and asked his visitor to give him a summary of recent developments in electrical experimentation in Europe. Speaking fluently now that he no longer had to rely on his limited knowledge of the English language, Karl told what was happening in the laboratories and lecture halls on the other side of the Atlantic.

Eickenmeyer was greatly impressed with his visitor's familiarity with electrical investigations in Europe, and the two men talked most of the afternoon. At last Karl brought the conversation around to the subject of securing a position.

"I am sorry, *Herr* Steinmetz," said the manufacturer, "but you must understand that I am not really engaged in the business of electrical engineering. My main interest is the making of hat machinery. Therefore, I regret to say that I do not have any job for you now. However, suppose you come and see me in about a week. Perhaps I will think of something for you by that time."

Karl went back to Brooklyn filled with high hopes, confident that he would soon be working. A week later he again made the trip to Yonkers and this time was hired as a draftsman at a salary of twelve dollars a week. He was told to report for work the next day! Before returning to his Brooklyn lodgings, Steinmetz went to the Federal Building and took the first steps toward obtaining naturalization papers. It was only two weeks since he had landed in America, but he said, "It is the least I can do for a country that has treated me so well."

Karl's joy at having secured a position was undimmed by

the fact that he was forced to get up at five o'clock in the morning in order to reach his drawing board on time. For some weeks he did routine tasks, unnoticed by any of his fellow workers or his employer. Then one day Eickenmeyer spilled some dye on his hand and was unable to remove the stain. Steinmetz went to the storeroom, poured some acid into a bottle, diluted it with water and handed it to his superior. "This will take the stain off your hands, sir," he suggested, and returned to his blueprints.

Eickenmeyer took the bottle, walked over to a washstand, poured the solution over his hands and watched the stain slowly vanish. "How did you know what to suggest, Steinmetz?" he queried. "Oh, I remember now, you studied chemistry at Breslau, didn't you? Perhaps you had better leave that drawing board and join me in the laboratory. Of course, you don't have to if you don't want to . . ."

Karl, whose English had greatly improved, broke in quickly, "There's nothing I would rather do than work with you in the laboratory! Just give me time to finish this drawing and I'll join you."

The two men became fast friends as they worked together in the small room set aside by the firm for research purposes. While engaged in the testing of various materials, they would argue about the future of electricity, and Steinmetz convinced his employer that experimentation would discover many new uses for electrical energy. Soon Karl had Eickenmeyer's permission to carry out any investigations he wished at the company's expense. He carefully arranged his schedule so that his scientific investigations in the laboratory would not interfere with his regular duties. As the weeks passed, Eickenmeyer slowly realized that his fellow German was the most capable man in the entire factory. As a result, he made him his assistant, and finally placed Karl in complete supervision of the entire plant.

Visitors to the Yonkers establishment were amazed when

they saw a gnome-like figure, all head and shoulders, with a shaggy beard, wiry hair, and sparkling blue-gray eyes, clad only in an undershirt and trousers, limping briskly from machine to machine and talking to the workmen in a harsh voice which seemed to come out of his nose. As they listened to him, the impression given by his unpleasant voice vanished under the fire and penetrating clearness with which he gave directions. New employees at the plant were always astonished at their first sight of the cripple.

One day a new worker looked up from his machine and demanded of his neighbor in a loud voice, "Who is that little runt over there?"

Everyone who heard the remark was greatly embarrassed, for they knew that Steinmetz had heard it, too. They tried vainly to warn the newcomer to stop talking. He paid no attention to their frantic signals, but roared, "Well, what's the story? Hasn't he got a name? If you want to know what I think, I'll tell you. Eickenmeyer ought to send him home. He doesn't belong in a place where grown-up men work!"

Meanwhile, Karl had not looked up from his task of adjusting a delicate piece of apparatus. In the silence that followed his remarks, the new worker realized that something was radically wrong and fearfully inquired, "Anyhow, who is that fellow?"

"That's Steinmetz, the assistant boss," was the answer. The loud-mouthed newcomer was dazed and looked it. He turned back to his machine, expecting every minute to feel a hand on his shoulder and hear the words, "You're fired!" Fifteen minutes later he did feel a hand, and looked up apprehensively to see Steinmetz peering at him over the rims of his glasses. Instead of the expected snarl, "the assistant boss" gave him a jovial grin, and reaching into his hip pocket, brought out a handful of cigars.

"Here, have a cigar. You'd better take another. Glad to have you working with us." Then, without another word,

Karl turned away. That was Steinmetz, never one to hold malice or use his position to harm others. After this incident, the workers at the Eickenmeyer and Osterheld plant practically worshipped their malformed, brilliant and lively superior.

Now Steinmetz began to show the genius which was to make him famous. Eickenmeyer, busy with other matters, had turned the firm's laboratory over to him completely, giving Karl the part-time assistance of one man. Steinmetz didn't get much help from him, however, for his aide was an expert at repairing hat machinery and was continually being called into the factory to make adjustments on one of the tools. Despite this handicap, Karl produced an improved electric motor for the Otis Elevator Company, thereby indirectly helping to make the erection of skyscrapers practical.

The ten-hour day at the plant was nowhere near long enough for Karl. He had so many ideas for improving electrical devices that he used to do the necessary paper work during the long trip between Brooklyn and Yonkers and return—saving the time he spent in the laboratory for experimentation. It was a tiresome journey: first, Steinmetz crossed over to Manhattan on a ferry and went uptown to Forty-second Street on an elevated train; then he took the New York Central Railroad to Yonkers and finally reached Eickenmeyer's after a long ride in a horse-car. Perhaps all these changes made him welcome the opportunity to work on an electric motor for streetcars, with the idea of making faster local transportation possible. Eickenmeyer had been asked to develop such a motor by Stephen D. Field, a nephew of Cyrus Field, who had laid the Atlantic cable. After discussing the problem with young Field, Eickenmeyer suggested that they turn the project over to Steinmetz.

Karl was thrilled with the assignment. He dropped all his other investigations and devoted his entire time to designing a motor for Field. Now there were no more ten-hour days —time meant nothing to Steinmetz as he worked. Long after everyone else had left the plant, he would be busy with his experiments. He soon realized that he could no longer waste the time spent in riding back and forth from Brooklyn to Yonkers; those hours could be used to better advantage in the laboratory. However, if he took lodgings nearer to his work, Karl knew he would lose the company of Oscar Asmussen. It was a difficult choice.

Steinmetz talked the problem over with his friend, and they decided that they would set up housekeeping for themselves. After looking around for some time, they finally found what they wanted in Harlem, not too far from Karl's place of employment. Then they worked out a schedule of household duties, agreeable to both. Steinmetz, who got up very early, would prepare breakfast; Asmussen, who was the first to come home in the evening, was to cook dinner. In theory this was an ideal plan, but it did not work out, as neither one of them liked to do dishes. The result was that the sink was constantly piled high with dirty plates, and the frying pan, which was the only cooking utensil they ever used, was never clean. For a while they tried paper plates, but that was just as unsatisfactory, for they forgot to throw them away!

Under these conditions it is little wonder that a family of mice who shared the apartment with them grew larger and fatter, but kindhearted Steinmetz would not let Asmussen set a trap. Soon there were so many mice that very few people would come to visit the Harlem flat!

This strange household was broken up when Oscar, who was now making eighteen dollars a week, announced that he had saved up enough money to send to Zurich for his betrothed. On her arrival, they were married and set up housekeeping in a house of their own. By degrees, the two friends stopped seeing each other and drifted apart, never to meet again. Steinmetz, the most companionable of men, could not live alone, so he made arrangements to board at the home of Edward Muller, a fellow worker at Eickenmeyer's.

Karl was extremely happy at the Mullers'. He was treated by the adults as a member of the family, and by the children as one of themselves. He delighted in playing jokes on the youngsters, and would often mount a broom and chase them, pretending he was a highwayman or a robber. When the girls went about their household chores, he would sneak up behind them and pull their apron strings and hide the mops and brushes. Yet if he were working on a problem he had brought home from the plant, he would fail to hear their chatter and would not notice them, even if they were playing noisily in the same room where he was working, so great was his power of concentration.

Living so near Eickenmeyer's, he could arrive at an early hour and do his routine tasks. He was then able to spend most of the day in the laboratory. There was only one thing about this arrangement that Steinmetz did not like; the weather had turned cold and the furnace was not yet in operation by the time he reached the plant. So he set up a small, pot-bellied stove in one corner of his workshop. More often than not, however, he would rush in and begin an experiment, forgetting all about lighting a fire in the stove. By the time he did think of it, the janitor would have the factory's heating system working.

Field, who spent a great deal of his time in the laboratory, had taken it upon himself to make sure before he left each night that the fire for the next day was laid in the stove. He also lit it if he came in early in the morning and found that Steinmetz had neglected to do so. Noticing this, Karl decided to play a trick on his associate. He soaked some kindling wood in linseed oil, and when Field put a match to the fire there was a tremendous explosion and the top of the stove went sailing through the air. The victim laughed as heartily as the prankster and suggested that they play the same trick on Steinmetz' helper.

"No, *Herr* Field, I've a much better idea," replied Karl. "It will also use linseed oil, however. That assistant of mine is always telling me how good my cigar smells. You know, not exactly asking for one, but hinting. Well, we'll give him a cigar, but we'll soak it first in linseed oil and let it dry. When he begins to smoke, it ought to be a sight worth seeing!"

With as much skill and care as if he were conducting a scientific experiment of the utmost importance, Steinmetz prepared the cigar, with Field's assistance. When it was ready, it was offered to the laboratory helper, who was tremendously flattered when his superior held a match so he could light it. The two conspirators anxiously watched the expression on the smoker's face, but it did not change. "Say," he exclaimed between puffs, "this is the best cigar I've ever smoked. How I wish I could afford cigars as good as this one!"

Steinmetz and Field looked at each other in stunned silence. Field gasped, picked up his hat and coat and left the laboratory, shaking his head in amazement. Karl merely shrugged his shoulders and went back to the task of designing a suitable motor for streetcars.

ʕ╞ ʕ╞ ʕ╞

Most electrical engineers of the period who were commissioned to develop a new type of motor would, as a matter of course, design one that ran by direct current, which flows continuously in one direction. Steinmetz was convinced, however, that if an efficient motor capable of supplying alternating current could be built, an entirely new field of electrical progress would result. The main obstacle to such an invention was the fact that very little was known about alternating current, although in theory it was simple enough. All the maker of an alternating current motor had to do was to place a metallic bar, usually of iron, inside a coil through which an electrical current was passed, and the bar would become magnetized. This bar, like the needle of a compass, which is nothing but a magnetized piece of steel, has both north and south poles; but if the current is reversed, the poles also reverse at the rate of one hundred and twenty times a second. Despite the great speed with which the alternating current motor changed directions, engineers knew that there was a delay in the reversal of the flow of electricity. They realized that the delay varied with the type of metal used for the bar and understood that, no matter how short a period of time was consumed before the current changed directions, the hesitation caused their motors to overheat, with a resultant loss of power and efficiency.

Research workers in engineering laboratories called this lag in the flow of current "hysteresis" and rightfully assumed that until an alternating current motor could be developed which would lose as little time as possible in reversing itself, the use of this type of electrical energy was not practical. Most electrical experts felt there was no possibility of finding an answer to the problem, and as a result avoided difficulty by designing their motors to operate on direct current.

Steinmetz, who read books dealing with engineering theory and the work of early scientists for relaxation the way many men rest their minds with detective stories, had perused everything published in German, French, Latin, Greek and English dealing with electricity. He decided to reread many of these volumes, hoping that in one of them he might discover a clue that would help him find a way to overcome hysteresis. His membership in scientific organizations made it possible to secure rare and out-of-print volumes from specialized collections, and the office boy at the Eickenmeyer plant staggered under the loads of books he carried back and forth from the public library.

Before he realized it, Karl was engaged in a course of study which covered the entire history of electricity. His studies showed that the Greeks and Romans had known about electricity and magnetism two thousand years before. "It seems to me," he muttered as he pored over a textbook, "that in two thousand years someone should have discovered an answer to my problem. All I know is that Field can't wait another two thousand years for his motor!"

A reprint of an ancient manuscript provided Steinmetz with fascinating reading as it described how it was a common practice for Greek ladies to rub their amber necklaces briskly, and then to pick up small objects, just as schoolboys use their fountain pens to attract bits of paper today. Another early volume told how soothsayers and doctors in Imperial Rome knew of the property of certain iron ores to attract other ore-filled rocks, and used this "phenomenon" to impress and "cure" their customers. These rocks, called loadstones, came from the province of Magnesia, and as a result their ability to draw other metals toward them was called magnetism.

Long after everyone else in the Muller household had gone to bed, Steinmetz would sit reading and smoking. Slowly the whole pageant of the development of electric heat, light, communication and power passed before his weary eyes. It was not, he reread, until the eleventh century that the attracting ability of the loadstone was put to practical use with the invention of the magnetic compass for steering ships. Straining his eyes, he managed to follow in facsimile reproduction the ancient Latin script of Peregrinus, a monk who had gone to the Holy Land by boat during the Crusades and had presented to the world, in 1269, in an illuminated manuscript the first scientific report dealing with magnetism. A lover of America and American history, Karl was delighted to learn that the knowledge that the direction in which the compass needle points varies with longitude was one of the results of Columbus' famous voyage to the New World.

More and more books were carried by Karl from the Eickenmeyer plant to his room at the Mullers' as he continued his study of the history of magnetism and electricity. Sometimes he would snort at the lack of scientific attitude on the part of early experimenters: at other times he would nod approvingly as he followed their activities. None of the pioneer investigators impressed him more than Queen Elizabeth's personal physician, William Gilbert, who proved that magnetism had absolutely no scientific value in medicine, and in the course of establishing this fact discovered that magnets have two poles—one of which seeks the north, the other the south. Gilbert also proved that like poles repel each other and that the earth is a magnetized globe, and he predicted that a magnetic needle would point vertically downward in the northern areas of the earth. Steinmetz knew that this forecast had been proven correct by the experience of Hendrick Hudson in 1608 as he sailed through the icy waters of the bay which bears his name.

Although he was learning nothing new, Karl thoroughly enjoyed re-reading Gilbert's book dealing with magnetism and electricity, which was first published in 1600. There was something about the pioneer scientist of England which made Steinmetz feel very close to him. For when the Elizabethan doctor found he needed a piece of apparatus to conduct an experiment, he did not give up the idea, like so many early investigators, but invented the necessary implements. That, Steinmetz felt, was the way a scientist should act. There was one thing for which he greatly envied Gilbert—the Englishman had added a word to the language—electric—taking it from the Greek word for amber, "electron." Little did Eickenmeyer's assistant realize that before he died he would have added several technical phrases to his adopted tongue.

When he came to the stories of Sir Isaac Newton, Joseph
Priestley, Luigi Galvani, Humphry Davy and Alessandro
Volta (from whose name we get the word volt), Steinmetz
read more quickly, for it had not been so long ago that he
had studied the life stories of these scientists as part of his
studies at Breslau and Zurich. As a well-educated engineer,
Karl knew that it wasn't until 1819 that Hans Christian
Oersted found a definite connection between magnetism
and electricity, showing that an electric current tended to
twist a magnetic pole around it. The work with currents and
magnets done by Ampere (who is remembered by the word
ampere) as well as Faraday's discovery that a wire carrying
a current could be made to rotate around the pole of a
magnet, which resulted in the building of the first electric
motor, were familiar to him, since they were comparatively
recent developments.

Poring over almost forgotten scientific reports, technical
papers, textbooks, biographies, and publications of learned
societies, Steinmetz found absolutely nothing new or helpful in his investigation into the problem of hysteresis. To be
sure, there were two relatively new books which contained
some promising material. One was written by Sir James
Ewing, who had studied the magnetic properties of various
materials in his laboratory in England. The other was the
result of the work in magnetism done by Gilbert Kapp in
Germany. As he studied these volumes, Karl soon found that
neither Ewing's nor Kapp's findings were valid, and as a
matter of fact, they contradicted each other in the data they
presented. Steinmetz had his choice of two procedures: he
could do what always had been done—build Field's motor
by trial and error; if it worked, very well; if not, build another and try again. On the other hand, by mathematics and
experimentation he might overcome the hysteresis loss and
design a workable alternating current motor.

Without hesitation, Karl made his choice. He would conquer the problem of power loss in alternating current motors! Dominated by the scientific point of view instilled into him by Professor Fechner during his student days at St. John's, Steinmetz tested every metal known to have magnetic properties. Carefully and painstakingly he compiled his data, filling pages in his notebook with complicated equations. When there were too many blots or erasures on a sheet, he would tear it out, take a long breath, light a fresh cigar and begin again. His task was made easier by an invention of Eickenmeyer's called the magnetic bridge, a device which measures the magnetic value of a material as simply as one can measure a piece of paper with a ruler.

Although he was perfectly content with his life at the Mullers' and in the laboratory, Steinmetz missed the association of men of similar tastes. Recalling the many pleasant evenings spent with his fellow members of the Mathematics Society in university days, he had joined the American Institute of Electrical Engineers and the New York Mathematical Society. No matter how busy he was with the problem of the alternating current motor, he never missed a meeting of either group. At first he took little part in the discussions, preferring to sit unnoticed at the back of the hall while papers were read and defended by their authors. Then one night Professor Thorburn Reid of Columbia University, later to become Steinmetz' good friend and colleague in the General Electric Company, delivered a report on *The Armature Reaction of Alternators*. Karl leaped to his feet the minute the speaker stopped talking and heatedly criticized the theory presented as being incomplete. Reid challenged Steinmetz as making the topic of discussion too complicated, but some months later admitted he was wrong when Karl offered a paper covering Reid's theory more fully.

Attending these meetings was the only break Steinmetz took from his investigations into hysteresis. Page after page of his notebook was filled with mathematical formulae and

slowly the fact emerged that hysteresis increases as magnetism increases. More investigation followed and at last he
had the whole problem reduced to an "empirical formula"
—or a general rule based on observation and experience,
which he expressed in an algebraic symbol.

Steinmetz announced his "Law of Hysteresis" to the engineering profession in *The Electrical Engineer* of December 9, 1891. Trial and error methods in the building of alternating current motors now gave way to a sure scientific
procedure, for thanks to Karl Steinmetz, engineers now
knew how much electricity was needed to magnetize a given
piece of material in order to assure the necessary magnetic
current, and how much loss there would be under actual
working conditions. Another result of Steinmetz' work was
the improvement in the quality of electrical apparatus as
well as the reduction in weight of electric motors and in the
cost of operating them.

With the publication of his discovery, Karl Steinmetz became world-famous. Barely three years previously he had almost been sent back to Europe as an undesirable alien; now
he was the foremost electrical engineer on this side of the
Atlantic. On the evening of January 19, 1892, he braved a
raging storm and went to a meeting of the American Institute of Electrical Engineers to discuss his investigations. His
feet soaking wet, Steinmetz rolled his pants up to his knees,
and explained his experiments. Most of what he said was
not understood by his audience, even though it included
the most brilliant electrical engineers in the United States.
But everyone present appreciated the fact that the "Law of
Hysteresis" doomed the use of direct current except for a
few highly specialized purposes—alternating current would
provide the world's electrical energy in the future.

Yet Steinmetz was not finished with his investigations
into magnetism. There were still some minor questions that
nagged him, and he was determined to find the answers—so

Charles Proteus Steinmetz in an unusual pose—all dressed up in a new gray flannel suit

The more at ease Steinmetz, at Camp Mohawk with his radio

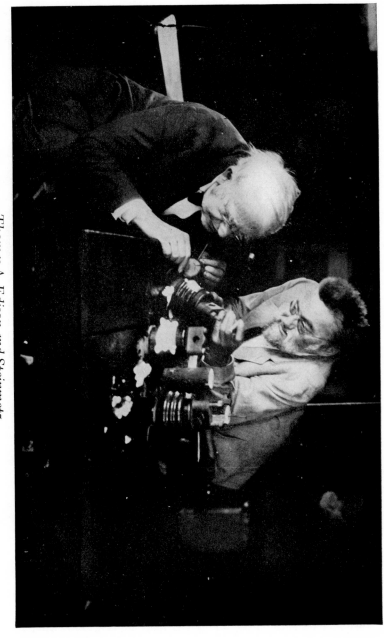

Thomas A. Edison and Steinmetz

Steinmetz in his canoe, "fishing" on the Mohawk River

TOP: *Steinmetz and Marconi, during the latter's visit to the Schenectady General Electric Works on June 26, 1922.* BOTTOM: *Dr. C. P. Steinmetz, J. W. Upp and E. B. Merriam*

Steinmetz examining the block of wood split by his lightning machine

he continued his research. By September, 1892, he had learned what he wanted to know and prepared another paper for presentation before the American Institute of Electrical Engineers. A capacity throng crowded into the auditorium to hear him speak, and loudly applauded when the chairman ended his introduction by saying, "His work in the past has been most important in its character, and this paper will fully support the reputation he has already earned." It did. In minute detail, Steinmetz explained to his listeners the amount of magnetism all known magnetic materials could carry and told of his experiments to find a perfect bar for use as the core of an alternating current motor. He admitted that, while he had found a combination of wrought iron and steel the best, he was not satisfied and suggested that additional experimentation be undertaken with cast steel.

The paper was warmly received and its author was given a rousing ovation when he was finished. *The Electrical Engineer* for October, 1892, commenting on the Steinmetz dissertation, summed up the feelings of the engineering profession: "He holds out to us the hope of our obtaining a full understanding of the phenomenon of magnetism in the near future." From Europe came cables of congratulation, and professional societies all over America honored the man who had made the use of alternating current motors practical. Steinmetz, naturally enough, was flattered by all this attention, but modestly pointed out that he could not have established the "Law of Hysteresis" and collated the other data if it had not been for Eickenmeyer's invention of the magnetic bridge.

Theoretically the motor Steinmetz built for Field as a result of all this study was perfect—it was the first alternating current motor to compensate for hysteresis loss. So on a Sunday afternoon, when there was little traffic—it would be ten years before daring men, driving "horseless carriages," would

stir up dust on New York streets—Eickenmeyer, Field and
Steinmetz attached the new motor to an old horse-car at the
Brooklyn car barns and tested it. The trial run was successful, but before the motor could be put into mass production, Field lost his interest in streetcar lines. Yet if he hadn't
gone to Eickenmeyer for help in constructing a streetcar motor, in all probability we would not have the widespread use
of alternating current today.

Eickenmeyer, who greatly appreciated the credit his brilliant assistant had given him for helping to develop the
"Law of Hysteresis," celebrated his assistant's achievement
by giving a dinner party. Dining with the Eickenmeyers was
no novelty to Karl, who had for months been a regular Sunday visitor at his employer's home, a large house known as
Seven Oaks. Sunday dinner at this spacious residence was
not a family affair. The manufacturer held open house for
his friends, and the cook never knew how many would sit
down at the table. Steinmetz had always been popular at
these weekly gatherings, but now he was honored as much
as old Robert Parkhill Getty, who could remember Yonkers
as a peaceful country village, with cows in every field, and a
pump in the middle of the square. Karl might spear a piece
of bread with his fork as the plate was passed, but everyone
at the table respected him for his scientific achievements
and ignored his eccentricities.

However, Steinmetz' greatest accomplishments were yet to
come. Nor was he to enjoy much longer the friendships of
the Eickenmeyer dining-room, the big brother relationship
with the Muller girls, and the familiar security of the laboratory at the plant. Tremendous changes were taking place in
the electrical industry, and Karl Steinmetz was to play an
important part in them.

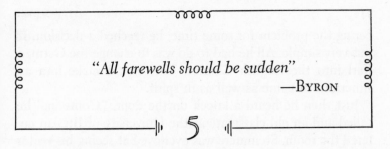

〳〳〳〳 IT WAS pay day at the Eickenmeyer plant. Karl stood in line in front of the cashier's window and when his turn came, took the envelope containing his salary, picked up a pen, signed the receipt required by the paymaster. As he did so, one of his fellow workers rudely leaned over his shoulder and read aloud as he wrote, "Karl August Rudolph Steinmetz."

"Now that's what I call a fine name for someone who is always talking about how American he is," jeered the paymaster. "Why, it's as German as it can be!"

Karl's face twisted into a frown, but he said nothing and returned to his work-table in the laboratory. Later in the day, he sat at his battered desk, doing the one duty he disliked—signing reports and requisitions for scientific material. As he wrote, he thought of the bantering conversation that morning in front of the cashier's cage. There was nothing Steinmetz wanted more than to be considered a true American. The death of his father two years before had severed the only strong tie with his old home. Suddenly, he reached a most important decision. If changing his name would help make him a better citizen of his adopted country, he would change it. There was only one difficulty, but it was a great one—what should he call himself? After pondering the problem for some time, he reached a decision. It was very simple. All he had to do was to change the German Karl into the English Charles. This would make him an American in name as well as in spirit.

Just then he heard a knock on the door. "Come in," he called and an old classmate at the University of Breslau entered the room. Steinmetz was overjoyed at seeing his visitor and plied him with one question after another. Had he been to a meeting of the Mathematics Society recently? Were all the old professors still teaching? What had become of Lux and all the other members of the Socialist Party?

"Wait a minute, please," pleaded the caller. "One question at a time!"

Steinmetz listened eagerly to the news from his native town. He was delighted to learn that the "foxes" still performed, and that the meals at Liechtenstein's were as delicious as ever. They spoke of his father, and the knowledge that some of his former instructors had also died saddened him. He was greatly impressed, however, to learn that his old astronomy professor, John Galle, was still actively engaged in celestial observations at the age of eighty-one. As for the fiery Lux, he continued to advocate a more democratic form of government for Germany, and had become one of the leading political reformers in Steinmetz' homeland.

It was almost dark when the two men finished talking. The visitor from overseas had to leave, and as he put on his hat and coat, he asked Charles if he would mind writing down the directions for reaching a chemical plant on the other side of New York City.

"Why, not at all," said Steinmetz, and pulling a pad of paper toward him, wrote down the requested information, and then, on the bottom of the sheet, he scrawled for the first time, "Charles Steinmetz."

"Thank you very much, Proteus," said the grateful caller.

"I won't have any trouble finding my way across the city to-morrow with these instructions in my hand. When are we going to . . ."

"Wait a minute," cried Steinmetz excitedly. "Give me back that paper! I just thought of something important. To be really American, I must have a middle name. You've suggested the perfect one!"

While talking, he was busy rewriting the directions. When he was finished, with a flourish he signed the name which was to become known from the rude settlements in the African jungle to the teeming cities of the civilized world: "Charles Proteus Steinmetz."

Absolutely content in the small laboratory of the Eicken-meyer plant, Steinmetz paid little attention to the news that the Edison Light Company, founded by Thomas Alva Edison, had announced its merger with the Thompson-Houston Electric Company of Lynn, Massachusetts, and had formed a new organization which was to be known as the General Electric Company.

"Just think, my boy," Eickenmeyer remarked one day, "Edison paid thirty-five million dollars for that plant in Lynn. The man is a genius and before he is through he will completely change the electrical industry. Why, it is less than six years ago, when Edison was dissatisfied with the excessively high tax rate in New York City, that he took over two empty factory buildings in Schenectady, in upstate New York, and moved the Edison Machine Works there. Now he has eight hundred people working for him! With this purchase of the Thompson-Houston plant, I tell you Thomas Edison is going to dominate the manufacturing of electrical apparatus!"

Steinmetz did not even look up from the experiment on which he was working. He had listened politely to his superior, but he was not interested in the formation of the General Electric Company. What difference did it make to him? Let Edison buy as many electrical companies as he wished and set up as many new factories as he wanted. Charles Proteus Steinmetz had far more important matters to consider. There was, for example, the problem of the transmission of alternating current from one point to another—how could it be done efficiently and cheaply? So he was quite indifferent to the news which was the main topic of conversation among those engaged in the field of electrical investigation and development.

Shortly after this conversation in the laboratory, a stranger was seen entering Eickenmeyer's private office, where he remained for several hours. Everyone in the plant wondered who he could be and what the subject of the conference was. Wild rumors flew from machine to machine. From one end of the factory to another, workers asked if anyone knew what the boss was talking about, and to whom? There were, of course, dozens of theories. Only Steinmetz continued his work, heedless of the meeting that had all the rest of the employees in suspense. At last Eickenmeyer threw open the door to his office, and sent a passing workman to the laboratory to get his assistant.

Annoyed at the interruption, Steinmetz quickly hobbled down the corridor and entered the office. He sat down in his usual chair beside Eickenmeyer's desk and looked inquiringly at his employer. "This gentleman is a representative of the General Electric Company," explained Eickenmeyer to the indifferent Charles. "He has, on orders from them, offered to buy my electrical patents and machinery for making electrical products. Frankly, the price they mention is an excellent one, and I have decided to sell. However, there is something else. General Electric wants you to come and work for them."

Steinmetz was stunned. Leave the Eickenmeyer plant! He had never thought of such a move. Why should he? His duties at the factory were very simple ones and had been reduced to a pleasant routine; and what was far more important, no matter what he wanted to do in the field of electrical experimentation, he was never questioned.

"A job with General Electric?" he asked. "I have one job. Why should I want another? I have absolutely no desire to work for any other firm but this." With that flat statement, he lurched to his feet and returned to his laboratory.

The representative from the General Electric Company followed him and asked if they could not discuss the matter further. "I have the authority," he began, "to offer you a larger salary than you are earning now. General Electric wants . . ."

"I don't care what General Electric wants," came the heated reply. "I only know what I want. I don't want to leave Eickenmeyer's. I refuse to discuss your offer. Now, sir, if you will please excuse me, I have work to do."

Eickenmeyer, who had listened to the conversation, threw his hands helplessly into the air, and pushed the General Electric man aside. Steinmetz, already deep in his experiment, had immediately forgotten all about the sale of the plant and the invitation to join Edison's company. "Look here, my boy," pleaded Eickenmeyer, "I don't want you to think that I want to get rid of you, for I don't. The thing for you to consider is this: working for a large organization like General Electric will enable you to carry on in a laboratory far more complete than anything either of us has ever seen. We couldn't afford one half as satisfactory here, even if we had a million dollars to spend equipping it with apparatus. With such implements and unlimited funds, who knows what electrical problems you might solve?"

This was the best possible argument. Dreaming of new discoveries, Steinmetz agreed to reconsider his absolute rejection of General Electric's proposition.

It was late in 1892 when E. Wilbur Rice, later to become president of the General Electric Company, arrived in Yon-

kers to supervise the final details of the purchase of the
Eickenmeyer patents and oversee the crating of certain machinery for shipment to Lynn. The directors of Rice's firm
had instructed him to talk to Steinmetz, and to offer the
discoverer of the "Law of Hysteresis" any necessary induce-
ment to join the research staff of their newly organized corporation. They were anxious to have the talents of the young
genius at their disposal—he was blazing the trail of electrical
development in this country, and they wanted to follow him.
Rice was determined to carry out his assignment.

Years later, he remembered his first meeting with the great
electrician and said, "I was startled, and somewhat disappointed by the strange sight of a small, frail body, sur-
mounted by a large head with long hair hanging to the
shoulders, clothed in an old cardigan jacket, cigar in mouth,
sitting cross-legged on a laboratory worktable!

"My disappointment was but momentary, and completely
disappeared the minute he began to talk. I instantly felt the
strange power of his piercing but kindly eyes, and as he continued, his enthusiasm, his earnestness, his clear conception
and marvelous grasp of engineering problems convinced me
that we had made a great find. I was delighted when, without a minute's hesitation, he accepted my suggestion that
he come with us."

The decision to leave the Eickenmeyer plant, the friendly
home of the Mullers and all his Yonkers associates was not
an easy one for Steinmetz. Mr. Rice might have thought
that there wasn't "a minute's hesitation," but the gifted engineer had spent many a sleepless night walking the floor,
debating whether or not he should change employers. It was
only the knowledge that he would be able to work in the
world's largest electrical laboratory that finally made him
decide to accept General Electric's proposition. It seemed to
the melancholy Charles Proteus Steinmetz that his entire
life had been spent in parting from friends and familiar sur-

roundings. First Breslau, then Zurich, and now Yonkers. Was he never to find a permanent home? It would have to be somewhere in America, there was nothing for him in Europe, now that his father was no longer living.

So with high hopes, early in 1893, Charles Steinmetz packed his meager belongings in a battered suitcase, carefully stowed his vast piles of calculations and books into dozens of boxes and took the train to Boston, where he made connections for Lynn. Before he left Yonkers, he went to the office of the *Yonkers Statesman* and inserted an advertisement in the issue of February, 1893. It read:

Leaving Yonkers, I wish herewith to say goodbye to all my friends.

CHARLES PROTEUS STEINMETZ
Lynn, Massachusetts.

⚑ ⚑ ⚑

Lynn is one of the oldest cities in the Bay State, having been founded in 1629, one year before the Puritans settled in Boston. The first smelting works in New England was established there in 1643. Early in the seventeenth century, the manufacture of women's shoes was begun, and it soon became the leading industry. When Steinmetz arrived, Lynn ranked second among the cities of the United States in the making of boots and shoes, and it was a teeming, thriving place.

It didn't take the newcomer long to find out how crowded Lynn was. For hours Steinmetz hobbled down one street after another, looking for accommodations in a rooming-house. Weary, hungry, and very lonesome, he was sorely tempted to go to the railroad station and take the first available train back to Yonkers and Eickenmeyer. Just as he was on the verge of giving up his exhausting search for a place to stay, he saw a grimy sign advertising rooms to rent above a small grocery store on the corner of Commercial and Common Streets. Even Steinmetz, who cared little for physical comfort, realized that the neighborhood was poverty-stricken, but he had no choice. He willingly paid his first week's rent in advance, returned to the railroad terminal and collected his belongings, which he transferred to his new lodgings. Then he fell across the uncomfortable bed, fatigued and very unhappy.

Early the next day he went to the General Electric plant and was immediately ushered into Mr. Rice's office. Rice, who had reported to his superiors that he had been greatly impressed with Steinmetz' originality and intellectual power, greeted the newcomer warmly and personally escorted him to the laboratory assigned to the calculating department. There the new employee was introduced to his chief, H. F. Parshall, who was in charge of the staff of ten outstanding engineers responsible for the task of solving all the mathematical problems that arose in the company's development of electrical power and energy. Parshall and his assistants made every effort to make Steinmetz feel that he was welcome. After some general conversation, the engineers went back to their work and Rice left. Parshall led Steinmetz to a desk and told him that this was where he would work, then took him for a tour of the laboratory.

As they inspected the various apparatuses, Parshall told Steinmetz how valuable the "Law of Hysteresis" had proved to the Lynn plant. "We're looking forward to having you in the department," he said. "If you want anything, just ask me or any of the others. You'll find this lab a very friendly place."

Immediately most of Steinmetz' fears and loneliness vanished. "Perhaps," he reassured himself, "Lynn won't be so unpleasant, after all Parshall seems to be as kindly a man as Eickenmeyer, and the engineers in the calculating department appear to be very sociable fellows. There's a good

chance I'll be just as content here as I was in Yonkers."
Turning to Parshall, Steinmetz said, "I'm ready for work.
What do you want me to do first?"

With a quick smile and a welcoming handshake, the head
of the calculating department replied, "Design a more practical and efficient transformer."

A transformer, as every boy who has ever owned a set of
electric trains knows, is a simple apparatus with no moving
parts, which is capable of changing electrical energy from
one electric pressure to another. Many have seen the outside
of one. The metal boxes on the top of utility poles are a
familiar form. The use of alternating current is impossible
without a transformer, and until a perfect one could be developed, the newly formed General Electric concern realized,
economical distribution of electricity was impossible. Steinmetz had long held the opinion that alternating current
could be sent from powerhouses through cables carrying high
voltage, for hundreds of miles from where it was generated,
if an effective transformer could be developed.

Electrical engineers had agreed for some time that the
transformers made by the firm of Osterheld and Eickenmeyer were the best in the country. Based on the pioneer
work of William Stanley, of Great Barrington, Massachusetts, who had built the first transformer, the Yonkers organization had designed and developed transformers capable
of converting alternating current from various pressures to
the one most suited for a required use. These ranged from
the extremely low voltage needed to ring a doorbell, to the
high voltage necessary in the electric welding of steel. In
fact, the outstanding reputation that the Eickenmeyer transformer had earned was one of the main reasons why the
General Electric Company had acquired the electrical machinery and patents of the famous hat manufacturer.

Steinmetz, of course, knew every detail of the Eickenmeyer technique, and had, for some time, been working to

improve transformers. It was obvious that the task of "stepping-up" voltage at the powerhouse and "stepping-it-down" at the point of use could be done by making a more efficient transformer. But how? What mathematical formula could be worked out to make the widespread use of alternating current possible? Unless such a method could be discovered, the long-distance transmission of electrical energy was absolutely impossible, and thousands of people could not enjoy its benefits, for direct current could not be transported very far from the place where it was generated.

This was the type of problem in which Steinmetz delighted. Joyously he set to work with notebook, logarithm tables, a jar of freshly sharpened pencils, and a pocket full of cigars. Some of the papers he had so carefully packed and brought from Yonkers were now invaluable to the mathematical genius as he filled page after page with shorthand notes. Steinmetz had been working on transformer theory ever since his establishment of the "Law of Hysteresis," realizing that his original investigations were of little value until alternating current was put into universal use. Unless electrical power could be received by the user at 110 volts, it had little commercial importance, so he had begun his investigations into the mystery of the transformer early in 1890, but now, after three years of research and study, he was no nearer a solution.

Weeks and months passed as Steinmetz toiled on the problem of designing a more efficient transformer. A lesser man would have admitted the assignment was far too difficult, but he was positive that mathematics would furnish the key that would solve the problem. Page after page of equations filled his notebook, but none of them presented the slightest clue toward finding the answer to the process he was seeking. "If calculating alternating current were only as easy as calculating direct current," he complained ruefully one day to Parshall, "how simple this job would be. Direct current is so elementary. It has direction and a value which can be measured with a meter. My difficulty is that alternating current has no definite direction and no value; its direction and value are constantly changing, making measuring its flow a terrifically complicated task. I'll find a mathematical solution to this problem, however—you just wait and see!"

Parshall was not the only one who waited. The entire electrical industry was marking time, waiting for someone to develop a means of mastering alternating current. There seemed little likelihood that this strange force could ever be controlled. Even Edison had come to the conclusion that alternating current would never be tamed to do the bidding of engineers. Researchers in the field frankly admitted that alternating current was dangerous to handle, while newspaper headline-writers scared their readers with screaming "banners" above their reports about the users of alternating current being electrocuted. Steinmetz paid no attention to the scholarly opinions of his associates or to the journalists, but continued to carry out his investigations and write down his equations. There had to be an answer somewhere, and once it was discovered, power plants would be able to send electrical energy thousands of miles across the countryside to those who could use it for turning the wheels of industry or making their homes more livable and attractive. Others might feel that whatever progress there could be in electrical development would come through the use of direct current, but not Charles Proteus Steinmetz. So he continued his seemingly useless and time-wasting experiments.

Then as the International Electrical Congress gathered in Chicago, Illinois, for its annual meeting, it was rumored in the electrical industry that Steinmetz of General Electric had a most important paper to read. He did. The directors of the Congress were greatly impressed with his modest statement that he had, at long last, reduced alternating current calculations to a "simple algebraic problem," and gladly allotted him an hour in which to explain to electrical engineers from all over the world the method he had developed to control this powerful force.

On the evening of Steinmetz' scheduled talk, outstanding electrical technicians representing private firms and governmental agencies crowded the hall. None of them really expected that the speaker would present a workable theory, but, after all, this was the man who had overcome the problem of hysteresis, so it wouldn't hurt to listen to him. The audience gasped with astonishment when they saw the bulky manuscript Steinmetz carried under his arm. It was over a foot thick! Their amazement turned to mental numbness as the dwarfed cripple continued to explain his formula of "The General Number." One by one the engineers left the auditorium. When the allotted hour was over, Steinmetz asked the chairman for an extension of time, and he was given ten more minutes. When that was used up, he requested, and was granted, ten additional minutes. At last he was forced to stop. Picking up his papers, he arranged them in a neat pile on the table, bundled them under his arm, smiled wistfully at the few remaining listeners who had tried in vain to follow his explanation and remarked, "Thank you, gentlemen, for listening to me. I hope you have found what I have had to say of interest. I only wish I had more time to continue my explanation. You see, I am but half way through my introduction!"

The engineers were definitely interested in what Steinmetz had said. The only difficulty was, they didn't understand one word of it! Even his fellow-workers in the calculating department of the General Electric plant in Lynn had trouble following his reasoning, and they had heard it many times. To most electrical engineers, the theory of "The General Number," or "The Complex Number," as it is sometimes called, was unintelligible. The very few who under-

stood it at all agreed that on paper the theory seemed flaw-
less. They had only one question. Was it workable?

It did not take long for Steinmetz to prove to his associates in the engineering profession that the theory of "The
General Number" was practical. He used it to design and
build a transformer that would work under all conditions,
and which was adaptable for every purpose. Now long-
distance transmission of electrical energy was assured, and
extensive electric systems could be established. Meanwhile,
the scientist had gathered together all his notes and had ex-
panded them into a manuscript three feet high, entitled
Theory and Calculation of Alternating Current Phenomena.
He asked the International Electrical Congress to publish
this work, along with the other papers which had been read
at the Chicago meeting of the organization. Unfortunately,
the Congress did not have enough money in its treasury to
pay for the printing of such a massive report. As a result,
Steinmetz' great discovery did not become available to engineers in book form until four years later, when a private
publisher issued the text. By that time the theory of "The
General Number" was accepted in every country in the
world that knew the benefits of electricity. The high voltage
lines that stretched between poles marching up and down
the earth's surface were proof of this—and Steinmetz' three
volume work sold well. Even today, they are considered absolutely necessary for any good engineering library, and
workers in the field consult modern revised editions frequently.

Not yet thirty years old, Charles Proteus Steinmetz had
solved two major problems in the development of the generation and distribution of electricity. Internationally famous, he modestly continued his work in the calculating
department of the Lynn Division of General Electric. Everyone there recognized him now, although for months he was
unknown outside the laboratory, except to a few engineers

who had met him in the course of routine conferences.

In fact, until his development of the theory of "The General Number," Steinmetz was so inconspicuous a person at the works that he almost starved to death! A short time after he joined the company, one of his associates in the calculating department, concerned with Steinmetz' appearance, asked, "What's the matter with you, Charles? Why, you're getting as thin as a piece of copper wire and you look as if you have received a violent electric shock."

At first Steinmetz would not admit anything was wrong. Finally, after a great deal of hesitation, he explained his difficulty. He had not received a single cent of salary since coming to Lynn! As a result, he had been unable to pay his room rent or to buy food. Parshall was immediately informed of the situation and rushed to the accounting office to demand an explanation. A check of the records showed that, through a clerical error, Steinmetz' name had never been placed on the payroll! The matter was adjusted at once, and Charles, his pockets bulging with back pay, hastened home to settle his bills and eat his first complete meal in several weeks.

Now that alternating current had been controlled, Steinmetz was ready to undertake another assignment. Before he could engage in any complicated research in the laboratory, however, he was drafted to do the routine mathematical work on designs for generators to be used to convert the tremendous water power at Niagara Falls into electricity. These generators were totally different from any that General Electric had ever built before, and the firm was most anxious to get the contract. Steinmetz' work was satisfactory, but a competitor received the order. Years later, General Electric did get an order to supply machinery for the electrical power project at the Falls, and Steinmetz' original designs were used.

In May, 1893, an economic depression swept the United

States and a panic resulted. Banks and brokerage houses failed by the hundreds and business throughout the nation drifted to a halt. No city was hit worse than Lynn. One by one, the shoe factories were closed and long queues of unemployed men stood patiently in line to receive donations of bread and milk for their children. In the General Electric plant, only one hundred vital workers were kept on the payroll, and they got only six days of work a month. Parshall's calculating department was cut to three men. One of them was Steinmetz. There was nothing for these experts to do, so the engineers idled in the silent laboratory for hours, smoking, telling stories, and playing jokes on one another. In more serious moments they would sit silently at their desks and wonder how long they would continue to draw their salaries, or which one of them would be the next to be fired.

Steinmetz knew that he was not going to be discharged when the firm sent him to the World's Columbian Exposition in Chicago. This display of industry, science and art, from every nation in the world, was the first "World's Fair" to be held in the United States. Manufacturers from many lands had sent their products to be displayed, in order to show them to the general public and win awards for excellence. Included in the exhibition were many foreign electrical devices, and General Electric wanted Steinmetz to report on any worth-while engineering developments their rivals had made. He wandered from building to building, enjoying the excitement, crowds, music and exhibits, but found nothing of value to report to his employers. To Steinmetz, the most enjoyable part of the whole Chicago trip was the opportunity to meet and talk with electrical experts he had not seen since his stay in Yonkers as Eickenmeyer's assistant.

One day, while walking through an exhibition hall, he was heartily greeted by his former helper at the Eickenmeyer plant, the young German mechanic Tischendorfer, for whom

Steinmetz and Field had painstakingly prepared the cigar soaked in linseed oil. Tischendorfer had gone back to Germany shortly after his employer had sold out his electrical patents and machinery to General Electric, and was at the Columbian Exposition displaying a searchlight for a European firm.

For a few minutes Steinmetz stood in front of the booth, talking to his old friend. Suddenly the latter said, "*Herr* Steinmetz, we don't have to stand here talking. Come, follow me." Wonderingly, Charles followed the young man to the back of the booth. Tischendorfer opened a door and led him down a narrow flight of stairs to the cellar. Here the clever youth had fitted up a most comfortable room in which he could entertain his friends, and had, by tapping the electric light wires of a neighboring exhibitor, flooded the room with light!

Steinmetz chuckled as his fellow German explained how he had rigged up the lights at no expense to himself or his firm. It was the kind of joke the engineer appreciated and he began to laugh. Then a thought struck him—was it possible that his one-time assistant had known that the cigar had been doctored and had turned the tables on Field and himself by pretending it was a pleasing smoke? Any chap whose sense of humor would lead him to tap someone else's electric supply line very well might—Steinmetz was just about to ask if Tischendorfer had or had not known that the cigar had been soaked in linseed oil, when a party of men came tramping down the stairs. Most of them were old New York friends of Charles and they laughed when he told them how he had been trudging from exhibition hall to exhibition hall, looking for them.

"Steinmetz, you sit right where you are," they told him. "Don't move, and sooner or later you'll see everyone in the electrical engineering game in this room."

Charles took their advice and during the rest of his stay

in Chicago, he spent most of his time in the cool, comfortable and cosy secret meeting place underneath the German searchlight display. Steinmetz had a wonderful time talking to fellow workers in the field of electrical investigation from all parts of the civilized world, and the time to return to Lynn and the empty plant came all too soon. When he thought of his dreary boarding house, Charles shuddered with disgust. As the train puffed East, he made plans to find living quarters in a more respectable neighborhood.

Steinmetz needn't have worried about more comfortable accommodations, or even about living in Lynn. On reporting to the plant, he was told that the company was transferring the operations of the calculating department to Schenectady, New York. So, once again, Charles Proteus Steinmetz was being forced to carry his genius and his baggage to a new home. Although he did not know it, this was the last move he was to make, and the happiest years of his life were still before him.

> *"The mathematician has reached the highest rung on the ladder of human thought"*
> —HAVELOCK ELLIS

6

"COME IN," called Eickenmeyer in answer to a loud knock on his office door. As it opened, he looked up from the papers on which he was working, jumped quickly to his feet and roared delightedly, "Steinmetz! Isn't this wonderful? Don't stand there, man. Come in and sit down! Here, take your old chair. It seems twenty years since you last sat beside this desk. Oh, but I've missed you, my friend, and the long talks we used to have in the laboratory. You'd laugh if you could hear me bragging that the Steinmetz who is the talk of the electrical industry was once my assistant, but I am so proud of the fact that you started your career in this plant, that I—enough of this chatter, though. Tell me, why aren't you in Lynn? There is nothing wrong, I hope."

"Everything is perfect," Steinmetz assured his former employer as he sat down. "I have come to Yonkers to spend the Christmas holiday season with my old friends. Between the lack of orders because of the depression, and waiting for the calculating department to be transferred to the Schenectady works the first of the year, there is absolutely nothing to do at the plant. So, remembering that I haven't had a vacation since I came to America, I decided that this was the best possible time to take one, and here I am!"

"You'll stay with me, of course," Eickenmeyer declared. "Oh, I know you'll want to spend a night or two with the Mullers, but the rest of the time you've got a room at Seven Oaks. Now, tell me all the news."

Between such happy reunions and much gay talk, Christmas week of 1893 passed all too quickly for Steinmetz. Before he realized it, the time came for him to leave for Schenectady. Just before the New Year he boarded a train for upper New York State and his new home. The move did not frighten him nearly so much as the others he had made. This time he was making the change in the company of a group of men he knew and liked. Moreover, he would not be a stranger when he arrived at the General Electric works. Modest as he was, Charles knew that everyone there had heard of him.

Legend states that Schenectady was once the location of the chief village of the Mohawk Indians. It was purchased from the tribe by Arendt Van Curler in 1661. The price paid was "600 hands of good Whyte Wampum, six Koates of Duffels, 30 Barres of Lead and Nine Bagges of Powder." For a great many years the settlement was the richest in the colony, becoming a lively river port with the opening of the Northwest. When De Witt Clinton built the Erie Canal, new wealth came to the community, and boat building developed into a leading industry. Schenectady grew in importance when, in 1831, it became the terminal point of the first steam railroad in New York State, and one of the largest locomotive works in the world was established there.

Yet, despite the bustling activity of the city on the Mohawk, there was much that reminded Steinmetz of Breslau. As he walked along the tree-shaded streets, lined with seventeenth-century houses, searching for lodgings, he could imagine, without effort, that he was in his native city. The quaint Dutch architecture recalled almost forgotten memories, and the Mohawk River, as it wound by the city on its way to join the Hudson, looked very much like the Oder. Standing on the bank of the Erie Canal, Steinmetz watched the sturdy mules trudging along the dusty towpath, straining against the traces as they drew heavily loaded barges, and he observed with keen professional interest the workings of the locks. He was sure that once he had found a place to stay, he was going to be happy in this city, which in so many ways reminded him of his former home.

After searching unsuccessfully for some time for the type of accommodations he desired, and hating the thought of living alone, Steinmetz suggested to a fellow engineer at the General Electric works, Ernst Berg, that they take an apartment together. Berg readily agreed, and the two set up housekeeping on Washington Avenue, near the plant. Now that Steinmetz had a place to live and—what was just as important to him—someone to live with, he was ready to go to work.

His first assignment was one of the most difficult he ever received in his entire career. Ordered to explain the theory of "The General Number" to the engineering staff of the Schenectady division of General Electric, he set up a classroom and turned teacher. His method of making calculations with alternating current was simple enough to Steinmetz, but terribly complicated to everyone else. So, despite the fact that the pupils in his classroom included the most brilliant engineering minds in the United States, it was necessary for him to repeat his explanation of the theory over and over again. Patiently and slowly he would present his facts, outlining every step in detail, pause and ask, "Has anyone a question?"

Every member of the class had one. They were all the same. How did one use the theory of "The General Number" in calculating the direction and value of alternating current? Lighting a fresh cigar, Steinmetz would smile encouragingly at his students and begin his explanation all over again. At a meeting of the class, one of the members, embarrassed at his inability to grasp the theory, apologized for "asking so many foolish questions."

Steinmetz lifted a hand in angry protest and exclaimed heatedly: "There are no foolish questions. No man becomes a fool until he stops asking questions. The science of education is the science of helping people find out what they want to know. Now, let's go over the whole subject once more."

In time the theory was more or less understood, and Steinmetz' pupils returned to their drawing boards and laboratories. Using their newly acquired knowledge, the engineers developed fresh methods of bringing power and light to the homes, farms and factories of America. Often while working on a new design, they would find the necessary calculations too difficult, and go to Steinmetz for help. He always gave it to them willingly, telling them to come to him any time he could be of service. So whenever engineers in any department of the General Electric plant were baffled by seemingly impossible mathematical problems, they would lay them before Steinmetz, confident that he would solve them. They were never disappointed.

One day, after many weary and tiresome hours of unproductive figuring, a group of engineers came into the calculating department. Steinmetz greeted them and asked what they wanted. Their spokesman frankly admitted that they had worked unsuccessfully on a problem and were no nearer an answer than when they had started. "Would you please help us?" he asked.

"Certainly, if I can, gentlemen," came the prompt reply. "Tell me, what is your difficulty?"

"What we wish to know," said the leader of the delegation, "is the cubic content of the metal which is removed from a cylindrical rod two inches in diameter when a two-inch hole is bored through the rod separating it into two pieces."

To the stunned amazement of his visitors, Steinmetz did not sit down at his battered desk and begin to figure. They looked at each other in astonishment. Should they stay or leave? Steinmetz said nothing, reached into his pocket, stuck a fresh cigar into his mouth, lit it and wrinkled his gnome-like face into a smoke-wreathed scowl. Then, after a moment's silence, he grinned broadly and said between puffs, "I think I have it, gentlemen. Yes, I am sure of it. The answer is 5.33 cubic inches. Is there anything else?"

No, there was nothing else, excepting their dumbfounded admiration for the marvelous mathematical skill of the dwarf who worked in the calculating department. Most of the engineers had once heard Ernst Berg assert that "Steinmetz can do equations in his head that ordinary men can't do on paper," but they hadn't believed it. Now they did. In fact, they were absolutely sure that there was no mathematical problem that he couldn't solve. Look at the ease with which he had answered their puzzling question—it should have taken him hours and reams of paper before he figured out the answer—but he had done it in his head in less than a minute!

Once Steinmetz had graduated his students in the theory of "The General Number," he again turned his inventive genius and mathematical skill to the mysteries of alternating current. His investigations in this field were to continue all his life, resulting in patents covering more than fifty types of electrical apparatus. Meanwhile, Parshall, his immediate superior at the plant, was sent to England by the General Electric Company to supervise the organization of the calculating department of the British division. At the time, it was thought that he would remain overseas for only a short time. However, he decided to stay in England and eventually became one of the most important figures in that nation's electrical industry. The officials of the Schenectady works wasted no time in choosing his successor; Steinmetz was placed in charge of the calculating department the same day that the news came that Parshall was not going to return to America.

Before he assumed his new position, Steinmetz took a few days off and went to Yonkers on a most important errand. Five years had passed since he had taken out his first papers, and now he was eligible to become a full citizen of the United States. Swearing allegiance to his adopted country was far more important to him than assuming the full responsibility of the calculating department and enjoying the raise in salary that went with the promotion. So he went to Yonkers, appeared before a Federal judge, answered pertinent questions dealing with the history and constitution of America, and walked out of the courtroom a citizen of the United States, far more proud than he had been about the high honors given him for his two great electrical discoveries.

No foreign-born citizen had a greater love for America than did Charles Proteus Steinmetz. His youthful dreams of a world in which all men had an equal opportunity to achieve fame and fortune could come true here. He himself was proof of this. His deep affection for his country is best illustrated by a letter he wrote within six months of becoming a full naturalized American citizen. It was written to Eskil Berg, brother of his roommate and associate at the General Electric plant, Ernst Berg. For some time Eskil, who was also an engineer, had been writing to his brother, saying that he was seriously thinking of leaving his native Sweden to seek his fortune in the United States. One evening Ernst handed Steinmetz a letter from Eskil which had arrived in the mail that morning and inquired, "What do you think he should do, Charles? I think he should come over, don't you?"

Glancing at the letter, Steinmetz replied, "I certainly do. In fact, I'll write him a note and tell him so. After all, I came to America with no brother waiting on the dock to give me shelter and help in finding a job, or to show me the way I should act. Anyone can succeed in this country. There's no reason why he should hesitate—why, he can get a job right here in Schenectady."

At the plant the next morning, Steinmetz sat down and wrote to Eskil Berg before he did anything else. After reporting what was happening in the electrical industry in America and the many opportunities that awaited a trained engineer here, he urged Berg to make immediate preparations to leave Sweden. In closing, he wrote: "Now the matter is this: come over at once, without wasting any more time in Europe. There is nothing to be got there, everything here. You had better start with the idea that you will never go back except for a visit. I never saw a sensible man who has lived in America a few years who was willing to go back to Europe to stay. By the way, you will have to work here, and a good deal of it, but there is plenty of time left to have a good time, so do come over at once!"

As engineer in charge of the calculating department, Steinmetz was head of a staff of five men. All of his assistants were exceptionally gifted individuals, but often when confronted with a complex problem, they would be forced to spend hours poring over reference books or filling sheets of paper with equations, seeking a solution. Their chief would watch them for a while and then ask diffidently, "Can I help you chaps?" Sighing with relief, the staff (which had been longing to hear those words) would tell Steinmetz their difficulty, and usually without any hesitation, he would rattle off the mathematical formulae for which his assistants had been searching in vain.

He was the most lenient of superiors, never giving his underlings an order. In fact, he regularly would do himself the routine tasks that, as head of the calculating department, he should have assigned to others. Steinmetz thought that his men should be as free as he wanted to be, and in the four years that he headed the calculating division he never interfered with any investigation undertaken by members of his group. He was, however, always willing and ready to help them in any way he could.

About 1897 Steinmetz and Berg moved to a sprawling house on the corner of Liberty and College Streets. It was just the place they had been looking for, with plenty of room, a large stable and a spacious yard. Their house soon became the gathering ground for all the young engineers at the works. One of these who had majored in English literature at college, in addition to studying technical subjects, christened the place "Liberty Hall," after the house of Squire Hardcastle in Oliver Goldsmith's classic comedy, *She Stoops to Conquer*. In the play, the Squire's residence is, through a series of humorous errors, mistaken for an inn when he tells two strangers, "This is Liberty Hall, gentlemen; you may do just as you please here."

"Liberty Hall" it was. The hard-working scientists welcomed the chance to throw over their heavy responsibilities and enjoy themselves in pleasant surroundings. They would meet early and stay until very late, thoroughly happy in the genial company of the man who, during working hours, was held in awed respect. Ernst Berg has left a graphic and vivid picture of the activities at "Liberty Hall" in a manuscript now in the files of the Alumni Office of Union College: "As I look back on those times, it seems extraordinary that so much real work was done because we played so much. While some years older than the group of young student engineers with whom he associated, Steinmetz was, in reality, the most playful of us all, and one of the chief plotters of our numerous activities. Our mischief took all kinds of forms. Sometimes we would be busy at night shifting signs, so that in the morning the dispenser of beer would find a dry-goods sign over his door and vice versa. We had all kinds of races on the Mohawk. A swimming race was our chief sport. I recall one when we went swimming dressed in frockcoats and silk hats. Then we had sailing, rowing and canoe races very frequently, and Steinmetz was the starter and official recorder.

"During the summer months we frequently took long bicycle excursions—once in a while as far as Lake George, sixty-five miles away. Steinmetz was usually trailing behind a mile or two, but always caught up at the end. During the autumn, he often joined us in our duck hunting, although he himself never did any actual hunting. He was, however, a fair rifle shot.

"Every few weeks we had a small dance at our house, and Steinmetz would usually pick out the prettiest girl and, with her, watch our antics in the hall from the staircase. He had an eye for beauty and enjoyed the company of girls quite as much as we did."

ΓΓΓ

Gifted at once with the cool head of an engineer and the bold imagination of an artist; concerned only with the achievement of results, Steinmetz, the most democratic of men, was utterly lacking in all the traits of effective leadership. He found it simply impossible to assign work to his assistants and to maintain a constant check on their output. Moreover, he disliked the routine paper work that went with the directorship of the calculating department; all he wanted was to conduct experiments in the laboratory. His attitude toward his helpers and the all-too-frequent waiting for vital reports that he carelessly buried under personal papers on his littered desk were most annoying to the management of General Electric.

All of the plant officials fully realized that Steinmetz, the little wizard of electricity, was by far the most valuable member of their research staff, but they simply could not tolerate the gross inefficiency of the department under his direction. After one particularly important report was "lost" for several days while he worked on a perplexing problem of high-voltage power transmission, the directors of the General Electric Company decided that, much as they regretted the step, they would have to discharge Steinmetz.

Determined to get their unpleasant task over as quickly as possible, two of the directors went to the calculating department laboratory. Steinmetz was not there. While they were waiting, the pair heard one of the engineers say to another, "I don't think that it is possible to reduce this to a mathematical formula. There's only one thing we can do—we'll lay our problem before the 'Supreme Court.' "

Just then Steinmetz walked into the room. He did not see the men who had come to fire him and stopped to speak to his confused associates. They told him that they were absolutely stumped. Their chief bent over the laboratory work-table on which they had spread their calculations, picked up a pencil and looked at the problem. "If you will put your y where you now have your x and place x in place of your y, you'll be perfectly all right," he told his assistants after a minute's intense concentration.

The directors looked at each other. This was the man they were planning to discharge! What was it the engineers had called him? The "Supreme Court"? That was the solution! Relieve Steinmetz of the routine work expected of him as head of the calculating department and let him do nothing but experiment and find the mathematical solutions to the complicated problems which baffled his associates. So, without saying anything to him, or even taking the title of head of the division away from him, they gradually relieved him of most of his former duties, with the result that the necessary reports were always finished on time and available when wanted. Now Steinmetz was free to follow any line of electrical investigation he wished and act as the "Supreme Court" when other staff members required help. As consulting engineer for the entire plant, Steinmetz was given a fully equipped laboratory of his own, and an unlimited expense account with which to buy materials and to build apparatus. This arrangement proved ideal for both the scientist and the firm that employed him.

In the meantime, Eskil Berg had taken Steinmetz' friendly advice and had left Sweden to come to America. His qualifications as an engineer were excellent and he had no difficulty in securing a position with General Electric. Eskil, as a matter of course, became a permanent resident of "Liberty Hall." The young Swede soon became one of the most popular members of the lively group who used the house as a meeting place. Although he could give Steinmetz keen competition in a chess game, he was an active young fellow, full of fun and very fond of animals. Steinmetz, who delighted in jokes and the company of pets, considered him an ideal companion and spent many hours with him, engaged in building pens in the back yard to house a private menagerie. The inhabitants of "Liberty Hall" never took a bicycle trip through the countryside, or a boating trip on the Mohawk, without bringing back an animal or two to add to their zoological garden. Soon the back yard of their house looked like a circus. Almost everyone in Schenectady had a horse or a dog, but only the Bergs and Steinmetz could point proudly to a collection of raccoons, skunks, woodchucks, snakes and rabbits. While the horse remained in his roomy stall, the other animals roamed and hopped through the house without any fear. Visitors became accustomed to the routine of pushing a snoring raccoon off a chair before they could sit down.

Steinmetz' favorite pets were two crows, which had been found when fledglings by a neighbor and given to him. Schenectady folk were always bringing him animals of one type or another for the zoo at "Liberty Hall," but John and Mary, as he named the two birds, were his special interest. Through patience and kindness, he had tamed the pair so well that it was not necessary to keep them in cages. They were allowed to fly freely around the city. This freedom was thoroughly enjoyed by John and Mary—but not by the residents of the neighborhood! The birds, like all crows, were fascinated by anything shiny and they would fly into open windows and steal watches, keys, scissors, pieces of jewelry and buttons. If they were caught in their thievery, their victims could get back the loot by shouting at them, for the frightened birds would drop what they had stolen and fly erratically to the safety of "Liberty Hall." Often, however, John and Mary would do their pillaging early in the morning, before their victims were awake, and carry their plunder back to their roost. When this happened, Steinmetz would wait patiently for a visit from an irate neighbor, hand over what his pets had stolen, and apologize for their perfidy.

John and Mary were always in a near-by tree when Steinmetz came home from the plant, and would caw excitedly when he entered the yard. He would wave at them, whistle loudly and the birds would swoop down and come to him. If he were on his bicycle, they would perch on the handlebars and ride to the stable with their owner. When Steinmetz was walking, they would light on his head and shoulders, and remain there as he entered the house.

One day the scientist read a scholarly article by Ernest Thompson Seton in which the world-famous naturalist stated that crows had a definite language and listed some of their "words." Steinmetz devoted an evening to memorizing this vocabulary and practicing the various calls. From then on he would sit at his bedroom window for hours, carrying on a "conversation" with John and Mary as they strutted back and forth on the window-sill. The crows would answer him

and Steinmetz insisted despite the scoffing of the Bergs, that
the birds and he understood each other perfectly. This happy
association came to a sad conclusion when one of the crows
was killed by a prowling raccoon, and the other soon died
of grief. The broken-hearted Steinmetz had the birds stuffed
and kept them all his life.

When not tending to his many pets, most of the engineer's leisure time was spent in experimenting in the well-
equipped laboratory he had set up in his room. Before long
he decided that the place was not large enough, nor completely furnished to do the advanced type of investigation
he wished to conduct, so he announced his intention of converting a section of the stable attached to "Liberty Hall"
into a more adequate laboratory. The Bergs agreed that the
proposed move was an excellent one, and assured him they
would gladly help to set up the scientific apparatus in its
new location. They took great care to hide their delight at
their roommate's plan, for it was the best news they had
heard in months. Although the Bergs were engineers and
quite accustomed to acrid laboratory smells, they were weary
of the overwhelming stench that steeped all over the house
from their companion's room, as he mixed acids and burned
out the wires on electric motors by deliberately overloading
them. In fact, it is extremely doubtful if even patient *Grossmutter* Steinmetz could have put up with the stains and
burns her grandson made on the floor and furniture as he
carried on his adult experiments!

There was no doubt about it, Charles Proteus Steinmetz
was something of a problem to his roommates. Often, pre-
occupied with his work at the General Electric plant, he
would start to leave the house incompletely dressed, and one
of the Bergs would have to send him back for the missing
clothing. Then, too, he might or might not appear at the
table at mealtime, to the intense annoyance of the cook,
who threatened weekly to quit because "her cooking wasn't

appreciated." And it took both Bergs an entire evening of soothing assurances to keep her from walking out of "Liberty Hall" the night one of the raccoons stole her carefully prepared dinner off the dining-room table! To be sure, after their frantic urging, she had agreed to stay, but made it plain that if "Mr. Steinmetz didn't stop filling the house with those horrible smells and nasty smoke and critters," she would leave. The brothers, therefore, gave Steinmetz' plan to set up his laboratory in the stable their full co-operation. Nothing, thought the Bergs, could be much worse than having to eat their own cooking—except to be forced to sit down to a meal prepared by Steinmetz! The laboratory was soon set up and the oblivious experimenter, the Bergs, and the cook were all happy.

Soon, however, there was another problem which demanded attention. The scientist's teeth were causing him a great deal of pain, but he refused to go to a dentist. "I doubt," Ernst Berg once wrote, "that even at twenty-five he had a single tooth that was not decayed. His was a good-looking head except for the teeth which had been neglected since childhood. Yet he got along with them. I tried vainly to persuade him to go to the dentist and get a set of false teeth, but he was afraid of taking gas." The reason for Steinmetz' fear of gas is unknown, but it is entirely possible that, even at this early date, he had been warned by a doctor that his heart was not as strong as it should be, and kept this information to himself.

Steinmetz rarely spent any money on personal needs, except for cigars and an occasional suit of clothes. The latter purchase he actually had to be forced to make. His gray flannel suits were always cut from the same material and made in the same style. New suits soon looked like the oldest ones in his closet, for he would carelessly wear them while experimenting, and never thought of having them cleaned and pressed. Nor could any tailor make his twisted body look attractive. "His legs seemed long in proportion to his height, and the waistline was so distorted that to keep the trousers in proper place was always a problem and required constant attention."

There was only one thing in which Steinmetz indulged himself. That was the conservatory which he had erected near his stable-laboratory. Malformed himself, he delighted in the outlandish, weird and strange shapes of cacti, and grew hundreds of species in pots and beds. Yet he also had a great love of beauty, and expressed it by raising vividly colored orchids. Buying plants and heating the conservatory to tropical temperatures when the cold winds roared down the Mohawk Valley from the Rotterdam Hills took most of his surplus salary, but he did not regret a single penny. Money was something to which he paid very little attention. Give him a place to sleep, one simple meal a day, a pocketful of cigars, a pair of baggy pants and a fully equipped laboratory, and his wants were satisfied.

Between his work at the General Electric plant, his investigations in the laboratory attached to "Liberty Hall," his activities in the conservatory and the care of his pets, Steinmetz was the busiest of men. However, no matter how occupied he was, he always found time to act as a kindly guide whenever a group of school children came to the house and asked to be shown the animals. To the rest of the world Steinmetz might be the mathematical genius who was, more than anyone else, responsible for the truly miraculous advance in electrical engineering, but to the youngsters of Schenectady he was "that nice man who has so many animals."

In the winter of 1895–1896, the carefree life of "Liberty Hall" was brought to an abrupt halt when Clara, Steinmetz' half sister, arrived from Germany. She came to Schenectady "to visit" and before long had established herself as housekeeper. Her open disapproval of the way her brother and the Bergs conducted themselves was never so pointed as when, on opening a bill from the butcher, she angrily snorted, "What a household! Your meat bill for your pets is larger than for yourselves! What kind of way to run a house is that?"

The trio said nothing, but something had to be done. Clara, with her insistence upon careful accounts, spotless housekeeping and regular hours, had completely changed the atmosphere of "Liberty Hall." In fact, now there was no liberty! Naturally enough, the Bergs looked to Steinmetz to think of a plan to get rid of the unwelcome guest. After all, Clara was his sister. He loved her, but he agreed with his roommates that her criticism of their way of living could not be tolerated. For days he thought of various ways to force Clara to leave without causing a breach in their relations. Every plot he devised he talked over with the Bergs, but they found a flaw in one after another. Finally, they agreed on an ideal scheme. One night at dinner, Ernst Berg looked across the table at Clara and solicitously asked, "Don't you feel well? Your face appears to be quite flushed."

Clara, who was perfectly well, looked at her questioner in amazement. Before she had time to reply, her brother and Eskil also expressed their concern over her appearance and suggested that she go to bed immediately. Convinced against her will that she was ill, the bewildered woman went to her room. The next morning, the trio stood at the side of her bed, and woefully shook their heads. There was no doubt about it, they assured her, she was suffering from scarlet fever! After some talk, the men "remembered" that in cases of communicable disease, the occupants of the house were always placed in quarantine. None of them could be spared from their duties at General Electric—they were sure Clara would understand if they left her before the doctor arrived and placed everyone under confinement. With hasty good-bys, the conspirators rushed out of the room.

Left alone, Clara Steinmetz lay in bed, confused and fearful. She felt there was nothing wrong with her; and she was sure she had no temperature, but after all Charles had studied medicine. Perhaps she was sick! Then suddenly she saw through the plot, packed her bags in amused anger, and took the next train for New York City, where she became a familiar sight in the art galleries. Clara was a very competent portrait painter, and once painted an excellent likeness of her brother.

With Clara gone, the Bergs and Steinmetz went back to their normal, gay way of living. That spring they formed the "Mohawk River Aerial Navigation, Transportation, and Exploration Company, Unlimited." The unlimited in the title of their organization meant that anyone who had the two dollars necessary for the initiation fee was welcome to join! Most of the engineers at the General Electric plant became charter members and enthusiastically went to work turning out the product which the company had been formed to manufacture—gliders. This group was, incidentally, the first gliding club in the United States. Despite the social aspects of the association, Steinmetz had serious plans to market their aircraft, but unfortunately, none of them worked. It was not until the outbreak of World War II that aviation engineers saw the value of gliders to carry men and supplies to otherwise inaccessible places, but Steinmetz' imaginative genius had sensed their possibilities years earlier.

Those members of the "Mohawk River Aerial Navigation, Transportation, and Exploration Company, Unlimited" who had failed to attend one of the meetings of the organization held in Hoffmans, a town just outside of Schenectady, gasped with astonishment when Steinmetz showed them a picture of one of the gliders in the air. At last, they were going to make their fortunes! Then one of the absentees remembered that at every meeting Steinmetz had been actively engaged with his camera, and realized that he was playing a joke on his fellow club members. By means of clever trick photography he had produced a picture of a soaring glider!

Another club in which Steinmetz played a very active part was also composed of a group of his associates at the plant. They met every Saturday at "Liberty Hall." The high-sounding name of this organization was "The Society for the Equalization of Engineers' Salaries." Its title was most misleading; the members met, not to discuss methods and plans by which they could get larger pay checks, but to play cards. Steinmetz' mathematical mind controlled his card playing, and he would never go against the odds. As a matter of fact, he didn't care particularly if he won or not, but only joined in the games because he enjoyed the company of the other players and feared that, if the host sat on the sidelines, the group would meet somewhere else.

Not all of Steinmetz' social activities were confined to meetings with his fellow workers, although he enjoyed their company the most. The Krugers, who lived on Liberty Street, were frequent visitors in his house, having met him through his friendship with their two children, Carl and Gretchen. In the fall of 1900, when Eskil Berg left "Liberty Hall" to set up his own apartment, and was followed soon after by Ernst, Steinmetz became very friendly with the Krugers. Although he found plenty to do working in his laboratory, as well as caring for his plants and pets, he was lonely at mealtimes and got into the habit of eating with his neighbors. During this period, Clara came to see him several times and spent most of her visit cleaning house. He saw little of her, as he was spending every available minute in his laboratory, working on a very complicated experiment.

Then one night the stable-laboratory burned down. The cause of the blaze was most likely an overheated wire and definitely Steinmetz' fault. Without the prompt and efficient work of the Schenectady Fire Department, the house would have been destroyed as well. The landlord threatened to sue for damages, but the scientist paid little attention to his ominous statements. "Let him sue," he told the Krugers one night at the dinner table. "I don't care. I really should sue him for not owning a fireproof stable. What if he does collect for his loss? It is a minor one. I'm the person who has suffered the most. My scientific equipment is ruined and the valuable notes I had on my desk are completely destroyed. The stable can be rebuilt, but where am I going to get equipment to replace what I've lost, and who is going to supply copies of my lost calculations?"

When Steinmetz tried to explain to his landlord that he thought the loss of its contents was much worse than the destruction of the stable itself, the situation became even more unpleasant. The landlord was furious at his tenant's attitude that his troubles were the greater, while Steinmetz was enraged that the man failed to appreciate what the burning of the laboratory apparatus and notebooks meant. The whole affair came to a satisfactory conclusion, however, when General Electric entered the argument and offered to pay for the ruined stable and to equip another workshop for its chief consulting engineer. This generous help was thankfully accepted.

Now Steinmetz had only the problem of finding a place to erect his new laboratory. He decided to build a house at the same time, drawing up the plans himself so as to include the features he considered necessary. Then, with a pocket full of cigars, he went walking up the streets of Schenectady, looking for a suitable lot. Charles Proteus Steinmetz was about to become a man of property and position.

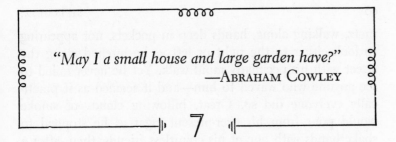

𝄢𝄢𝄢𝄢 THE gnomelike genius of electricity held a continual reception as he hobbled through the streets of Schenectady, looking for a lot on which to build his house. By this time, there was hardly a person in the entire city who did not know Steinmetz by sight, and many knew him well enough to call him by name. So, as he walked along almost everyone stopped to say a few words to him. Those who did not feel that they knew him well enough to speak to him, or who were on the opposite side of the street, would wave, and he would answer their salutations by raising both arms above his head and shaking his own hands in midair.

Steinmetz was not only greeted by those who were walking on the street, but also by the storekeepers, who would pause in their task of sweeping the entrances of their shops or arranging outside displays, to speak to him. Little children always stopped their game of jacks or halted their imaginary ponies to say "good morning," and ask how Jenny the monkey and the other animals were. Steinmetz would always answer their friendly inquiries in detail, stopping as long as was necessary to give them the information they wanted about his pets.

In fact, to the citizens of Schenectady, there was no more familiar sight in the city than that of Charles Proteus Steinmetz, walking along, hands deep in pockets, not appearing to look either to the right or left as he lurched along the street with his peculiarly rapid walk. Yet he never failed to see anyone who waved to him—and it seemed as if practically everyone did so. Great, billowing clouds of smoke would pour from his ever-present cigar as he stopped to shake hands with one of his countless friends, then, after a brief conversation, he would set out again, only to be halted a few yards further on to speak to someone else.

Sometimes Steinmetz would go hunting for his house lot on his bicycle. Often both hands would be off the handlebars simultaneously as he waved to passers-by on opposite sides of the street. If he saw someone to whom he particularly wanted to talk, he would ride his metal steed along the sidewalk curbing, so he could more easily carry on a conversation. At times he would become so engrossed in the subject under discussion that he would forget to turn a corner, or cross the street at the proper point. Completely absorbed, he would continue to ride along, talking, until he discovered too late that he was nowhere near his destination!

Ever since those youthful years in Breslau when, in company with his nature-loving father, he would wander over the hills outside the city, looking for brilliantly colored rocks and birds' nests, Steinmetz had enjoyed walking, despite his physical handicaps. The long hikes into the country to see the sunrise after the Friday night meetings of the Mathematics Society were among the most vivid memories of his university days. So it was only natural that he walked so much in Schenectady, even though he could now afford a horse and carriage. Unlike most of the other engineers at the plant, he usually walked to work. It was only in extremely cold weather or when it was raining that he took a streetcar. Once aboard, he would make his way to the front and take the seat nearest the motorman.

Everyone in Schenectady recognized the fact that this

particular seat "belonged" to him. If someone were sitting in it, he would get up and ask Steinmetz, "Would you like your seat?" With a grateful smile, and a gracious "thank you," the engineering genius would accept the offer immediately. Once in his favorite place, he would lean forward, elbows on knees, and stare intently at the instruments in front of the motorman as they fluctuated while the car's speed was increased or decreased by means of the controlling handle. Eyes firmly fastened on the vibrating needles, the scientist would think back through the years, recalling the weary months of ceaseless investigation in the laboratory of the Eickenmeyer plant when he had toiled for long hours, trying to design a practical alternating current motor for Field to use in streetcars. How simple it was to provide city dwellers with fast, safe, and economical transportation now, he would think, as the trolley rumbled and swayed on its way toward River Road and the General Electric works. Yet he was not quite sure that the best method of carrying people to work had been developed. Streetcars were adequate, but something more suitable might be produced if someone would study the problem. Perhaps one of these days he would see what he could do. Meanwhile, he had far more pressing matters demanding his attention.

One stormy day Steinmetz hobbled off a streetcar, waved good-by to the motorman, lit a cigar, and walked toward the main entrance of the General Electric plant. As he reached the gate, the uniformed guard on duty, instead of saluting and passing the engineer in with the usual hearty "Good morning, sir!" held up a restraining hand.

"I am sorry, Mr. Steinmetz, but you'll have to throw your cigar away," announced the guard. "Our instructions are not to admit anyone who is smoking. Orders have been posted all over the plant that no smoking is allowed in any of the shops, offices or yards."

Steinmetz came to a sudden stop, took a few quick puffs

on his cigar and blew the smoke through the gate, looked at its guardian and calmly replied, "Very well." Then, turning on his heel, he retraced his steps to the streetcar stop and rode back to "Liberty Hall."

For three days he did not go near the works. On the fourth day a representative of General Electric was sent to bring him back to the calculating department. The engineering division had become stalled on a difficult problem and were unable to continue their work without Steinmetz' help.

The company messenger rang the doorbell, and after a few moments' delay, Steinmetz came to answer it.

"When are you coming back to the plant?" inquired the emissary.

"Never, I suppose."

"What's that? Never? Why not?"

"No smoke, no Steinmetz!"

"Well, come back today, anyway. You can smoke if you do."

That afternoon Steinmetz returned to the works and walked through the gate, blowing smoke-rings. Shortly afterward, he sat down at his desk, listened to a group of engineers explain what was holding up production and in a very few minutes had solved the problem for them.

The next day the directors of the General Electric Company posted a bulletin announcing that in the case of one employee, and one employee only, the rule against smoking did not apply. That one employee was Charles Proteus Steinmetz.

☞ ☞ ☞

Despite this incident, the scientist was not an absolute slave to the tobacco habit. Visiting him one night, Dr. Ernst Berg watched silently while his associate checked his apparatus and wrote down some figures. As Steinmetz paused in his calculations long enough to light a cigar, Berg remarked,

"My friend, you are smoking far too much. Since I've been here you've consumed three cigars. You ought to cut down."

"I ought to cut down on smoking!" exploded Steinmetz. "You're a great one to even suggest such a thing. Why, I'm sure that you smoke more than I do. What's more, I could stop smoking, but you never could."

"Oh, is that so?" came the heated reply. "You know, I think I will take you up on that foolish statement. Meanwhile, you should try to see how long you can make a cigar last instead of smoking like a factory furnace."

"I already know how long I can make a cigar last," Steinmetz informed his friend. "I experimented with a great many different brands until I found a long, thin, mild one which would burn just as I wanted it to. You see, I taught myself to smoke scientifically, my good doctor. First, I only took a couple of puffs, then a dozen, then a quarter of a cigar, then a half, next three-quarters and finally a whole one."

"Always the mathematician!" Berg laughed. "Charles, you've reduced everything in life, except friendship, to a mathematical formula. Now let me tell *you* something. I'll bet you a dinner at Nicholaus' that I can swear off smoking for a year, but that you can't. What do you say to that?"

"What do I say? Just this. You are going to pay for the biggest meal of goose-liverwurst I ever enjoyed in Schenectady! Swearing off smoking for a year—what's that? It is such a simple thing to do. Look! I throw my cigar away without even a farewell puff and won't smoke again for a year. You, Berg, will be smoking within two days!"

The two engineers shook hands, sealing their wager. Days, weeks and months passed, and by degrees people became accustomed to the sight of Steinmetz without a cigar in his mouth. On the day the year was up, Berg was out of town, supervising an electrical installation. So Steinmetz sent him a telegram, stating that now he had proved he could swear off smoking, he was going out to buy a box of cigars and begin all over again. Five minutes later, a plant messenger entered the office of the chief consulting engineer and handed him a telegram. It was from Ernst Berg and contained almost the identical message!

The lease on "Liberty Hall" had run out in May, 1900, but Steinmetz, after much difficulty, had secured an extension from his landlord, who had never quite forgiven him for burning down the stable. By autumn Steinmetz was frantically walking and pedaling up and down the streets of Schenectady, looking for a house lot. At last he found it. The General Electric Company had recently bought a vast area of land in one section of the city, with the idea of selling it off in small parcels for residential use to its employees. In order to accomplish this, an organization called the General Electric Realty Company had been formed. Among the very first visitors to this firm's office was Steinmetz. One of the house lots they offered was just what he wanted, but he kept this information to himself.

With a sales representative of the real estate office, Steinmetz went out to Wendall Avenue. As the two walked up and down, the engineer casually pointed to a large lot on the opposite side of the street. "That's an attractive house site," he remarked, "but isn't it unfortunate that the land slopes so steeply on one side?"

"That's right, sir," agreed the agent. "We are going to have a great deal of trouble selling it. For, you see, not only does the land slope, but there is quite a bog at the foot, extending the full length of the adjoining lot. I guess we'll have to lose money on the house lot with the slope and give up any idea of selling the swampy piece."

"W—ell," said Steinmetz slowly, "I might be interested in both lots if they were cheap enough. Having no family, I don't have to worry about youngsters falling into the bog, and buying it will assure me privacy. The slope on the other piece won't interfere with my laboratory. What do you want for them?"

The amazed salesman looked at his companion in bewilderment. Was this man the most brilliant engineer employed by General Electric? Why, he couldn't be! No person with even the slightest amount of common sense would want to buy a house lot next to a bog. A sale was a sale, however, and perhaps this would be the only opportunity the realty organization would ever have to get rid of the unattractive property. Consulting his papers, the agent named the price.

"Frankly, that's a little more than I feel I can afford," declared Steinmetz. "I think we had better forget the whole thing."

"I've a better idea, sir. Why don't you let me consult my office before you stop considering the purchase of these lots?" suggested the wily salesman. "My superiors realize that not everyone would be interested in a piece of land that slopes, and they know that a swampy lot has very little value to someone who is planning to build a house. Perhaps they will be willing to make an adjustment in the price, and we can come to an agreement."

The General Electric Realty Company was more than willing to make a concession. The amount of money they asked for the lots was very reasonable, and Steinmetz quickly signed a contract to buy them, afraid that the Realty Company would change its mind, for the slope and the swamp lot were exactly what he wanted! With very little work, the bog could be made into a beautiful glen full of water lilies, swamp grasses, lady slippers, and other marshland perennials. Along the slope he could build a natural rock garden. Little did the sales personnel in the real estate office realize that what seemed to them the two most unattractive lots in the entire development were ideal for the engineer's purpose. He let them think they had got the better of him in the transaction, but he had a most difficult time restraining himself from bragging to his friends about how he had made the General Electric Realty Company cut the purchase price of "the only two good lots that they had to sell in the whole area."

The money Steinmetz saved on the buying of this land meant absolutely nothing to him. His real pleasure in the negotiations came from the fact that he had played a trick on the men in charge of the sales of the lots. In money matters he was a strange mixture. Wealth meant nothing to him, but at the same time he would go miles out of his way to save a few pennies on purchases. Shortly after setting up housekeeping in "Liberty Hall," he wrote to one of the daily papers published in the near-by capital city of Albany, taking a year's subscription at the advertised price of five dollars. A few weeks later he again wrote the paper's circulation department, heatedly demanding an explanation of why it was possible to have the same journal delivered to his front door each morning by a local newsboy for twenty-five cents less a year!

This was the man who graciously and willingly contributed to any charitable cause and never turned down a request for funds from needy individuals. No one in Schenectady was a more staunch supporter of the Christmas fund of the Salvation Army than he, but Steinmetz did not permit a public record of his contributions. On the other hand, he would wait until "double coupon days" at the chain tobacco store to purchase his cigars, in order to get twice as many of the brilliantly colored slips of paper which could be traded in for valuable premiums. Then he would distribute the coupons among the children in the neighborhood who were collecting them to exchange for dolls, bicycles, or sporting equipment! It was not until some years after his death that the residents of the city of Schenectady learned that the mysterious "Santa Claus" who provided a gift for every child in the city's orphanages at Christmas time was a crippled St. Nicholas, whom they all knew and admired.

≤≤≤

Once he had acquired a house lot, Steinmetz began to design his home. The plans for the laboratory had been made months before, and construction of that building was begun immediately. E. W. Rice, who had persuaded the scientist to leave Eickenmeyer's and join the engineering staff of General Electric, and who was now president of the company, had listened with great interest to Steinmetz' description of the workshop he planned to erect, once he found a suitable location. Realizing that the electrical wizard would engage in experiments and investigations of the utmost value to the firm, Mr. Rice suggested that General Electric build and equip the laboratory at cost. Steinmetz wasted no time in accepting this gracious offer.

While workmen poured concrete and raised the framework of the laboratory building, progress on the house itself was very slow. The main reason for this was the fact that Steinmetz kept changing his mind as to what he wanted. His first tentative drawing of his new home was made in 1901, and the final brushful of paint was not applied until the fall of 1903. The results of these three years of constant changing of designs and plans was an ornamental red brick house, with high peaked gables, whose entire interior was finished in dark wood. If the building could be said to fall into any one class of architecture, it was nearer Tudor than anything else. In the rear, off the reception hall, was Steinmetz' office. This room was completely filled with treasures, which ranged from an exhibit of the various types of electric light bulbs to cases of Indian arrowheads. Shelves and display racks reached from floor to ceiling, and to make it easy for the malformed Steinmetz to reach these objects, a ladder fitted with wheels ran around the room on a track.

Long before his house was ready for occupancy, Steinmetz had transferred his orchids and cacti to a new conservatory which was built in two sections, one much larger than the other. In the smaller of the glass rooms there was a pool about ten feet square and five and a half feet deep. At first Steinmetz used this pool to swim in during the winter months, or on summer days when he was too busy to go to a favorite spot on the Mohawk River. As he grew older, he changed the swimming pool into a water-lily bed and found the matted roots of these aquatic plants excellent hiding places for the fry of the exotic types of goldfish with which he populated it. He built a most attractive bridge arching the pool, and when weary or confused, would stand on it, elbows on the rustic guard rail, peering for hours into the flower-studded water, watching the flashing forms of the fish as they darted from one end of the pool to the other. Then, relaxed and refreshed, he would return to his calculations.

One of his favorite dishes was terrapin soup. A terrapin is an edible species of tortoise which inhabits the fresh waters of central North America. Often after eating a large bowl of terrapin soup in his favorite restaurant, an old-time German eating place called Nicholaus', he would leave the table, go out to the busy kitchen and look over the cook's stock of terrapins. He would buy all of the creatures the management was willing to sell, then tucking them into his already bulging coat pockets, hurry home to the conservatory. Once on the bridge, he would pick the terrapins out of his pockets and drop them gently into the pool, observing with intense delight the way they climbed upon the lily pads, perfectly content with their new home.

When Steinmetz stood on the bridge above the pool, he was able to reach and care for the baskets of orchid plants that hung in profusion from the ceiling. There were hundreds of varieties, from every tropic region of the world, including some of rare horticultural and scientific interest. He liked nothing better than attempting to cross two standard species of these flowers and develop an unrecorded hybrid. As a result, the area above the pool was a mass of brilliant variegated color.

In the larger of the conservatory rooms, he raised his cacti. Unlike the section in which the orchids were raised, this space was kept as hot and dry as possible to simulate the arid regions in which most types of cacti grow. Looking at the beds, one could see succulents of every type and of every conceivable shape—some of them were ribbed like melons, others were flat as a piece of paper, a few looked like columns, while still others resembled balls. Many of these plants would bloom, displaying large, showy blossoms with exceptionally high coloring, in which scarlet, crimson, rosy-pink, orange and yellow predominated. If visitors gasped at the sight of the beauty of the orchid room, their host would remark quietly, "This is nothing. Wait until you see my cacti in the other room."

What he didn't tell his callers was that his planting of the natives of the hot, arid desert regions of the earth was the largest collection of cacti in the world, with the exception of Kew Gardens, the famous botanical park maintained under royal patronage in London, England. As a matter of fact, Steinmetz was as famous among horticulturists for his cacti collection as he was among engineers for his investigations. Realizing this, newspaper editors would regularly assign reporters to "get a story about that conservatory of Steinmetz'."

Paul Waitt, one-time Sunday feature editor of the Boston *Herald*, took this assignment himself when Steinmetz came to Boston to address a meeting of businessmen. In the course of their conversation, which took place in the lobby of the hotel where the scientist was staying, Mr. Waitt asked, "Doesn't beauty in a flower have any appeal to you at all, Mr. Steinmetz? I mean in flowers beside orchids."

"No," replied the engineer as he looked intently at the throngs of people rushing through the convention-jammed hotel. "Take the rose. Most people think it is beautiful; I don't care for it at all. I much prefer the cactus, for the simple reason that it has a far more interesting personality. The cactus has wonderfully adapted itself to its surroundings; and we human beings can learn much from its ability to adjust itself to unfavorable conditions."

"Most gardeners keep a record of their activities in order to see how one season compares with another. Do you also make notes on 'how your garden grows'?" inquired the editor-turned-reporter.

Waving his cigar in a wide circle in response to a greeting from a passer-by, Steinmetz replied, "Mr. Waitt, I never keep any record of my experiments and investigations. My memory files all things away conveniently and reliably. I should say though, I do not encumber it with a lot of useless matter. I remember only the things that interest me and facts of which I intentionally make a mental record. Names and faces, for instance, do not interest me, so I never remember either. But if a man says anything or asks anything that interests me, that is what I will remember him by, and that will recall his personality."

Steinmetz' fondness for cacti, with their clusters of spines, bundles of bristles and tufts of barbs, was closely related to his own physical handicap. To him, these plants, capable of surviving without much nourishment and very little water, were a symbol of his struggle to convince the world that his crippled body did not hamper the workings of his mind. For all too often he had noticed the look of pity or dismay on the faces of those who saw him for the first time. Then, too, despite his recent successes, he could remember all too well the surly engineer at the Edison works who had turned him down when he applied for a job, shortly after his arrival in America, and how that individual had paid no attention to his letter of introduction, but had thrown it in the waste-basket. Steinmetz was sure that this refusal to give him a chance to show what he could do had been due to his malformity. While most of his visitors never paid the slightest attention to his infirmities, there were a few who pitied him, he felt. In order to teach these folk a lesson, he delighted in planting an ordinary flower in the same pot with one of his cacti. Later on, he would call attention to the plant, now completely withered, and chortle, "See, cacti may be ugly and deformed, but they can live and flourish, producing flowers of great beauty under the worst possible conditions."

In this fashion he would express his kinship with the prickly, misshapen cacti. He gave them loving care and attention, finding his reward in the glorious blossoms they sent forth. Perhaps to his kind and understanding friend and former employer, Eickenmeyer, the twisted body of Steinmetz may have seemed like a cactus, whose flowering was his brilliant discovery of the "Law of Hysteresis." Appearance is so often deceptive. It is almost never the measure of a man's ability.

Once his many varieties of plants had recovered from the shock of transplanting and were established in their new home, Steinmetz turned his attention to his new laboratory. It was connected to his conservatory by a basement passageway, which was later used by the builders as part of the foundation of the house. He wanted the laboratory to be big enough for every possible type of experiment, so he had it built two stories high. There were three rooms on the ground floor and two smaller rooms above. No sooner had the workmen finished the shell of the building than Steinmetz left "Liberty Hall" and moved into his new workshop. He made himself perfectly comfortable with a few odds and ends of furniture, and then set to work installing the scientific equipment he had ordered through Mr. Rice.

Although no one else in the world would have been satisfied with such a collection of household goods, Steinmetz, who never cared about physical comfort, was quite content with the furniture in the laboratory—a rickety bed, a scarred table, a badly damaged chair or two and an assortment of broken and cracked dishes. When the General Electric Company had installed him as chief consulting engineer for the firm, great pains had been taken to fit up one end of the calculating department with easy chairs, a wide desk and filing cabinets so that the dwarf-like genius could work in comfort. The first time Steinmetz walked into his new quarters, he called for some porters. Pointing to the luxurious furnishings, he ordered, "Take that stuff out of here! I don't care where you take it, but take it out!" The puzzled workmen stripped the room of the new furniture, and under Steinmetz' direction carried in a battered desk and a plain wooden chair. At last he was satisfied. Looking around, he rubbed his hands with glee and said, "Thank you, boys. Now I can work here!" He did, however, leave one overstuffed chair in the room. No one ever saw him sit in it, but he insisted that it be kept dusted, and when he died it was in as perfect condition as the day it was bought.

So it was natural enough for Steinmetz to be happy with nothing but the plainest furniture in his new laboratory at Wendall Avenue. He never even considered the need of a stove—after all, he always could cook his meals on a Bunsen burner!

What he lacked in the way of household goods he made up for in scientific equipment. The laboratory was a maze of wires, switchboards, armatures, generators, batteries, motors and other electrical devices. Three or four laboratory worktables were scattered through the room, and all of them received ample light from the numerous windows. Within easy reach of the crippled experimenter, on wide shelves above the workbench that ran along the wall, various supplies were stored. At first boxes, vials, cartons and cans were neatly arranged, but before long the shelves were piled every-which-way with chemicals, small parts and hand tools.

Just before Steinmetz moved into the laboratory to live, his sister Clara came to pay another of her visits. He did not spend as much time with his guest as he did in supervising the building of the new house. Then, too, setting up his laboratory and caring for his plants and pets kept him very busy. His collection of animals had grown over the years and it was almost a full-time job to tend them. Feeding the alligator was no easy task—it had grown old and lazy, and it was necessary to have help to force the ration of raw meat down its throat. The scientist would ask any caller to push the meat down the reptile's throat while he held its jaws open. This was not, as can well be understood, one of the more popular entertainments at Wendall Avenue.

Then one day the alligator, warmed by a few days of pleasant weather, seemed to regain his vitality. Somehow he wandered out of the conservatory, made his way across the lawn and started down the sidewalk. His progress was seen by most of the neighborhood, but no one had courage enough to capture him. By the time Steinmetz came home from the works, the reptile had completely vanished. Immediately, the entire city of Schenectady was in a state of alarm! Children were warned not to go swimming, and very few citizens dared venture forth at night. At last the alligator was corralled and brought back to Wendall Avenue, seemingly none the worse for his adventure. However, he refused to eat, and in attempting to force-feed him, Steinmetz pushed too large a piece of meat down his throat and the poor creature choked to death.

While her brother was engaged in his various activities, Clara was not idle. "Liberty Hall," where she was staying, hadn't had a thorough cleaning since her last visit. When she complained to the scientist, he merely shrugged his shoulders and asked gruffly, "What difference does it make?

After all, I don't live here any more, and just as soon as my new house is built, I'll remove the furniture. So why should I clean it—for that landlord of mine? I haven't forgotten how he laughed at the loss of my notebooks when the stable burned down."

Poor Clara could say nothing. To the world at large her brother was a genius. To her he was the same impossible boy who had been such a problem in the old days in Breslau. So she washed floors, polished furniture, cleaned windows and spent hours trying to convince Karl—for she still called him by the old name—that she could prepare better meals than the griddle cakes and eggs which he insisted upon cooking for himself on a Bunsen burner, and eating on a laboratory worktable. It was a hopeless task.

In order to soothe Clara's ruffled feelings, Steinmetz occasionally did come to eat dinner with her and spend the night at "Liberty Hall." On one of these rare evenings, the doorbell rang. Two young men had come to call on the engineer. One of them, a fellow-worker at the General Electric plant, had never met the chief consulting engineer of the firm; the other knew him well, having often dined with him at the Krugers'. Clara greeted the two visitors and conducted them up the stairs to the second-floor hallway, which was used by her brother as a sitting room. He was playing with one of his parrots when they arrived, but he immediately put the bird back on its perch, thanked his sister, and turned to his guests. The stranger was introduced to him as Joseph LeRoy Hayden, an engineer who had just been transferred to Schenectady from the Lynn plant of General Electric, where he had been engaged in experiments aimed at improving street lighting.

Steinmetz was attracted to young Hayden at once. Not only did he like the youth's personality, but he was greatly impressed with his knowledge of electrical engineering. What began as a short social visit lasted for hours, as the

two men discussed the problem of making city thoroughfares brighter at night. When Clara made it clear that the
callers should go home so that their host could go to bed,
Steinmetz held out his hand and said, "Be sure to come and
see me again, Mr. Hayden. I have enjoyed our little talk
immensely. If I am not here, you will find me either in my
conservatory or laboratory on Wendall Avenue. Perhaps,
now that you are on the staff here, we can work together on
your street-lighting problem. It interests me very much."

Hayden left "Liberty Hall" in a daze. The greatest electrical engineer in the world had suggested that they collabo-
rate! Indeed he would come again! The young man soon
became a constant visitor, and as the weeks went by, the
older man and his youthful associate grew closer and closer
together. Steinmetz, the genius with a warped and twisted
body, was essentially a lonely man, and this new found friend
gave him the comradeship he had sought in vain all his life.
Roy Hayden, on the other hand, discovered in the experienced Steinmetz an inspiration and a closer kinship than
he had ever felt toward any other man. The time was not
so far distant when their relationship would become even
closer, for eventually Steinmetz legally adopted Roy. Their
association was a most happy arrangement for a fancier of
terrapins, crows, parrots, alligators and monkeys who had
never heard the voice of a wife or child in his home. Now
Steinmetz had a son!

"The night comes down, the lights burn blue"
—JOHN HAY

╫ **8** ╫

〽〽〽〽 LATE in the fall of 1903 the house on Wendall Avenue was finally finished. Instead of being delighted with the idea of having a home of his own after long years of living in poorly furnished rooms and rented apartments, Steinmetz was not happy. In fact, as he hobbled from one room to another, he wondered why he had ever considered building the house at all. Standing in the downstairs hallway and looking up the stairwell, he asked himself, "Why do I need all this space? The conservatory was different; after all, I had to build a place for my orchids and cacti. I've no regrets on that score. Nor am I sorry that I accepted Mr. Rice's friendly assistance and designed such a large laboratory. Those two buildings should have been all. I knew I needed them, but I certainly didn't need this house. Roy and I are perfectly comfortable in the laboratory."

He really did not require a house. With his plants sheltered and a place where he could work, a house was an unnecessary expense. To this devoted scientist, no better place could be found in which to live, sleep and eat, than in his beloved laboratory, surrounded by electrical and chemical apparatus. Everything he needed and wanted was within easy reach in his spacious workroom, but it was very evident that in this large house that he had so foolishly built, he would be lost as the glow from a firefly during a thunderstorm.

"Now that I have built my home," he complained one day to Mr. Kruger, "what am I going to do with it? You can see that it is much too big for my needs. Actually, I haven't enough furniture to put in the rooms—even if I could use all of them. Surely, you'll admit it would be downright foolish of me to go out and buy more beds, chairs and tables when I don't really want them. I've got all the household goods I want and need in the laboratory, and after all, when I go to sleep one bed is enough—there's another one for Roy, of course. In fact, those extra rooms are of no use to me at all. Frankly, I am afraid I will have to admit that the whole idea of building this house was a foolish one. While I'm so comfortable in the laboratory, I've no intention of moving, anyhow, so why did I build it?"

As a result, the new house stood silent and empty while its owner continued to live happily in his old quarters. From time to time, one of his fellow engineers at the General Electric plant would spend the night with him, sleeping on one of the many cots he kept for visitors. Despite the fact that these cots were far from comfortable, guests never complained. Tossing about in a lumpy bed, surrounded by humming generators, was an exceptionally cheap price to pay for the opportunity of spending an entire evening with one of the world's greatest scientists, discussing complicated theories of electrical engineering.

Not everyone who came to call at Wendall Avenue was honored with a cordial invitation to spend the night on a cot in Steinmetz' laboratory. A visitor had to be capable of two things in order to be welcomed: first, he must be able to contribute something worth-while to the conversation during the evening; and, second, he would be wise to have the ability to appreciate a practical joke.

Most of the workers at the General Electric plant who

were in the habit of visiting Wendall Avenue were, by training and experience, capable of meeting the first requirement
demanded of an overnight guest, but many failed miserably
on the second test. As Steinmetz considered a broad sense
of humor in a man an even more important possession than
vast technical information, callers who did not know how to
laugh at themselves were never welcome at his house, no
matter how great their knowledge of science might be. For
busy as he was pursuing investigations into new uses of electrical energy, Steinmetz always found time to engage in
pranks. He had learned to laugh at his own troubles, and
found in elfish escapades a relief from the severe mental
and physical strain of long hours of calculation and experimentation. Others, he reasoned, should learn to laugh and
enjoy life as much as he did. If they didn't know how, he
would attempt to teach them. If they were unwilling pupils, they did not have to come to school.

His favorite trick was to electrify every metal object in the
laboratory so that when an unsuspecting victim touched one
of them, he would get a harmless but startling shock. By
means of an extremely clever system of wiring, Steinmetz
made sitting in any of the laboratory chairs a very risky process. When those callers who were constant visitors learned
by sad experience not to touch anything in the laboratory,
and always, before sitting down, to turn their chair over and
carefully disconnect the wires fastened to it, the impish scientist decided it was time to develop a new system of jolting
his guests. After some thought, he placed a small storage
battery in one of the pockets of his baggy, gray-flannel pants,
and ran an almost invisible wire down the inside of his right
arm. In this way he was able to give a shock to anyone with
whom he shook hands.

The more dignified the caller, the more Steinmetz enjoyed playing a trick on him. One pompous engineer, who
was associated with the scientist in a research project at the

General Electric works, took great care to avoid touching anything in the laboratory, always refused to sit down, and pointedly avoided shaking hands with his host when he came to discuss the progress of their investigation. For weeks Steinmetz plotted, trying to figure out some means of upsetting the stiff, unbending manner of his fellow worker. At last he conceived an ideal method. Just inside the door to his workroom, he set up an electrified metal plate and carefully camouflaged it. When his victim entered the room one evening, Steinmetz slyly turned on the current. Dignity vanished as the caller leaped into the air in shocked amazement.

Some weeks later, the same visitor came to spend another evening. Smirking wisely, he stood on the doorsill, gathered his legs under him, and jumped, landing three or four feet inside the room. Pretending that he had not noticed his guest's unusual and very undignified entrance, Steinmetz greeted him and cheerily asked him to make himself comfortable. Proud of having turned the tables on the prankster, the visiting engineer strutted toward the center of the laboratory. Suddenly he yelped with terror and shot into the air! Steinmetz had cannily reasoned that his caller would, by one means or another, avoid the metal plate placed just inside the door, and had rigged up another in the middle of the room. Then he had waited for the proper moment to send an electrical charge through it!

Fun and practical jokes, however, did not take up all of the time of the gnome-like genius. Far from it. Both at the Wendall Avenue laboratory and at his desk at the General Electric plant, Steinmetz was devoting long hours to the problem of improving street lighting. Ever since 1668, when the citizens of London had been commanded "for the safety and peace of the city to hang out candles duly to the accustomed hour," a workable method of installing adequate lights on city streets had been an objective of civic authori-

ties. In this country, long before the Revolution, New York
and Boston had attempted to find a solution to the problem
of providing people with light as they went from one place
to another after dark, by passing laws requiring every seventh householder to place a lighted candle in his window at
night. As early as 1789, during the meetings of the Consti-
tutional Convention, Philadelphia had a few street lights,
and the first gas-lighting company in America was organized
in that city in 1815. By the time that Steinmetz had begun
to devote his energy and talents to finding a means of using
electricity to brighten city streets, gas was the accepted
method of lighting thoroughfares.

Like the boy in Robert Louis Stevenson's poem, in *A
Child's Garden of Verses*, youngsters in every large city envied the lamplighter with his torch and considered no public
official as important as the man who turned the gas lamps
on in the evening and shut them off at dawn. Steinmetz had
no such ideas. To be sure, gaslighting was far better than
candles, whale or oil lamps, but it was not good enough.
Electrical power was the answer to street lighting. The only
question was how to use it to best advantage.

Steinmetz had been keeping in close contact with H. W.
Hillman, who was in charge of the experiments being conducted in street lighting by various specialists at the Lynn
plant of General Electric. As a matter of fact, long before
Roy Hayden's first visit, the great scientist had planned an
investigation of the problem. He had tested the electric arc
lamps that were being developed by his firm and which were
slowly coming into use in progressive cities—and thus had
welcomed the chance to talk to one of the engineers who
had helped design them. These lamps, Steinmetz discovered,
were a decided improvement over the original electric arc
lights, but they were far from perfect. Dismantling one of
them, he found that they consisted of two hard, hollow car-

bon rods baked under high temperature in a die. The hollow core was filled with a soft carbon powder. These carbon electrodes were then placed beneath a reflector and subjected to a flow of direct current. One rod being positive, the other negative, the electric current jumped from one carbon to the other, causing them to burn brightly in "a most brilliant ascending arch of light, broad and conical in form in the middle." Research had established that most of this light came from the positive carbon and showed the temperature of the arc to be between 6000 to 7000 degrees Fahrenheit—equal to about one-tenth the brightness of the sun!

One of the difficulties experienced by users of the lamps produced at the Lynn works was the constant attention needed to set the carbon rods near enough together to strike the arc, and at the same time to keep them the proper distance apart so as to burn properly and give the maximum light. As the lamps were used, the carbons were consumed, making the space between them greater. When the distance between the electrodes became too great, the arc would fail and the lamp would go out. By the clever use of an electromagnet, lighting engineers eventually overcame this handicap.

Although the electric arc lamp was the latest in a long line of devices invented by mankind to overcome darkness, it was still based on a centuries-old technique—burn something and get light. Because the carbons were exposed to the air, they were quickly destroyed. Edison and other scientists who worked on the electric filament lamp were motivated by this fact. They sought to break away from the traditional method of getting light by developing a means of lighting that would prevent the oxygen in the air from reaching their carbons. The result of their attempt to avoid the rapid burning of the rods was the invention of a light completely enclosed in a vacuum, thus making the electrically charged filaments glow, instead of burn. This was because the glass bulb prevented contact with the air.

From that day late in 1809 when Sir Humphry Davy made the first practical carbon arc lamp in his laboratory, down to Steinmetz' time, experiments were constantly being carried on to prevent oxygen from reaching the carbons by enclosing them. As early as 1846, Staite announced a successful demonstration of restricting the flow of air to the electrodes by covering them with a large glass globe. Through the years, his method was gradually improved. When Steinmetz began his study of the problem of lighting city streets, the General Electric plant at Lynn was producing an electric arc lamp which was surrounded by a glass container in which the carbons were consumed ninety per cent more slowly than in the open type arc lamps. This enclosed arc lamp was not quite as brilliant as any of the open arc types, because the lack of a free flow of oxygen prevented the formation of a seething "crater" on the tip of the positive carbon.

This flaw in the performance of the closed arc lamp was overlooked by cities seeking to improve their street lighting, because these lamps did not require the frequent renewal of burned-out electrodes. One of the enclosed carbon arc lamps made by General Electric could burn for a period of one hundred hours without adjustment, thus giving several weeks of satisfactory service before having to be "trimmed"—as replacing the carbons was called. The enclosed arc had another advantage over open arc lamps for in order to be absolutely sure that the latter would provide light when needed, their manufacturers equipped them with two sets of electrodes. The additional pair was so regulated as to start automatically in case the original carbons should burn out during the night. This feature made open arcs more expensive to purchase and more difficult to service.

After subjecting the closed arc lamps developed at Lynn to a series of tests, Steinmetz declared himself perfectly satisfied with their operation. Deciding that he couldn't improve on the lamp itself, he set about finding a more suitable material than carbon to use as electrodes. He realized that if he could find a substitute for the commonly used carbon rods that would not burn out so quickly, he would overcome the high maintenance cost of street lighting by electric arc lamps—a factor which prevented many tax-conscious city governments from switching from gas to electricity. Then, too, if his replacement provided more light than did carbon, he would do away with the objection of lighting engineers that closed arc lamps had less luminous efficiency than open arcs.

Steinmetz started his work on this problem in his usual fashion. Before beginning any experiments, he first studied the scientific reports of all those who had ever worked on the problem of the electric arc. He did not have to read nearly so many volumes dealing with this subject as he had when preparing for his investigation of hysteresis, for the electric arc had been known to scientists only since 1800, coming into commercial use three-quarters of a century later. The work of Charles Francis Brush, the pioneer American worker in carbon arcs, was so recent that Steinmetz was very familiar with it. Every technical school freshman knew how Brush, experimenting with the possibilities of combining lampblack and ground-up pure coke for use as carbons in an arc lamp, had molded them in the family kitchen, using his wife's cooking molasses as a binder; then baked the rods in the kitchen stove, while the rest of the household hungrily waited for him to finish so that dinner could be prepared. The library at the plant furnished a complete record of this experimenter's successful lighting of the Public Square in Cleveland, Ohio, with arc lamps run by electricity furnished by a dynamo of his own invention. This happened about two years before Edison's perfection of the carbon-filament lamp, and Steinmetz read about it thoroughly.

Once he had completed his research, Steinmetz began to experiment. After investigating the possibilities of many different materials, he decided to use magnetite as a substitute for carbon rods in his lamp. Magnetite is a hard, black, opaque mineral with a metallic lustre. Composed of 72.4 per cent iron, it is very magnetic. This property of the mineral had been recognized in very early times, and was described at length in the first century of the Christian era by Pliny, the Roman naturalist and author. After several months of investigation and testing, Steinmetz perfected a magnetite arc lamp that promised to replace those with short-lived carbon electrodes.

However, he did not immediately inform his superiors at General Electric of the results of his experiments. He continued to conduct a series of trials and make improvements until he was absolutely sure his lamp would give complete satisfaction under all working conditions. At last, he felt that the bright, bluish light given off by the burning magnetite was as luminous as anything he was going to develop, and he gave an official demonstration. Everyone agreed that he had created a totally different and more efficient arc lamp; yet it had one very obvious flaw. In a period when all improvements in the field of electrical energy, light and power were dependent on alternating current, Steinmetz' arc ran on direct current.

When one recalls how long and patiently Charles Proteus Steinmetz had worked to advance the use of alternating current by the electrical industry, it seems most strange that he developed the magnetite arc lamp, for, although there was no doubt that his interest in the problem of lighting cities at night had resulted in the best method yet invented of turning dark thoroughfares into avenues of light, it was, paradoxically, a direct current arc. Eventually electric arcs were engineered to operate on alternating current, but by the time they were placed in widespread use, the perfection of the incandescent lamp made them obsolete. Not all of the uses of arc lamps were taken over by filament lamps, however. They still are used for certain specialized purposes, such as airport beacons, searchlights, in lighthouses and in the projectors of motion picture theatres. Another important use of the arc lamp is for medical purposes. Various types of arc lamps are employed by physicians to treat skin eruptions, tuberculosis, bone diseases and other ills.

Before arc lamps were discarded, along with candles, lanterns, and gas lights, as a means of lighting city streets, Steinmetz' improvement over the old carbon electrode arc lamp was subjected to further refinements. In its final form, the upper or positive electrode was made of a solid cylinder of copper, which burned very slowly because of copper's ability to conduct heat, thus keeping the cylinder relatively cool. The negative electrode was composed of an iron tube containing three parts of magnetite and one part of titanium oxide. Magnetite, being an excellent conductor of electricity, vaporized quickly in the arc, resulting in a large flame made extremely brilliant by the titanium, a very hard mineral named after the Titans of Greek mythology, who were gigantic in size and power. Before long, due to its exceedingly bright bluish flame, the magnetite arc was known among electrical engineers as "the luminous arc."

All the time Steinmetz was working on his arc lamp, Roy Hayden had been closely associated with him, both at the plant and at the Wendall Avenue laboratory. A bachelor, with no family responsibilities, Hayden had gradually changed from a frequent overnight visitor to a permanent resident of the workshop-home of his superior. As their work progressed, the two men took over one of the upstairs rooms for a bedroom, leaving cots in one of the crowded downstairs shops for their overnight guests. Because he had been active in the electric arc investigations at the Lynn works, Roy was an ideal assistant as Steinmetz experimented with magnetite. Moreover, Hayden had an excellent sense of humor and greatly enjoyed the pranks in which Steinmetz constantly engaged. The young man would keep his face absolutely straight, even though he was bursting with inward laughter while the mischievous cripple explained to someone who was staying overnight for the first time, "This is our hot water heater. We don't run it all night, because it isn't necessary—but would you do me a favor? Seeing that you are sleeping downstairs, it will be easier for you to light it first thing in the morning. If you do, we'll all have plenty of hot water to wash and shave, with enough left over to do the dishes. You don't mind, do you?"

Who could object to such a simple request? Nobody. What the visitor didn't know was that the hot water heater was very apt to blow back in the face of whoever lit it, if not perfectly adjusted—and only Roy or Steinmetz knew how to regulate it. Many an expert in engineering jumped precipitately back from the exploding heater; then, wanting to be helpful, tried to light it again—with the same result. Most of them stopped only when they heard loud shouts of laughter coming from the upstairs bedroom.

When Steinmetz was completely satisfied with his magnetite arc lamp, he suggested to the directors of the General Electric Company that they secure permission from the city of Schenectady to test the new light on Wendall Avenue. "It will be the best possible advertising for the magnetite arc," he argued, "if we set poles along the sidewalk and light the area with the lamps. You can use my back yard as the location of the Brush dynamo, and young Hayden can watch it. We'll make a civic celebration out of the affair. I don't think you'll have any trouble with the city officials. After all, they will be getting a section of Schenectady brilliantly lighted at night without any cost!"

Arrangements were soon completed for the lighting of Wendall Avenue by the new electric arc lamp. Hayden was assigned the task of supervising the Brush power plant, which a crew of workmen set up in Steinmetz' back yard, between the conservatory and the laboratory. Roy's job was not a simple one—the generator was very apt to get out of order and had to be watched constantly. Steinmetz had wanted his young assistant to be in charge of the machine because he wished to avoid the risk of a power failure that would spoil the public test of his new invention.

On the night when the lamps were turned on for the first time, a tremendous crowd gathered in front of the scientist's house. Everyone of importance at the General Electric works and in the city government was there, along with hundreds of sightseers. After a few brief speeches, the lamps were turned on, and a new era in street lighting was begun.

Steinmetz was extremely happy. Not because his lamps with their bluish glow made Wendall Avenue the brightest street in the world; he had known that they would do this. His joy came from seeing so many of his friends all at once. He hobbled through the crowd, shaking hands, handing out cigars, greeting strangers and acquaintances. Before he was through, he had spoken to almost everyone on the street.

"You know," he said to Hayden with a grin, "I haven't had so much fun in years. Why, I've met people tonight that I haven't seen in months. This is much better than announcing the results of an investigation to a group of engineers at a meeting of a scientific society. The members just sit and applaud politely. These people are different. They cheer at the top of their voices, and go out of their way to tell me how wonderful they think I am. I don't know whether I have done anything remarkable or not, but it is very pleasant to have your friends and neighbors compliment you."

"Stay here and listen to the praise, sir," replied the courteous Roy. "I had better go back to that contraption of

Brush's. If it stops, there won't be any plaudits from the crowd or from the bosses at the works for either of us! Oh, will I be glad when someone develops an arc that runs by alternating current which can be supplied from a central power station, instead of by a source of direct current that has to be watched every minute."

"You've not long to wait, Roy," Steinmetz promised with a smile. "I have been thinking about that problem and I feel I have a solution to it."

Waving his hand in farewell, Hayden returned to his power plant. Steinmetz stuck a fresh cigar in his mouth and walked toward the people on the sidewalk. As he went across the lawn he noticed that the shrubs planted in front of the house did not show up to advantage under the magnetite arcs. Immediately he was dissatisfied with his latest creation, and decided to develop an even more brilliant light. He would begin work on it tomorrow.

That was the trouble. There were so many things to do tomorrow and not enough hours in which to do them. There was always some complicated problem at the plant that needed attention, and he was not spending the time he should with his orchids, cacti and pets. Of course, Roy was a most capable assistant and he had grown so used to his companionship that he wondered whether he could ever face living alone in the laboratory without him. Yet even with the help of Hayden and the services of specialists at the plant, Steinmetz could not find sufficient time to undertake all the investigations into the mysteries of electricity he desired.

All he could do was to try to accomplish as much as possible. "I'll just do the most important things," he said to himself. "The other projects will have to be forgotten. The future will have to take care of itself. I'm not going to worry about it. There is only one thing I wish I could forget, and that is this house. It is ridiculous to have it standing empty.

Building it was my most unsuccessful experiment."

Meanwhile, Roy Hayden had also been doing some thinking about the future. The young man had become engaged and Steinmetz was vitally interested in the progress of his assistant's love affair and liked to discuss it with him. In fact, on the nights when Roy went to call on his future wife, the scientist would wait up for him, anxious to find out whether everything were going smoothly. If anything were wrong, the older man and his companion would have a serious talk, Steinmetz giving words of advice as to the best way of winning a lady's hand and heart!

Roy, of course, was in no hurry to get married as he was quite happy living and working in the laboratory with Steinmetz. There were, however, a number of things about their relationship which Hayden found unpleasant. The scientist's interest in and knowledge of chemistry gave Steinmetz the delusion that he was an excellent cook. But no one who ever ate a meal cooked by him agreed with this opinion! Painful memories of meals prepared by Steinmetz had been one of the reasons why the Berg brothers had begged the cook to reconsider when she had threatened to leave "Liberty Hall." They knew what kind of food would result when their roommate took over the kitchen.

In addition to Steinmetz' painful efforts with stove and pan, he would often develop a strange fancy about food, and try to convince everyone that his new theory on eating was the key to healthful living. During the experimental lighting of Wendall Avenue by the magnetite arc lamps, the scientist was insisting on preparing meals according to color! "I've been doing some serious thinking, Roy," he announced one evening, "and I have come to the definite conclusion that foods that are yellow in color are the most healthful."

With that statement came the start of a series of meals consisting of nothing but scrambled eggs, griddlecakes and cornmeal. Just when Hayden was ready to rebel, Steinmetz decided that the most suitable food for himself and his companion was steak and potatoes. As a matter of fact, potatoes were the only vegetable that he seemed to know anything about—at least he never cooked any other kind! This menu, while far more appetizing than what Roy called "the yellow diet," soon became unpalatable, and once again Hayden had more than enough of a food monotony. This time he did speak out.

In an interview published many years later, he told a reporter: "Life in the laboratory was all right, but I was getting sick and tired of steak and potatoes every day. I couldn't stand it. So I said, 'I'm going out and get married!' Steinmetz said, 'You'd better go ahead.' So I married and went to live on the other side of town. About the first night Mrs. Hayden and I were back from our wedding trip, someone knocked on the door. It was the Doctor. We asked him to stay for supper, and he did. He dropped in nearly every day, and pretty soon he asked us to come and live with him. You see, he wanted friends around the house. We moved in as soon as we could get some furniture, and from then on I always called him 'Dad.'"

At last the house on Wendall Avenue was occupied. Steinmetz was delighted with the arrangement. No longer did he refer to his home as an "unsuccessful experiment." With the Haydens in the house, it did not seem too large and cold for the ever-lonely electrical genius. Always happiest when surrounded by young people, he gladly moved from the laboratory and chose the bedroom in which he was to sleep until he died. After many unsatisfied years, he really had a home of his own, and in it a family which was to grow dearer to him daily. When the three Hayden children were born, he requested and received permission from the court that they be considered his grandchildren by legal adoption. For twenty years the Haydens and the crippled genius shared the same roof in absolute harmony.

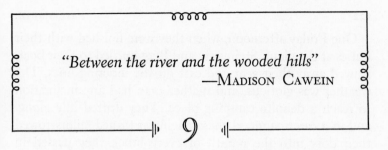

᚛᚛᚛᚛ ALL the difficulties Steinmetz had experienced in designing and building the house on Wendall Avenue seemed worth while once the Haydens were settled there. As a matter of fact, though he should have had no trouble in deciding just what type of house he wanted and how big it should be, because this was not the first house he had erected from his own plans. Long before Steinmetz had the slightest idea of having a city home, he had built a rustic camp on the banks of the Mohawk River, where he spent his summers and every week end during the fall and spring.

The beauties of the Mohawk had been familiar to Steinmetz almost from the beginning of his residence in Schenectady. In company with other General Electric engineers, he swam in its waters, explored its shoreline and sailed over it in hired boats. Sometimes it was impossible to rent a boat, so when Ernst Berg joined Steinmetz at "Liberty Hall," the two men decided to ask a local boat-builder to find them a dory for their personal use. On Friday afternoons they would go down to the dock where their craft was moored, get aboard, and cast off with no particular destination in mind. After sleeping underneath the stars and cooking their meals in the open air, they would return to the city early Sunday evening, refreshed and rested.

One Friday afternoon, when they were finished with their duties at the plant, Steinmetz and Berg hurried to their boat, stowed away their gear and cast off the mooring lines. The weather was glorious, and neither man had any inclination to reach a definite camping place. They drifted idly along, and in a carefree mood these engineers-turned-sailors rowed their dory into the mouth of every brook they passed in order to see how far they could navigate without going aground. Sometimes they were able to reach inland a considerable distance; at others they would be forced to turn back after a little way. Frequently the pair had to go over the side and push their craft off a sand-bar or mudbank, but since they wore bathing suits, this was a simple matter.

Just before sunset, Steinmetz called his companion's attention to a large stream that made a junction with the Mohawk by cutting through a high bank. "Let's camp here, Ernst," he suggested. "We'll never find a better place. I think this is Viele's Creek, but the name doesn't matter. Isn't it beautiful here? How would you like to have a house on that bank? What a view, and just think, swimming and boating right in your front yard!"

"Never mind how I would like a house," grumbled Berg. "All I am interested in right now is something to eat. After my stomach is full, I'll be in a better mood to enjoy the beauties of nature. Come on, let's beach the boat on that sand-bar and camp for the night."

While Steinmetz tied the boat securely to a black-alder sapling to keep it from rubbing on the sand, in case a wind should come up during the night, Berg gathered driftwood for a fire. By the time his companion had finished making the boat shipshape and had unpacked their gear, Ernst was boiling coffee and frying steaks. The smell of the food put Berg in a more agreeable frame of mind. From his kneeling position in front of the fire, he looked around. The sun set-

ting behind the Rotterdam Hills had turned Viele's Creek
and the Mohawk into ribbons of vivid red, and the view
was superb. "I won't wait until after I eat to tell you that
this is the most beautiful spot I've ever seen in America,"
he admitted. "It reminds me— Look out, the coffee's boiling
over! Come on, let's eat."

When they had finished their supper, the two engineers
sat beside the fire, smoking and talking. Weary from their
day's work at the plant and the long row up the river, they
soon spread their blankets, doused their campfire with several bucketsful of water, and made themselves comfortable
for the night. Cigars aglow, they lay silently listening to the
sounds that came from the river fifty feet below them. The
bass voices of frogs mingled with the soprano chorus of
crickets and the occasional splash of a rising fish. From time
to time the mournful hooting of an owl could be heard as
it called its mate back from a hunting expedition in the bul-
rushes that lined the river. With a final puff on his cigar,
Berg ground it into the sand beside him, mumbled a drowsy
"good night," pulled his blanket closer, and went to sleep.

Hands locked behind his head, Charles lay on his back,
looking at the stars. Although he was tired, he could not
sleep. How happy he was out here by the river— If only he
might live in the country, what a wonderful garden he could
have. Instead of keeping pets in cages, he would tame wild
animals to come and eat out of his hand. Suddenly he was
struck with an idea. Why not build a permanent camp on
this bluff at the junction of Viele's Creek and the Hudson's
longest tributary? In his excitement, Steinmetz reached over
to wake Berg and tell him of his plan, but decided it might
be best to wait until morning. "I don't believe I'd think
much of the scheme if someone should rouse me out of a
sound sleep to tell me about it!" He chuckled quietly and
fell asleep to dream of "Camp Mohawk."

As dawn broke, the two men sat up, rubbed their eyes, and without saying a word, sprinted down the bank for a dip in the river. Then they began preparing breakfast.

While they were eating, Steinmetz asked his companion, "What would you say if I told you I have decided to build a camp on this spot?"

"Why, I'd say that it was a splendid idea," replied Berg enthusiastically. "We've been up and down the length of the Mohawk, and this is definitely the most attractive camping spot we've seen. It isn't too far from town, and I wouldn't be surprised if there isn't a road near by that you could use to get here, if you didn't want to or couldn't come by water."

"Then what do you say if we don't go anywhere else this week end? Suppose we camp here and find out who owns the land—the nearest farmer ought to know—and see if there is a road? If the land can be bought or leased, and there is a road by which building materials can be brought out from town, I am determined to erect a camp on this bluff. Of course, if you don't want to stay on here now, we'll leave getting all the information for another time. It is entirely up to you. Do you mind?"

"Don't be foolish," Berg assured Steinmetz. "I don't care a bit. There is, however, one condition to be met before I agree to your suggestion. Once you have the camp built, you have to give me your promise that I can spend week ends out here!"

"Have no worries about that," Steinmetz laughed. "As of this minute you have a formal invitation to come here as often as you wish—providing I can acquire the property."

Breakfast over, the two engineers clambered over the bank, looking for the best place to build. Scientific knowledge gave way to pure enthusiasm as they paid more attention to such details as the best possible view and the easiest way to get to the water. Flushed with excitement, Steinmetz actually drove sticks into the ground to represent the four corners of the proposed camp. He even began to draw rough plans in the sand and was busy calculating the dimensions of the various rooms, when Berg jolted him into reality by suggesting that they hike along the meadowland above the river and look for a farmhouse, so they could inquire whether the land was available or not.

"There's no need of getting all worked up about this project, my friend, until you are sure you can obtain permission to build," he pointed out. "Come on, let's go exploring."

Cutting across the meadow, they entered a narrow belt of scrub timber, found a path and followed it until they came to a road. "Which way shall we go, Charles?" asked Ernst. "To the right or to the left?"

"Technical training is of no help at all at this point," admitted Steinmetz. "However, I can assure you that we should go either to the left or to the right! Seriously, I haven't the slightest idea what we should do. One of us could, I suppose, go one way, and one the other, but there is no guarantee that such a system would work out successfully. I know what to do— Let's approach this matter in a true scientific manner—toss a coin!"

Berg spun a coin in the air. "Heads left; tails right," he called.

It was heads. The two friends sauntered along the dusty, winding road, which was little more than a wagon track, and finally reached a farmhouse. Over a tin cup of cold water, they introduced themselves and asked if their host knew who owned the bluff where Viele's Creek joined the river.

To their surprise, the farmer replied, "Why, I do! Any special reason you want to know?"

Steinmetz explained his interest. After a short conversation, he completed arrangements to lease the land, with the option of buying it at a later date. The transaction was sealed with a handshake, and while the two principals were making plans to meet at a lawyer's office in the city to draw up the necessary legal documents, the farmer's wife handed Berg a paper bag full of freshly laid eggs.

After saying good-by, the engineers returned to the river, taking turns at balancing the eggs. As they descended the bank, Berg remarked, "I would call that a most successful walk, Charles. We found out that there is a road at the edge of the meadow and that it runs through the woods to the main road to Schenectady, you got a lease on this piece of land on which you can build your camp, and we had lunch given to us. You'll want these eggs scrambled, I suppose?"

"Always thinking about eating, Ernst, aren't you? I don't want anything until I finish my plans for 'Camp Mohawk' and definitely decide where I am going to build."

Berg shrugged his shoulders, carefully tucked the eggs under some bushes, and then joined Steinmetz. He found his friend pulling up the stakes he had driven into the ground earlier that morning. "Now that I know I can build here," he explained, "I can really lay out the location of my camp. Sooner or later, the lot will have to be surveyed, of course, but, meanwhile, let's go to work locating the four corners of the building."

It was dark when the two men had finished their task. Even Ernst was too weary to eat much. Backs against a comfortable log, cigars drawing freely, they discussed the best method of putting up the proposed camp. Finally, exhausted, they slipped between their blankets and were soon asleep.

The next morning found them anxiously awaiting the arrival of their new friend, the farmer, who drove across the meadow in a swaying buckboard. "Figured I might as well start making a road 'cross the medder," he said. "You'll be needing one. Say, you boys have got your camp all staked out— Now all you have to do is start building!"

"Speaking of building, you don't know anyone who would be interested in the job, do you?" asked Steinmetz.

"Well, if you don't want any of that fancy cabinet work, I reckon I can handle a saw and hammer well enough to build a camp. Don't want to talk someone else out of a chance to make a dollar, though."

"Don't worry about that. I won't even speak to anyone else. How soon can you go to work?"

Before the farmer left, arrangements for securing the necessary building materials and the rate of payment were settled on the spot. Steinmetz and Berg then took a quick dip in the river, packed up their gear, shoved their dory off the sand-bar and headed for Schenectady.

In its final form, "Camp Mohawk" consisted of a large main room with several surrounding bedrooms, covered with a gabled roof. Located on the top of the bluff, fifty feet above the water, it overhung the bank, the front half being supported by a series of wooden posts. At first glance, it looked as though the entire building were on stilts. In fact, Steinmetz the engineer was not nearly so pleased with the completed structure, as was Steinmetz the camper. His knowledge of stresses and strains made him wonder if the uprights underneath the large porch which faced the Mohawk could withstand the weight placed upon them. There was only one way to find out. Do as he had always done when confronted with a technical problem—conduct an experiment.

This was to be no laboratory test but an actual trial of the building. Using the excuse that he wanted to have a gala housewarming, Steinmetz invited all his fellow members of "The Society for the Equalization of Engineers' Salaries" to spend the week end at the newly completed camp. "Come Friday night and stay until it is time to leave for work on Monday morning," he said. "On Friday night I am going to

have a band and we will have a song-fest. There will be loads
to eat. Nicholaus' restaurant has promised to supply all the
refreshments we want. Saturday we'll go swimming and
boating all day—and then have another party at night. We
can spend Sunday resting up for work!"

Everyone accepted, and early Friday afternoon the engineering staff of General Electric could be seen making its
way to the junction of Viele's Creek and the Mohawk. Some
of the younger men came by canoe and rowboat, others rode
bicycles, while still others piled into hired carry-alls and
drove along the river road until they reached their destination. Steinmetz greeted them in his usual genial fashion,
showed them where to change their city clothes for the
"official uniform of Camp Mohawk"—bathing suits for all.

After an invigorating swim, the men changed into dry
suits and gathered in front of the camp. Their host made a
brief, humorous speech of welcome, and with a wave of his
hand invited the company to inspect his property. By this
time the six-man band had arrived and had been shown
where to set up their music stands on the porch. The evening was extremely warm and the punch bowl had been
placed at the *far* end of the refreshment table, making it
necessary for the thirsty engineers to walk the full length of
the porch every time they wanted a cold drink. Throats dry
from singing, groups of them would stand around the re-
freshing punch-bowl, looking out at the moonlight dancing
on the Mohawk.

Enjoying themselves, none of the guests thought of Steinmetz. If they had gone in search of him, they would have
found their host on the beach, watching the uprights, keeping a careful count of the number of people who were on
the porch at one time. At last, satisfied at what he had observed, he threw his cigar into the water and walked up the
bank to the camp, murmuring, "I guess if those timbers can
support all those people at once, my porch is safe enough."

Back in the house, he proved that he had complete faith in his building calculations by walking out on his porch for the first time since the camp had been built!

The house-party was a tremendous success. From that time on, the most sought-after invitation in Schenectady was Steinmetz' hearty, "Why don't you come out to my place on the river this week end?" Even the wives of the General Electric engineers looked forward to spending a day or two on the banks of the Mohawk. Everything was so pleasant there. Moreover, one didn't have to worry about what to wear. Everyday summer clothing was considered perfectly proper, and all you had to pack for the menfolk were two or three bathing suits. From the time you arrived you didn't have to do a thing: the men did the housework while Steinmetz cooked all the meals. To be sure, the food was not very fancy, but hours in the open air made even his culinary efforts tasty.

When there were women guests, Steinmetz' former neighbor, Mrs. Kruger, and her daughter Gretchen, acted as hostesses. However, most of the parties at "Camp Mohawk" were masculine affairs, for while Steinmetz made the ladies welcome, he was happiest when surrounded by just his fellow workers. The outings would begin Fridays, as soon as his guests could arrive by boat or horse-drawn vehicles, and continue until late Sunday afternoon. Steinmetz himself spent every week end at the camp, except in the middle of winter. Before his marriage, Roy Hayden, who did not have to report to the plant until eight o'clock on Monday mornings, stayed over with his host, spending Sunday night cleaning up the beach and helping "Dad" with straightening up the house.

Visitors at the camp needed no alarm clock to awaken them. Early in the morning they would hear a "tap-tap" and know that their host was hitting his barometer and making his weather observations. Steinmetz really didn't need to strike the instrument, but used the gesture as an excuse to rouse his guests. He never slept late in the morning and saw no reason why anyone else should! According to Emil Remschied, who worked with him for years in many different capacities, the electrical wizard always kept a daily weather record. As was to be expected, he did it by means of a mathematical formula which he wrote in the upper right-hand corner of his diary. Everything was taken into consideration: temperature, humidity, wind velocity, amount of sunshine, type of clouds and visibility. A perfect day was given a rating of 10+ while 10— stood for a severely stormy day—and the figures between this maximum and minimum were allotted to other days, depending upon the weather conditions. The last thing Steinmetz did at night before going to bed was to look at his barometer and tap it—which was a polite signal that it was time for everyone to retire.

No matter how cold the weather, he never wore anything but a bathing suit and knee-high rubber boots when at camp. One summer day in 1910, a group of visiting Russian scientists who were touring the General Electric works requested the honor of meeting "the great engineer who has made the use of alternating current possible." It was a very awkward situation. Steinmetz was never at the plant during the summer months, and would be furious if his privacy were invaded. On the other hand, it would have been most impolite to refuse the foreign delegation's request. So Mr. Rice, president of the company, hoping for the best, hired a carry-all and had the party driven out along the river to "Camp Mohawk," in charge of Roy Hayden.

On arriving at the camp, the Russians, dressed in gray striped pants, cutaway coats, stiff-bosomed shirts, Ascot ties and tall silk hats, gingerly made their way down the steep bank to the beach.

Roy cupped his hands and called loudly, "Dad! Come here, I want you."

The distinguished scientists from the other side of the Atlantic looked at each other in amazement. What was this young man trying to do? Suddenly, from around the bend came a canoe paddled by Steinmetz. "What ho, Roy!" he shouted.

With a few powerful strokes of his paddle, Steinmetz ran his canoe up on the sand, and stumbled out of his craft. Dressed as usual in bathing suit and boots, he was a fantastic sight as he came forward to meet his formally attired guests. In a few minutes the group was chatting excitedly in German about the possibilities of utilizing water power to generate electricity, neither the Russian scientists nor the crippled genius paying the slightest attention to their absurd contrast in appearance.

Steinmetz' favorite method of reaching camp was to paddle up the Mohawk in a specially designed canoe. In the fall of the year, this was quite a chore, as the water in the river was so low that the sand-bars stuck up high enough to block his passage. The most difficult of these obstructions ran out of the mouth of Viele's Creek, and a group of his closest friends decided to repay his hospitality by building a dam there that would assure enough depth of water so he would not run aground. If a construction firm had been obliged to pay the salaries of the crew which worked on this project, it would have gone into bankruptcy, for the finest engineering brains in the country spent three summers hauling rock, laying boulders, and cementing them in place. Yet despite all their technical knowledge, the dam was frequently washed out by spring floods, and repairs had to be made almost yearly. The men would laugh at their inability to erect a dam strong enough to withstand the rush of melted snow, but secretly they were exasperated and spent hours trying to figure out a way to improve their original design, in order to overcome the damage done during the period of high water. They were never able to win, and it became a tradition to devote one week end every spring to repairing the dam. Steinmetz took no part in the project, but would sit in his canoe, talking to his "workmen" while they piled more rubble behind the stone walls and pointed cracks in the cement. When the dam failed to hold back enough water to cover the sand-bar, he would ride out to camp on his trusty bicycle. As he grew older, he would often make the trip in his electric automobile.

For years the water held back by the dam was used by the campers as a swimming pool. Then Viele's Creek was filled in and the Mohawk was widened as part of the New York State Barge Canal project. Steinmetz, who was always in favor of progress, did not approve of this development. The reason for his displeasure was that the use of the river as a link in the Barge Canal made swimming in front of the camp too dangerous, because of the increased depth due to dredging. This meant that the Hayden family no longer spent all summer long at "Camp Mohawk." Their parents feared for the safety of the three youngsters, Joe, Billy and Marjorie. They did, however, continue to come out on week ends, and the two boys were Steinmetz' constant and eager companions all the time they were there.

Despite the deepening of the Mohawk, the camp was still a favorite resort of everyone from world-famous scientists to children. In August, 1907, Rudolph Eickenmeyer, Jr., son of the man who had given Steinmetz his first job in America, came to spend the week end. As so often happens in summer, a cold spell made outdoor living very uncomfortable. Bundled in coats and wearing two pairs of pants, young Eickenmeyer did not stir from the warmth of the fire, but Steinmetz still went around clad in his bathing suit and boots!

By now "Camp Mohawk" had been enlarged considerably, but it was still a rambling structure, plain as the man who owned it. Steinmetz was happier there than anywhere else, and whenever the weather permitted he would take his calculations "out to the camp." On arriving, he would change into his bathing suit, place four smooth boards across the gunwales of his canoe to use as a table, and shove off, carefully balancing his pencil box, logarithm tables and pad of paper. Once in midstream, he would let his "office" drift, and work contentedly on an engineering problem. If it were rough, before leaving the beach he would pick up a stone or two with which to weigh his papers down, and never notice how the canoe rocked and bobbed on the waves.

One Saturday morning Steinmetz gathered his papers together and said, "I am going fishing, Roy." Hayden smiled to himself. "Dad" always called his long hours floating around in his canoe "fishing." It was well known that he never took a rod and line with him when he went out on the water, but merely used the word to keep curious folk from asking why he spent so much time in his canoe. Those who knew realized that his "catch" was far more valuable than anything he could pull up from the waters of the river.

Returning to his Schenectady office the following Monday, Steinmetz handed his secretary the results of his week end "fishing" trip. It was the solution to a very intricate problem which could only have been worked out by the use of logarithm tables.

"I never expected to have this to type," exclaimed Cecile Rhein, who was one of the few people who could read her employer's private shorthand. "Just after you left Friday afternoon, I noticed that you had forgotten your logarithm tables. I ran after you, but by the time I got to the gate, you were disappearing pedalling like mad on your bicycle."

"Yes, I know, I forgot them, *dummkopf* that I am. You shouldn't have bothered to chase after me. But I suffered for my forgetfulness. I had to rule up a sheet of paper and make out a table of logs before I could get my work done."

Miss Rhein was not surprised to hear that Steinmetz had

been able to compile his own table of logarithms. She knew that he carried the table up to one thousand in his mind and could even recall the extension of it to the seventh place! Often she had seen him multiply large numbers by each other in a matter of seconds, while puffing on a cigar.

"Camp Mohawk" was always the scene of some exciting event. One week end Steinmetz astonished his guests by announcing that he had installed an electric lighting system. Everyone knew that there was no power line near the camp, and that their host had not set up a generator. Curiously, they crowded into the main room and waited for the engineer to explain. He pointed to a small bulb attached to some wires and said, "I've connected that light to the battery of my electric automobile. If someone has to take it to the city on an errand, we'll have to go back to oil lamps. But while the car is here, I can promise you modern lighting!"

In order to show their appreciation of his kindness in letting them use his camp as the site of an office party, a group of General Electric employees left a radio set on the porch for Steinmetz. Through an oversight, no note accompanied the gift, and the genius had the mistaken idea that the present had been given to him by the president, Mr. Rice. As a matter of fact, Rice knew nothing at all about the radio. Meanwhile, Steinmetz took great pride in pointing out the set to his guests, saying it was a "gift from the president"— leaving his visitors to wonder if he meant, by any chance, the head of the United States government. The real donors of the present enjoyed his little two-sided joke so much that they laughed to themselves and never told him the truth.

Life on the Mohawk was never so pleasant for Steinmetz as when his sister Clara came to visit him in Schenectady. He would leave her in the Wendall Avenue house, explaining that he had some very important calculations to do and could work better in the peace and quiet of the camp. On one of her visits, Clara insisted on having a companion, and asked for one who could help her improve her use of English. Anxious to please his sister, Steinmetz promised to find a young girl who could combine the duties of companion and tutor. After much correspondence, he found just the person he was seeking in Doris Bramson, a student at the famous Dorothy Dix School for Stage Children, in Boston.

Considered to be a very beautiful girl, Doris Bramson, although only in her teens, was making a reputation as an outstanding actress. In addition to her theatrical studies at the Dix school, where she boarded, and her appearances in local theaters, she was also a student at Girls' Latin School in Boston, one of the most difficult high schools in the country. One day, on her way home from classes, a man dressed in a flowing black cape and a sombrero stopped her and asked her name. Terrified, she started to run, frantically increasing her speed when she saw that she was being followed and never stopping until she arrived breathless at the front door of her dormitory.

As she burst into the hallway, the headmistress, Miss Whipple, stopped her and cried, "Is that any way for a young lady to enter a building? Your conduct is most disgraceful, Doris!"

Panting, the frightened girl explained how a strange man had stopped her, asked her name and then started to chase her. "Look!" she shrieked, pointing through the glass in the door. "Here he comes now!"

Miss Whipple stalked toward the entry, determined to put an end to this nonsense, once and for all. Just as she placed her hand on the door-knob, she recognized the intruder. Throwing open the door, she bowed graciously and said, "Come in, Mr. Sargent. This is indeed a great honor."

Doris' pursuer nodded his head curtly and blurted out, "Good day to you, madame. Please do not stop me. I saw a young lady come into this building, and I must find her. For weeks I have roamed the streets of Boston, seeking a girl to pose for the murals I am painting for the Public Library, and when I find her, she runs away. Where is she?"

Miss Whipple acidly explained that she trained her pupils not to speak to strange men, but agreed that she would call Doris. Secretly, the headmistress was delighted that John Singer Sargent, the most famous painter of his day, wanted to use the girl as a model. The final result of this chance meeting can be seen the next time you are in Boston. On the top floor of the main building of the Boston Public Library in Copley Square, you will find two of Sargent's most famous works: *The Old Testament* and *The New Testament*. The angel holding the scroll above the handmaidens of the Lord in the latter picture is the painter's portrait of Doris.

So it was only natural that when Miss Whipple was asked to send a lively girl with an excellent command of English to act as companion-tutor to Clara Steinmetz, she should choose Sargent's model. Now a well-known lecturer and dramatic coach, Doris Bramson Whitehouse recalls her summer in Schenectady with mixed emotions:

"I met Charles Proteus Steinmetz in 1901. His letter asking me to teach his sister Fräulein Steinmetz English, in return for her teaching me German and my expenses, was charming. I arrived at Wendall Avenue quite nervous, for I did not know what to expect—and I never quite got over my nervousness! In the first place, to a teen-age girl used to the light and warmth of the theater, the house itself seemed weird and unfriendly—and frankly so did Mr. Steinmetz himself. From the first day I was there, I had the feeling that he was not over-fond of his sister and greatly resented the fact that she had come to visit him in the summertime when he preferred to be at his camp. I also felt that he had asked me to act as her companion for the simple reason that if she were busy with me, he would not have to bother with her.

"Always an imaginative youngster, I never walked through

that sprawling house without feeling that some of the snakes Mr. Steinmetz had preserved in glass jars would come alive in the night, crawl upstairs and bite me! This frame of mind was not helped in the least by one of the tasks the Fräulein and I shared daily—feeding the fish and turtles. They ate well, finely cut tenderloin steak being the main staple of their diet. In fact, at times they ate much better than we did!

"Although Mr. Steinmetz spent most of his time at the camp on Mohawk River, he was engaging in a series of experiments with the electric stove at both the General Electric plant and his home laboratory. In order to test the improvements he designed at the works, he insisted that we do all our cooking on a duplicate stove set up in the kitchen of his house. Time after time he would reprimand his sister and me, in both English and German, because we would go off and leave the stove turned on—it had no lights or controls such as are found on modern electric stoves, and you could not tell whether it was on or off, unless you put your hand on it. He became so infuriated with us because we could not seem to use it properly that he finally forbade us to prepare any more meals in the house, but insisted that we go to a hotel to eat.

"The small pagoda type conservatory in the front yard was like a fairyland. I have never seen such beautiful flowers, even at a flower show. Whenever I had a moment to myself, I would wander up and down the narrow paths between the beds, admiring the glorious colors of the orchids or looking at the strange shapes of the cacti. Incidentally, some of these cacti were supposed to have exceptional medicinal qualities and Fräulein Steinmetz and I were continually answering the doorbell, as people came from miles around begging for a piece of a certain cactus to cure some ailment or other.

"Another task we had was to keep a close watch on Dr. Steinmetz' dog—I don't know what breed it was—but it was large and valuable. The animal was very dear to him and it was stolen again and again—and then returned for a reward. Looking back, I think the students at Union College made a practice of stealing the dog whenever they needed money for a dance or a football game, knowing that they would be paid for his safe return, with no questions asked. I think Steinmetz realized this, too, but was perfectly willing to make believe he knew nothing about it.

"Most of the time I was there, he was at his camp. I was there quite often, but he hardly spoke to me. He was too busy talking to his two parrots, who were very garrulous and seemed to understand everything their master said.

"His sister was the demanding and egocentric type, whereas he seemed very shy and retiring, and happiest when in the company of the Hayden youngsters. Just when I had overcome my fear of his beard, humpback, and piercing eyes, I was sent home. It all seems so silly now, but I cried all the way to the station. The reason for my dismissal was that Fräulein Steinmetz contended that I knew nothing about the English language since I said tough (tuff) was correct, but that dough was *never* 'duff.' She called me stupid in two languages and when I declared, 'I do not decide upon the pronunciation of these two words, but obey the rules as set down by the dictionary,' I was told to go home. Another reason—and I think the real one—was, and I quote her: 'Men look at you when we go to the hotel to eat, they never look at me—go home!'

"She was about forty at the time, I was fifteen!"

> *"A teacher affects eternity; he can never tell where his influence stops"* —HENRY ADAMS

⊪ 10 ⊪

༆༆༆༆ NO VISIT to Schenectady is complete without a tour of the beautiful campus of Union College. Established in 1795, Union was the first institution of higher learning in New York State north of New York City and it has long been recognized as one of the leading small colleges of the United States. Union is called the "Mother of Fraternities" by collegians, because six of them were founded there, including Kappa Alpha, the first Greek letter social organization in America. In 1902, the president of the College, Dr. Andrew Van Vranken Raymond, an extremely progressive educator, decided that the time had come to change the curriculum and provide students with a more rounded education.

It was Dr. Raymond's intention that every young man who attended Union should have an opportunity "to receive such training as is now considered essential for every educated man." Observing the tremendous strides being made in industrial development, he realized that the old purely academic course, with its emphasis on language, history, and literature, while important, was not meeting the demands of the times. From now on, it was evident, colleges had to pay more attention to technical education. To be sure, Union had long offered a lecture course in engineering, but President Raymond planned to expand the course into a department.

The General Electric Company, needing hundreds of engineers for its ever-growing plants, offered Union the unlimited use of materials from its stockrooms, three thousand dollars' worth of scientific apparatus—and Steinmetz, as their share of creating the new division. The engineer was to receive no salary from the College, and General Electric would assume most of the incidental costs of the project. This offer was immediately accepted, and at the annual meeting of Union alumni, held in New York City in December, 1902, Dr. Raymond announced the establishment of the new department and introduced its chief—Charles Proteus Steinmetz.

The little scientist spent the most pleasant years of his life as a member of the faculty of Union College. In his youth he had dreamed of being a college professor, and now he was one. In addition to his classroom work, Steinmetz spent much time in the newly-equipped engineering laboratory, engaged in a study of corona—the leakage of electricity during the transmission from one point to another. With the assistance of professors and students, he set up a transmission line, built to a scale, that represented two thousand miles of high tension wires. His experiments did a great deal toward enabling engineers to cut down on the loss of electrical energy as they sent power from the point of generation to its user.

Although Steinmetz, as usual, was perfectly happy in the laboratory, his contact with the students in the lecture hall, on the campus and at social events gave him the most pleasure. He was the most informal of teachers. Standing in front of the class, hands on a table, he would lean forward as he talked, punctuating his sentences with waves of his arms or by stabs with the ever-present cigar. From time to time he would rush over to the blackboard, write an equation in a crabbed hand that could not be seen by anyone who did not sit in the first row, hobble back to the table, find he had broken his cigar and reach for another without a pause in his explanation. Steinmetz' greatest fault as a teacher during his tenure at Union was that he thought that all his students had as great a mental capacity as himself, and thus expected too much from them. On the other hand, he had great patience and the ability to make complicated theories understandable.

The best word picture of Steinmetz the teacher is found in the files of the Alumni Office at Union. It was written by C. N. Waldron, one-time secretary of the institution:

"While not an engineer myself, I used to go into his classes now and then, for he was a fascinating lecturer, and I found him pleasant to listen to even when I did not understand the subject. Somehow you seemed to understand it while he was talking. I recall the helpless look in his students' faces when he would write an equation on the board, and then say, 'from this we get this.' He knew the steps from one to another and could solve it instantly in his mind, but to his students it was far from clear.

"The best story I remember has to do with the class roll-call. He taught in two-hour periods, with fifteen minutes in between for the boys to go out, smoke and relax. The roll was called at the beginning of each period. On days when he was talking far above their heads, many would not return for the second period, but their friends would answer for them on the second roll-call. Noting this one day, Dr. Steinmetz, with the characteristic gesture of tugging at the top of his gray flannel trousers, was heard to murmur, 'What a remarkable mathematical phenomenon, twenty-five people, but fifty voices.' "

A short time after assuming his duties at Union, Steinmetz was invited to become a member of the Phi Gamma Delta fraternity. The new professor of electrophysics was delighted and accepted at once. After his initiation, he became as active in the organization as any undergraduate, and never missed a meeting of the group. It was like the old days in Breslau and the Friday night gatherings of the Mathematics Society. Because the fraternity did not have a chapter house of its own, meetings were held in the home of Professor Frank Hoffman of the language department, who was faculty adviser to the group. The boys were very anxious to secure a building lot on the campus and erect a fraternity house, but for some reason the College authorities refused to grant this request, and it seemed as though Phi Gamma Delta would have to continue to use Professor Hoffman's home as a gathering place.

As a faculty member, Steinmetz had been given a piece of land on the campus on which to build a home, and he immediately turned the lot over to Phi Gamma Delta. The college officials told him that he was not permitted to give the boys the land. Steinmetz then sat down and wrote out his resignation from the teaching staff and handed it to Dr. Raymond. Not wanting to lose the services of the electrical wizard, the authorities agreed that he could deed his lot to the fraternity. The grateful students then made him chairman of the committee in charge of building the chapter house, and he gave freely of his time and money to the project. The building, one of the most attractive on the campus, was soon erected.

When the house was built, Steinmetz spent a great deal of time there. He could often be seen in an animated scientific discussion with graduate students, playing cards with members of his classes, or just enjoying the comradeship of the boys. At any time he was ready to help and encourage those who were having difficulty with their classroom work. He also was instrumental in securing excellent positions in industry for many students. His kindness and interest made him very popular, and before long the members of the fraternity were calling him "Daddy." Steinmetz was as proud of this term of affection as he was of the title he had received at the nickname ceremony at Breslau, so many years before.

While "Daddy" was always interested in all the men at Union, he had a particular concern for the students in the engineering course, and had definite ideas about the attitude these young men should have toward their professional careers. Speaking one day to a group, he said, "If a young man goes at his work as a means to an end, like getting a raise in salary or making a million dollars, I am not interested in him. I am interested, however, if he sets out to do his task for the work's sake and for the satisfaction it gives him. Success in life is to make a living at work that interests you."

In June, 1903, Union College awarded Steinmetz the degree of Doctor of Philosophy in recognition of his outstanding achievements in the field of electrical engineering. A year previously, Harvard University had honored him with the degree of Master of Arts. Dr. Charles W. Eliot, president of Harvard, presented the diploma to Steinmetz with these words, "I confer this degree upon you as the foremost electrical engineer in the United States, and therefore the world." These honors did not change Steinmetz. To the boys in the fraternity house, he was always the same "Daddy," and to the other students at Union, "Steiny." Only new arrivals on the campus and staid members of the faculty called him Dr. Steinmetz.

The corona experiments were taking so much time that Steinmetz could spend only three hours a week at the General Electric plant and deal with only vitally important matters. As his investigations into electrical leakage became more complicated, he found that he could not spare as much time as he wished to lecture at Union and he was forced to drop some of his classes. In his place he secured the services of experts in various fields from the plant. He did not lose contact with the student body, however. Any Union man was always welcome in his home, and most evenings he could be found giving a demonstration or an informal lecture to a group of "his boys" in the Wendall Avenue laboratory.

Busy as he was, Steinmetz always attended fraternity meetings. One night a group of the brothers expressed the desire to have a purple light in the main room of the chapter house—as that was the official color of Phi Gamma Delta. "Daddy" said nothing, but several days later entered the building carrying a very bulky box. He locked himself in the room, and in a short while threw open the door. The curious members crowded in and saw a delicate purple light flooding the walls and ceiling. "There you are, boys!" cried Steinmetz. "You wanted a purple light—I had nothing to do last night so I made one out of odds and ends in my laboratory. It's a mercury vapor lamp, and I think it may be just what you wish."

It was, and if you visit the chapter house today, you will see his purple light still in use!

"Steiny" and his bicycle were a familiar sight on the Union campus. He would pedal along the paths, waving to everyone he passed. The students could always tell if it were extremely cold, by the simple method of watching to see if Steinmetz wore a hat or not. If it were well below freezing, he would enter the College Yard wearing a coonskin cap and would be moving so quickly that the dangling tail would appear to be frozen stiff as it stuck out behind his head. On warm Sundays, he would ride his bike from his Wendall Avenue home to the fraternity house, park it against the steps, and sit on the porch for hours, talking with the boys.

During these sessions of talk and good fellowship, "Daddy" would give advice, lend money, tell what he was doing at the General Electric laboratory, and explain how his latest experiment with the transmission of power was coming along. Sometimes he would entertain the gathering with card tricks. Steinmetz was adept at magic—not the tricks where the hand works faster than the eye, but those involving card guessing and card calculation. He solved the most difficult "magic" problems with astonishing rapidity and accuracy, and spent hours developing new and puzzling combinations with which he would bewilder the students, to his great amusement.

One evening a group of his young friends visited "Steiny" at his home. He showed them the latest additions to his arrowhead collection, some newly arrived rare orchids and cacti, and watched with lively interest their attempts to wake up his pet Gila monster. As the boys were leaving, one of them said, "We've brought you a present, sir," and handed their instructor a cardboard box.

Opening it, Steinmetz found five white mice. He was delighted with the gift and immediately made his new pets comfortable in a warm home made from a glass aquarium. Soon there were dozens of fish tanks filled with mice. A mathematically inclined student counted them one evening and reached the astounding total of 500! Everyone told their proud owner that he ought to get rid of them, but he indignantly refused. "How could the poor things find anything to eat if I released them?" he asked. "You certainly don't expect me to destroy them, do you?"

The entire conservatory might soon have been filled with aquaria containing mice, if some of the students hadn't decided to do something about the situation. One day, while "Steiny" was busy at the college laboratory, they set all the mice free. For weeks afterward, residents of the Wendall Avenue area were complaining about "the number of mice we have seen recently." Steinmetz was greatly annoyed at the students, but forgave them when they apologized, although he often expressed the desire to know "if my poor mice are all right."

Whenever examination time came, "Daddy" would gather

all the boys at the fraternity house in the main room and give them a refresher course in order to help them pass. Other students would go to his house for special help on the night before tests. One evening some of them arrived at Wendall Avenue, explaining that they had just come to spend a social evening. Steinmetz, always pleased when in the company of young people, gave them a tour of the conservatory, allowed them to play with Jenny the monkey, pointed out the new fish he had recently placed in the pools, and called their attention to some exotic cacti which were in bloom. The boys expressed great admiration for everything they saw, and then, with great skill, casually brought the conversation around to the subject of the final examination in mathematics. "Daddy" pretended he had no idea why they should discuss such a subject with him, but admitted that if he were studying for the test, he would pay particular attention to certain things.

The students made mental notes of his suggestions, thanked him for a very pleasant evening and rushed back to Union, where they wrote down what Steinmetz had said. On the day of the examination, they found that "Daddy" had given them the actual questions. As a result, they all passed. Of course, Steinmetz was absolutely wrong in telling his class anything about the test. It was not fair to them, nor to the other students in the class. It was only because he was so interested in "his boys" and wanted to help them that he was guilty of such an unethical act.

Steinmetz was always playing jokes on the student body. When a new group of "pledges" was initiated into Phi Gamma Delta, he was placed in charge of the humorous part of the ceremony. Once he suggested that this portion of the ritual be held in his conservatory. "I think," he suggested with an infectious grin, "that it would be most interesting to see how long our new members can sit on one of my prickly cacti!"

Everyone agreed that "Daddy" had an excellent idea, and on the evening of the initiation the candidates were led blindfolded by a roundabout route to Steinmetz' house. Then they were taken into the plant-and-flower-filled building that was his pride. The cacti were placed in position, and one by one the "pledges" were told to sit down, and not to utter a sound or to move! When "Daddy" had decided that they could not sit still any longer, the boys were led to the edge of the big fish pool, where they were pushed in and ordered to "wash away the thorns!" After this, they were marched around some more, and finally taken to the laboratory, where the engineer had rigged up a static electricity machine. This outfit was capable of throwing sparks twelve to eighteen inches long, giving a harmless but startling shock to anyone who touched it. In preparation for the initiation, "Daddy" had wired every piece of metal in the room so that when the new members touched such things as doorknobs, sparks shot from their fingers. It was a ceremony that has never been forgotten by those who were present!

Steinmetz was just as ready to help his students as to play jokes on them. Leo H. Perry, one of his pupils, was writing a thesis dealing with arc lamps, and in order to gather the necessary data, worked on the Wendall Avenue installation, raising, lowering and helping repair the lights the electrical genius had set up in co-operation with the City of Schenectady. This experience enabled Perry to collect a great deal of material on the subject of arc lamps, which he outlined for use in his thesis. Organizing the pages of notes he had gathered was a most laborious task, and he soon found that it was going to be impossible to finish his paper within the period of time allotted to him by the college authorities.

"The thesis was due on a Saturday," Perry recalled at a celebration held in commemoration of the seventieth birthday of Steinmetz, "and I had the choice of struggling with it or going to a circus. The circus seemed far more important than arc lamps, so I asked 'Daddy' what I should do. He said I had no choice—I should go to the circus! During the afternoon, Steinmetz spent several hours going over my notes, and while I was enjoying myself at the circus with the future Mrs. Perry, he outlined my thesis for me. As a matter of fact, his suggestions were the thesis, and it goes without saying that Dr. Steinmetz approved it and I passed!"

All this time it was very evident to the trustees of Union that while Steinmetz was the most popular professor on the campus, he was expecting far too much from his students in the classroom. Yet it was recognized that his lectures were inspiring, and that personal contact with the leading electrical engineer in the world was something the boys would treasure all their lives. Even Dr. Raymond had heard, unofficially of course, the story of William Smith, a student who was majoring in mathematics. While on a week end visit to "Camp Mohawk," the young man informed his host that he would have to spend several hours working on an assignment given by his geometry professor. "It is a very difficult problem in analytic geometry, sir. That is, it is difficult for me, although the prof did say that he didn't think that any member of the class would be able to do it. So if you will excuse me for a while, I'll go to work."

Steinmetz, who was sitting on the bank, watching the Mohawk glide slowly by and admiring the clouds as they scudded over the top of the Rotterdam Hills in the distance, took the cigar out of his mouth and inquired, "What's the problem?"

Opening his notes, Smith read the figures aloud. "Steiny" took two or three quick pulls on his cigar and then asked quietly, "Got a pencil? Good. Very well, write down what I dictate."

Smith did as he was told. Simply and clearly, Steinmetz dictated to him the various steps in the solution of the problem. The next Monday in class, Smith was the only one who was able to report that he had finished the assignment. The professor sent him to the board and watched with astonishment as he wrote down a long series of complicated equations, all of which seemed to be correct. The amazed instructor went carefully over his student's work, but could find nothing wrong, and he was speechless when Smith returned to his seat, cheerfully and truthfully remarking, "I really had no trouble at all with this outside work, sir!"

It is doubtful if "Steiny" gave the ethics of doing Smith's assignment the least thought. To him, the proposition was a mathematical challenge, a temptation he could never resist. Even in his Breslau days he was considered the best private tutor of mathematics in the city, and the years had brought him additional knowledge—so without a second's hesitation, his brilliant mind went into action, and he did not have the slightest consideration of the impropriety of his act.

During the first part of Steinmetz' association with Union there was little official financial aid granted the various athletic teams. The expenses of the different sports were met by voluntary contributions from the student body. "Steiny" always gave generously to every campaign for funds to support the college teams, and enthusiastically attended all home games and meets. As a youth he had been unable to run like other boys and, although he could sprint with easy grace through mathematics and science, he could enjoy real sports only as a spectator.

Steinmetz became a Union tradition the night he attended a theatrical performance given by the student body at the Van Curler Opera House. It was a very formal affair: the women were dressed in evening gowns, the men in dress suits. Just before the curtain, "Steiny" appeared in one of the stage boxes attired in his usual baggy suit and a gray flannel shirt. Many a man in the audience, uncomfortable in stiff shirt and highly starched collar, envied Steinmetz' comfortable clothing, but not one of them would have dared to go to the performance in such an outfit. As for what the ladies in the theater thought of Charles Proteus Steinmetz —it is just as well that it is not recorded!

By now his experiments at Union, in the laboratory at the General Electric plant, and his home workshop were taking so much of his time that "Steiny" regretfully was forced to drop more of his classes. Looking around for someone to take his place, he asked Dr. Ernst Berg, his former roommate and close associate at the works, to join the college faculty. Berg accepted the offer, but was quite worried for fear he would not be able to make his lectures interesting enough to hold the attention of the students.

"Don't worry, Ernst," Steinmetz assured him. "You can use my system. As you know, I am doing a great deal of writing these days, dealing with electrical subjects—and as fast as I finish a chapter in one of my books, I read it to my engineering students. I judge whether it is interesting or not by the number of students who go to sleep. If only half of them nod, I am sure that my material is all right!"

"What do you do if a student disagrees with something you say in the classroom?" asked Berg.

"I am delighted!" retorted Steinmetz. "That's proof that at least one of the class is paying attention!"

No wonder Dr. Berg once wrote in appreciation of Steinmetz: "He saw things in a clearer way than anyone I have met, and he was able to make clear what he knew, to the ordinary mind. He was always anxious and able to be helpful."

In 1913 the great electrician was forced to give up his active association with Union. Ever since Berg had joined the staff, Steinmetz had managed to break away from his work long enough to give an occasional lecture, but now the time spent in the lecture hall, enjoyable as it was, could be used to better advantage in the laboratory. For ten years "Daddy" had been supremely happy as a college professor; but, after

all, he was a research scientist and there was so much to discover and so little time in which to do it. So, with great
regret, Charles Proteus Steinmetz turned his department at
Union College completely over to Dr. Berg, and devoted
himself to further investigations into the mysteries of electricity. From time to time, however, he would visit the college and take over a class. He also continued his habit of
welcoming the students to his home to discuss their problems and to help them all he could in their studies. No
wonder he was held in such affection.

THE mercury vapor lamp that Steinmetz had constructed for the Phi Gamma Delta fraternity "from odds and ends" was the direct result of his annoyance that his shrubs had not shown to advantage under the magnetite arcs during the experimental lighting of Wendall Avenue. In fact, he had begun to investigate the possibilities of developing a new type of lamp within a week of the gala ceremony in front of his house. Roy Hayden's worry about the Brush generator that had to be watched continually so that it would not break down under the strain of a full power load had sparked Steinmetz' thinking about the problem. But the fact that passers-by could not enjoy the lush greens of his bushes under artificial illumination shocked him into action.

Before he could start the experiments he had outlined, however, the engineer was forced to stay at his desk doing a routine task. At last a commercial publisher had decided to take a chance and issue in book form the *Theory and Calculation of Alternating Current Phenomena*. First written in 1890 and based on Steinmetz' paper read before the International Electrical Congress in Chicago, the original text was far too technical for anyone but its author to understand.

However, using his classroom experiences as a lecturer at

Union as a guide, Steinmetz completely rewrote the book in as simple fashion as he could, in order that students and workers in the field could follow his theories. The revamped volume was entitled *Theoretical Elements of Electrical Engineering,* and the author used it in his courses. He soon found out that, despite the revision and simplification, the average candidate for an engineering degree was unable to understand its pages. Seeking to find a reason for his students' inability to comprehend what he considered the bare rudiments of electrical knowledge, Steinmetz discovered that his pupils' difficulty arose from the fact that they had not received a sufficient background in mathematics before entering college.

An examination of the various books used in high schools throughout the country convinced him that there was a definite need for a basic text for those who were planning to take technical degrees, and he promptly filled it with the publication of his *Engineering Mathematics.* Over the years this volume has become a required tool for all electrical engineers. As his experimentation opened new fields, Steinmetz also enlarged the original *Theory and Calculation of Alternating Current Phenomena.* This is still considered a standard work.

With his manuscript on alternating current corrected and edited, Steinmetz was now free to devote all his attention to the developing of a new lamp. Ever since the announcement of Cooper-Hewitt in 1902 that he had successfully vaporized mercury and used it in an arc lamp, Steinmetz had been greatly impressed by all the varied uses of mercury. Always fascinated by unusual things, whether terrapins or cacti, he was intrigued by the liquid metal that in one form could provide the explosive power of bombs and cartridges, in another furnish some twenty-five preparations used by doctors, and in still another make the milling of gold and silver ore possible.

Well-read in the history of man's constant search for a better means of providing himself with light, Steinmetz knew that the first experiment in the use of mercury in an arc lamp had been conducted by J. T. Way in 1860. This scientist had poured a very fine spray of mercury from one metallic container to another, having first wired both vessels in series to an electric battery. The electric current split the jet-like stream of mercury into beads and formed arcs between them. There was, of course, no illumination from Way's arcs, but they furnished a basis for further investigations into the use of vaporized mercury as a gaseous conductor of electricity.

Steinmetz' contribution to the long series of improvements in mercury-arc lamps was in the field of street lighting. Thus he was able to keep his promise to his adopted son that he would invent something to overcome the inefficiency of the Brush generator, and at the same time produce a lamp which would be kind to his shrubs. He did this by developing a rectifier, which later engineers improved. However, because many colors are blotted out or are greatly changed in appearance when streets are lit by mercury-arc lamps, his invention never enjoyed widespread use. In other fields, mercury lamps of different types have become very popular. They have been found ideal for use in photographers' studios, in hospitals where ultraviolet energy is wanted, in television lighting and in other specialized situations.

Nor do lighting engineers feel that they have unearthed all the possibilities of the mercury lamp. They are still at work, experimenting, designing, and dreaming of a mercury vapor lamp that will provide ideal illumination—light with no waste of energy in the lamp itself, or in invisible radiant energy.

Yet if a modern scientist does achieve this goal, he could never be quite as pleased as was Steinmetz with his mercury-arc lamp. You see, the great experimenter found a use for his invention that only he could have thought of—no other electrical engineer would be apt to see in the mercury-arc the chance to play a practical joke! Once Steinmetz had observed how the bluish glare of his lamp showed off the shrubbery satisfactorily, he installed a set of them in the conservatory. One evening while escorting an extremely pretty girl through the orchid room, he noticed that her face and hands underwent a startling transformation because of the tendency of mercury lamps to distort color. Naturally enough, he had known this, but the sight of his guest's appearance gave him a puckish idea. Saying nothing to his family, he spent several hours the next day installing a mercury-arc lamp in the guest room of the Wendall Avenue house, where the ladies left their wraps and powdered their noses.

With deliberate intent, he set the light fixture in such a position that anyone who entered the room would be forced to look at his reflection in a full-length plate glass mirror that hung on the wall opposite the door. Of course, he didn't tell Mrs. Hayden what he was doing, for she would have scolded—not that anything that good woman would have said might have stopped him—but Steinmetz disliked upsetting her. Finally, the job was done and he was ready for his first victim.

He did not have long to wait. That evening the attractive daughter of one of his assistants at the plant dropped in with a book her father had borrowed. It was an extremely blustery night and the young lady's hair was wind-blown. "Dr. Steinmetz," she asked, "would it be all right if I stopped long enough to tuck my hair under my hat before going out again? I really look such a fright that I . . ."

"Why, of course, my dear. You are far too pretty to have even a single hair out of place—although if you will allow an old man to say so, you look beautiful just as you are. Go right in and make yourself comfortable," came the cheery reply.

With a word of thanks, her glorious blonde hair streaming down her shoulders, the grateful visitor entered the powder room and snapped on the light switch. Suddenly there was a scream of horror. The young woman had seen herself in the mirror—but what a sight! Thanks to the mercury-arc lamp her host had set up, her reflection showed her to have a *green* face and *dark purple* lips! Unable to believe her eyes, she had looked down at her hands and found, to her dismay, that they too were green! Sobbing with fright and shaking with terror, she rushed from the room and out the front door.

Mrs. Hayden and Roy had come rushing downstairs when they heard the scream. They stood open-mouthed as the terrified girl ran by them. "Dad, what in the world is the matter?" demanded Roy. Steinmetz was unable to answer the question. He was doubled-up with laughter, holding his sides while tears ran down his face. At last he was able to sputter an account of what had happened, punctuating his story with loud guffaws. "Now, don't get angry," he concluded. "You have no reason to be upset. You see, it was only an experiment. I wanted to prove that beauty is only relative."

Over the years Steinmetz did a great deal of research with mercury lamps, and in order to show what could be done with them often invited parties of newspapermen to Wendall Avenue. One reporter, after spending an evening in the laboratory, wrote: "Dr. Steinmetz' lamp is a long glass tube containing a few spoonfuls of quicksilver, and when an electric current is applied, the metal is vaporized and driven through the tube, giving out a strong green glare. It is an eerie sight to sit underneath it and watch your hands turn color and your neighbor's hair fade. You realize how strange you must look, for you can see how grotesque everyone else appears. Your host stands there laughing and explains the reason for your change in appearance by saying, 'Yes, it does make you look rather ghastly, because there is no red in the light.' "

In the same newspaper account there is a discussion of Steinmetz' annoyance at his inability to make the mercury lamp do everything he wanted it to do: "While a mercury lamp is the nearest thing to sunlight we have in artificial illumination, and does not tire one's eyes, its tendency to distort colors is its main drawback. Dr. Steinmetz illustrated this by showing how a red bandana handkerchief turned a dull brown when exposed to his lamp, and then asked if anyone in our group had a ring set with a colored stone. One of the ladies offered him an opal ring. Our host looked at it and commented, 'Nothing could be better! Under ordinary lamps or in daylight an opal lives up to Pliny's description of the stone—"in them you see the living fire of the ruby, the glorious purple of the amethyst, the green sea of the emerald, all glittering together in an incredible mixture of light!" ' Then he placed the ring directly under the lamp, and it turned a drab purple with flecks of yellow.

"Pointing to his feet, the scientist continued: 'Have you been looking at my shoes? I assure you they are not red; they are actually brown. But take this remnant of pink silk. Hold it as close to the lamp as you wish—and what do you find? It stays pink! That is one of the strange things about mercury lamps. Perhaps some day someone will develop a mercury lamp that will show all colors in their true shades— however, I don't think it is possible.' "

If Steinmetz had said, "I don't think it is possible" at the General Electric plant, no one would have argued with him. The matter would have been considered a closed issue. For with the passing of years "The Supreme Court" had become more and more important. To be sure, he never spent more than three hours a day in his office at the works, going there only by appointment to hold a conference on some complicated aspect of electrical or mechanical engineering theory. The rest of the time he was either in the laboratory or "fishing" on the Mohawk. Relentless in the pursuit of an idea, he would not and could not devote any more time than was necessary to office work. Although chief consulting engineer of General Electric, he was given all the freedom he desired to pursue his own inclinations—no other work was ever forced upon him.

From time to time, one of the directors of the organization would make arrangements to meet Steinmetz at the works. Armed with a long series of recommendations by other research experts, the official would ask the great scientist's opinion of the practicability of engaging in a series of investigations along a certain line. Steinmetz would listen politely, his face screwed into a frown while he puffed on a cigar, his legs tucked up underneath him as he sat on the top of a laboratory worktable. When his superior had finished, he might say, "That is impossible!"—and all plans to conduct experiments in that direction were thrown into the discard. If, on the other hand, he jumped to his feet and cried, "Say, that's a wonderful idea!"—no expense in men or materials was spared to conduct the proposed investigations.

His odd sense of humor never deserted Steinmetz, no matter where he was. Most of his associates, rightly enough, held the directors of the General Electric Company in awed respect. But not he. One winter day, when, thanks to a thawing wind, the weather had turned comparatively warm, he threw open the laboratory windows. A short while later a plant official, accompanied by a group of important clients of the firm, entered the room to discuss the design of an intricate piece of apparatus. During the conversation, the company representative, noticing that the visiting dignitaries were not comfortable in the draft, looked pointedly at Steinmetz and then at the windows. The scientist completely ignored the hint and went on explaining how the required machine could be built. Suddenly, impatient and annoyed at his employee's disregard of his frantic signals, the official broke in with a curt, "Dr. Steinmetz, I think that window . . ."

"Why, yes, of course—you feel it should be opened wider. Excuse me, gentlemen, while I do so," came the prompt reply and the elfish engineer threw the sash up as far as it would go!

He was just as much of a problem to Mrs. Hayden. Most of the time she could get him to do what she wanted, but in one thing he firmly refused to bow to her wishes. From his days at Eickenmeyer's, he had acquired the habit of working dressed only in trousers and undershirt. While he stayed in the laboratory, Roy's wife had no objection to this informal garb, but often he would come into the house seeking some book he had mislaid, or on some other errand, and seeing that there were visitors, politely stop and chat for a while. In vain the mistress of Wendall Avenue pleaded, "It isn't the right thing to do, Dad. You have no idea of what people will think of you dressed like that! Please, promise me that you will wear a shirt."

"I'll promise nothing of the sort," growled Steinmetz. "If those callers of yours have nothing else to do but to think how strange I look in an undershirt, I'm sorry for them. That's the way I like to dress when I work, and that's the way I'm going to dress! So let's have no more talk about it!"

There was a great deal more discussion, but it accomplished nothing. Steinmetz continued to dress the way he pleased, and Mrs. Hayden was forced to give up the unequal contest.

Nothing illustrates the independence of Charles Proteus Steinmetz more than an incident that occurred late one June. Production work on a turbine designed for overseas

shipment had come to a halt because of a technical difficulty. In vain the engineers in charge of the project tried
to find a way to solve their problem, but it was no use.
There was only one thing to do—ask "The Supreme Court."
A call to Steinmetz' secretary resulted in the discouraging
information that "he won't be in today, and I doubt if he
comes to the plant tomorrow. He is actively engaged in a
most important experiment at the Wendall Avenue laboratory."

"It makes no difference how busy he is," retorted the man
in charge of the turbine project. "As chief consulting engineer of General Electric, he should be available when
needed. I can't wait until he gets around to coming to the
works—I'm going out there and get his advice on how to
set that production line of mine working!"

Grabbing his hat and coat, the distraught technician
rushed to Wendall Avenue. He cut across the lawn and
went directly to the laboratory. The door was open and he
could hear a babel of voices. On entering, he saw Steinmetz
and the Hayden youngsters bending over a bench which was
littered with flasks of chemicals. Without a moment's delay,
the engineer explained his mission and ended up by saying
cuttingly, "As you can see, our difficulty at the plant is far
more important than what you are doing with these children."

"Oh, is that so?" replied Steinmetz testily. "Nothing is
more important than what is being done in this laboratory!
In fact, it is so important that your turbine will have to
wait until tomorrow for my attention. Don't you realize that
next Thursday is the Fourth of July?"

"Pardon me, but what in the world has that got to do
with it?"

"Why everything! We are making fireworks and if we
don't finish them today, they won't be ready in time. You
know, I'm sure, that such things as sparklers have to dry be-

fore they work properly—so please go back to the plant. I promise that I will come in tomorrow and see what I can do about your turbine."

There was nothing else for the technician to do but return to the works. Steinmetz wouldn't have disappointed young Marjorie, Billy, and Joe even if Mr. Rice himself had ordered him to report immediately to his office. After all, what was General Electric making that was more important than fireworks for the Fourth of July? The next day, true to his word, Steinmetz was at his office, and within a matter of minutes had eliminated the flaw in the turbine design.

As a matter of fact, the General Electric Company had reason to be grateful that the fireworks didn't take longer to manufacture, for if they had, Steinmetz would have stayed away indefinitely. The immediate happiness of any child was more important to this strange genius than solving the most baffling engineering problem.

It is difficult to say when he was the most relaxed: while investigating some untamed phenomenon of electricity, or playing with his adopted grandchildren. From their first day at school he took over the task of helping them with their lessons, instilling in them the idea that they should ask all the questions necessary until they completely understood the topic being studied, and insisting that they get excellent marks. Many a night when he should have been out in the laboratory, checking the performance of one of his new developments before turning it over to his employers to market, Steinmetz sat beside the Hayden youngsters, checking their homework, frankly admitting that he would rather help them than work on his invention.

Nor did he confine his interest in their activities to aiding them with schoolwork. He was never too busy to join the trio in staging a show for the neighborhood children, and would spend as much time preparing an electrical effect for the performance as he would over a technical paper he was to read before a gathering of distinguished scientists. Often, on coming home from work, he would join the young people in their games of hide-and-go-seek, scrambling up and down the bank to the glen, as lively as any of the teen-aged players.

Nothing the Hayden children did was wrong in his eyes. Even Billy's habit of picking flowers in the conservatory failed to excite him. Steinmetz would explain to the child that the flowers shouldn't be picked, but it was of little use —the boy could not resist the temptation. The scientist never picked flowers of any type, either in his greenhouse or in the woods near "Camp Mohawk," because he wanted them to go to seed so that they would produce even more blooms the following season. When Billy wasn't gathering a bouquet, he loved to help his grandfather plant seeds and set out new plants. The two transformed the bank behind the laboratory and the bog lot into a beautiful wild garden. Many of the plants were sent to Steinmetz from friends in the engineering profession, who dug them up in the various places to which their duties took them. One portion of the glen garden was filled with mountain laurel, gathered in the near-by Berkshire Hills. This range is famous as the location of the Mohawk Trail, which the Indians traveled when going back and forth between what is now Massachusetts and New York. It is one of the most scenic drives in the United States.

In order to try to impress upon Billy the fact that he should not pick flowers, Steinmetz gave all the Hayden youngsters certain sections of the back yard in which to plant their own gardens. Before these beds were seeded, "Dad" and the youngsters spent many hours going over flower catalogs, which were the scientist's favorite reading material. After much discussion, they filled out an order blank and the four of them walked to the nearest postbox and mailed it. When the package of seeds arrived, Steinmetz carefully checked them off, gave each child the varieties he had ordered, and said, "From now on I am not going to have anything to do with your garden. It is all yours—let's see what you can do with it!" The children agreed to take full charge of their plots and planted, weeded, and watered their flower beds. But when the first blooms appeared, Billy, as usual, was the one who picked a bouquet for the dining-room table!

The electrical genius' charming personality was never more evident than when he was with children. He understood the ways and minds of young people as easily as he appreciated the complexities of higher mathematics. The children in turn loved and admired him and showed their affection on every possible occasion. "Dad's" birthday was always a gala celebration on Wendall Avenue, and the traditional party was held in the conservatory. Adult friends might present Steinmetz with rare or exotic orchids, unusual specimens for his museum, or something of equal value, but nothing he received gave him as much pleasure as the simple gifts of the children—a pencil sharpener or a box of pencils. He would make a brief speech, thanking everyone for the gifts, then Roy Hayden would throw the switch and all the lights would go out—which was the signal for Mrs. Hayden to come across the bridge over the pool, bearing a candle-lit cake. Steinmetz would cut the cake, making sure that the younger members of the party received the largest pieces, and then, after a few gay songs, everyone would go to bed, for the guest of honor felt that the evening would be spoiled for the children if the grown-ups continued to celebrate after they were forced to leave the party. In this he showed a sensitivity totally lacking in his lusty, practical jokes, where he delighted in the discomfort of his victims. But youngsters easily melted his crusty heart.

"Dad" was always the last one to leave the conservatory

after one of these family affairs. If someone happened to look back to see what he was doing, he would find Steinmetz picking up cake crumbs and throwing them into the pool for his goldfish—they had to share the party too! Sometimes he would find pieces of frosting and carefully wrap them in a leaf picked from the nearest plant and place it in his pocket. On returning to the house, he would offer his gleanings to his parrots as a treat. He had one of these brilliantly plumaged birds on each floor of the house. He had tried to keep them both in the downstair hallway, but they were inclined to peck at each other, for he allowed them to fly freely about. He overcame the danger of a serious fight in mid-air by keeping the parrots isolated.

The Hayden youngsters were always bringing kittens home, and since Steinmetz was very fond of cats, the active little balls of fur, no matter how dirty, were always given a warm place to sleep and a saucer of milk. Whenever their master would stoop down to pat one of the kittens, the parrots would show their resentment by chattering and flapping their wings. He was always annoyed at the birds' reactions, for he wanted peace and quiet at all times—except when he began a violent argument for the sheer pleasure of yelling louder than his opponent, as when he lost a game of cards. Steinmetz didn't really mind losing at cards, for his losses were always minor ones, since the stakes were so low. But he would pound on the table in mock rage and accuse the score-keeper of cheating, in hopes that someone would take him seriously and answer him in the same way!

One afternoon Steinmetz picked up one of the stray kittens that had been brought home by Marjorie and carried it upstairs to one of his parrots. The bird began to jabber excitedly and started to peck at the intruder. "Now, now, no more of that," chided Steinmetz. "You have just got to stop this foolishness. Come on, make friends with this little puss. Stop that noise. Stop it, I say!" Instead of minding its owner, the bird cackled and made weird cries of rage. Meanwhile, the kitten had raised her back to an arch, curled up her lips and was spitting at the parrot. The more the kindly engineer tried to make the two become friends, the more they excited each other. At last, exhausted, he gave up the project and shooed the kitten down the stairs, ruefully remarking to Roy, "Now I can truthfully say I have conducted an unsuccessful experiment."

All Steinmetz' time was not devoted to household problems. He kept busy with a full schedule of work. In addition to his investigations into improving the mercury-arc lamp, he was spending a great deal of time writing scientific articles and lecturing to engineering associations. His addresses were considered so important that the committees in charge of program arrangements made it a practice to have his talk close the meetings. If he spoke earlier, most of the audience would leave after hearing it—having attended for the sole purpose of listening to what the "Wizard of Schenectady" had to say. A paragraph in a technical journal of the time best describes Steinmetz on the lecture platform: "resonant of voice, quaint accent, ultimate clearness and force of phrase, the close-knit reasoning advancing with rapid, but definite steps toward an unavoidable conclusion—that is Dr. Steinmetz thinking on his feet."

Not only was he writing scholarly reports and speaking to learned groups during this era, he was also taking an active part in professional societies as well. In 1901 he was elected president of the American Institute of Electrical Engineers. Just ten years before, as an unknown German immigrant, he had announced to that body his discovery of the "Law of Hysteresis"—and now he held the highest honor the organization could bestow upon him. When, after Steinmetz' death, Roy Hayden was going through "Dad's" possessions, he found the scientist's original membership card in the American Institute of Electrical Engineers, signed in the proper place by the president of the group. This would not have been remarkable, except for the fact that the signature was that of none other than Charles Proteus Steinmetz himself!

Many an engineer who could understand the theory of "The General Number" and other complex investigations undertaken by the clever cripple was unable to solve this mystery for Hayden. How could Steinmetz be president of the A.I.E.E. before he was a member? Despite the fact that no trained scientific mind has come up with a solution, it might be safe to guess that Charles Proteus Steinmetz, with his highly developed sense of humor, had used his knowledge of chemistry to obliterate carefully all traces of the original signature and had substituted his own. It is interesting that the great Steinmetz should be remembered, not only for his mathematical genius, but also as a genie of practical magic, for among members of the engineering profession this mystery of names is still talked about.

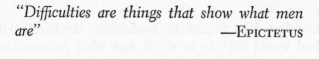

"*Difficulties are things that show what men are*" —EPICTETUS

12

NO OTHER scientist employed by a large commercial corporation ever was granted the freedom of action and thought that Steinmetz enjoyed. Not only was he allowed to come and go as he pleased, but no matter what line of investigation he wished to follow, he was at liberty to do so. In addition, any type of apparatus that he wanted for an experiment was immediately provided by the General Electric Company. While he never spent more than three hours a week in his office at the plant, he accomplished more in that short time than any other engineer—due to the fact that he worked long hours on various projects at home, and while "fishing."

From the moment he arrived at the works, until it was time to return to Wendall Avenue or "Camp Mohawk," a steady stream of department heads poured through his door, seeking guidance and help. Frantic at their inability to solve a technical difficulty, and fearful of the loss of their jobs if they held up production, the troubled engineers would stammer their requests for aid, and confess how upset they were. With a reassuring smile and a kindly pat on the shoulder, Steinmetz would pick up a pencil, pull a piece of paper toward him and say quietly, "Now don't get nervous. Tell me what you want to know. I'm sure we will be able to work

something out. It will be all right. Come on, stop worry-
ing."

Comforted by Steinmetz' confidence, the harassed individual would explain in detail just what information he
needed. Usually after a few minutes of intense concentration, the master mathematician would find in some complicated formula the means of overcoming any difficulty
that had arisen in the various divisions of the plant. Steinmetz would then wave away praise and thanks, and turn to
his next caller. His skill with figures was a constant source
of bewilderment to everyone associated with him, and as he
solved one problem after another, his fellow workers became
more firmly convinced that "The Supreme Court" could do
anything with mathematics—from figuring out the proper
ratio in a set of gears to squaring the circle. His reputation
for doing intricate computations was greatly increased when
a delegation of English scientists made the long voyage from
London to Schenectady, so they could place before the crippled genius a technical problem that had stumped them for
over a year.

The visitors from the other side of the Atlantic were prepared to spend some time waiting for the answer, and appeared laden with baggage holding enough clothing for a
two weeks' stay. They had been given an appointment with
Steinmetz the very morning of their arrival, and went to the
plant expecting to explain their difficulty, ask for help, and
be told to return at some future date for an answer. The
door to the engineer's office was open and they could see
Steinmetz hunched over a worktable, but they politely
knocked. The little cripple looked up from his figures and
boomed, "Why are you knocking? Don't you see that the
door is open? That means anyone can come in. If I want
privacy, I don't shut the door, gentlemen. I go home and
work in my laboratory. So please come in. That's fine! I understand you have come all the way from England to ask

me a question. Well, there's no time like the present. Ask
it!"

"Thank you, Mr. Steinmetz," said the spokesman of the
group and he explained the mission which had brought
them to Schenectady.

While the Englishman was talking, Steinmetz was making shorthand notes on a page of the ever-present notebook.
Almost before his caller had stopped talking, he said, "Gentlemen, the correct answer to your problem is——." Then ex-
cusing himself, he turned to help an engineer who had just
entered the room.

Stunned with amazement, the delegation staggered out of
the plant and started for their hotel. As they walked along,
one of them mumbled to himself, "By Jove! What a chap!
I say, now it will take us a year to find out how he got that
answer!"

When his conferences, appointments and correspondence
were finished, Steinmetz would pick up his papers and take
them to Wendall Avenue in the winter, or to his camp in
the summer. On arriving, he would look over the letters he
had brought with him, scrawl shorthand answers for his
secretary to type out the next day, then devote himself to
his real work—experimentation. Ever since his improvement
of the mercury-arc lamp, he had been devoting his time to
the problem of long-distance transmission of electricity. He
was determined to find some way to make it possible for
cables to carry the increased voltage being demanded by industry.

He had, of course, been working on this project at the
laboratory of Union College, and his interest in it had been
one of the reasons why he had to cut down on the number
of hours he spent in teaching. While the model transmission line he had set up at Union provided some information
about corona, or leakage in high-tension lines and its effect
on the generating apparatus in power stations, there was still

a great deal of investigation to be done before the problem could be solved. Steinmetz decided that he would have to erect another experimental hook-up, so he requisitioned materials and necessary labor from his superiors and built it in a corner of the plant yard. He spared no expense, and when he was through he had a complete high-tension line connected to a new-type transformer which was capable of raising the voltage in the cables to 220,000 volts—the highest load ever carried up to that time. For months he conducted a complicated series of tests, constantly checking the transformer and cables, and using his unique knowledge of mathematics, seeking a way to cut down on the leakage of electrical energy as it was sent from its source to the user.

The result of all this expenditure and effort was a new type of cable capable of carrying high voltage for great distances, and a new method of transmitting electric power. Of course the development in 1907 of a high-tension line which could supply 220,000 volts had no commercial value. It would be twenty years before that amount of electrical energy would be demanded by America's industrial plants. The greatest amount any factory needed at that time was but 80,000 volts. Thanks to Steinmetz, however, when those 220,000 volts were wanted, the General Electric Company was already sending 2,000,000 volts through its model transmission line.

It is interesting to note that, although Steinmetz' establishment of the "Law of Hysteresis" brought him his first fame, and his theory of "The General Number" made it possible for engineers to calculate the flow and value of alternating current and make it available for universal use, he was proudest of his work in the field of electrical transmission. Of all his two hundred patents, he considered none of them as important as the one that was given him for his development of improved cable and, in spite of his innate modesty, he was proud that his investigations made the widespread use of electrical energy possible.

The reason for his attitude is best summed up in a statement made by Philip Stern of the American Gas and Electric Company on the seventy-second anniversary of Steinmetz' birth, April 19, 1937. After lauding the scientist's work in alternating current—"The use of alternating current freed the hands of engineers and of the pioneer electric companies and they were able to extend their systems until today, in this country at any rate, we have a network of power lines extending into every community, no matter how small"—Mr. Stern offers a most satisfactory explanation of Steinmetz' pride in his improvements on methods of high voltage transmission. "His own physical weakness strengthened the scientist's normal aversion to back-breaking toil on the farm, in the mill, factory or home. He felt that this heavy labor could be performed with much less effort by electric power—and he, as much as any man, contributed toward the lifting of this burden."

While Steinmetz was busy with his corona experiments, he was also actively engaged on several other projects. About 1903 he became vitally concerned over the waste of the nation's coal resources, and he wrote and lectured that the time was not far distant when they would be completely depleted. He pointed out the dangers to our economy in such a situation. The rest of his life was to be devoted to a never-ending campaign to interest governmental and private agencies in the value of water power as a source of electrical energy. Another field of endeavor that consumed much of his time and talent was that of impressing well-fed Americans with the fact that the once rich soil of the world had, by constant cultivation over the centuries, slowly become exhausted. In spite of the scoffing of a generation which was unfamiliar with cultured molds which produce such boons to mankind as penicillin and brewer's yeast, he suggested that it might be wise for chemists to begin experimenting in order to find a "host" in which they could raise vast crops of microbes as a source of cheap food for a hungry world. He admitted that he did not know how to conduct this investigation, but was sure it could be done if it were undertaken by serious scientists.

He had an alternative plan for assuring a continual supply of food for mankind, in case laboratory technicians could not isolate eatable microbes and raise them inexpensively. This was to return to the worn-out soil the nitrogen which years of tillage had taken from it. For generations the only way farmers had known to overcome the lack of nitrogen in the soil was to spread either barnyard waste or sodium nitrate from Chile over their fields. The first method was not practical in many cases, and the use of the South American import was quite expensive. Steinmetz had a solution to the problem: "Let us supply the soil with nitrogen from the air, through electrical devices. If we do this, the United States will be able to feed the world. The result will be stupendous, wonderful, beyond all present view. I have talked this idea over with Thomas Alva Edison, engineer, wizard possessor of nearly all present electrical knowledge, sociologist, psychologist, geologist and the greatest living American, and he agrees with me."

As usual, Steinmetz was far ahead of his times. For although the industrial fixation of nitrogen from the atmosphere had its origin in this country—the first plant for this purpose being established at Niagara Falls—it was not until after the outbreak of World War I that this process was undertaken on a large scale. This was because the importation of Chilean nitrate became almost impossible, due to the diversion of merchant ships from the South American trade to the cross-Atlantic run. In 1913, the year before the conflict between the Anglo-French allies and the Central Powers broke out, 56.66 per cent of all nitrogen used in agriculture and industry came from Chile. Fifteen years later, slightly over sixteen per cent came from that source, thanks to the advance of science and the widespread use of electrical energy—thus furnishing concrete proof of Steinmetz' vision.

During this period, many honors were paid to the brilliant chief consulting engineer of General Electric. In 1913 he was awarded the Elliot Cresson Gold Medal, "In recognition of the first successful application of analytical methods to the solution of numerous problems of first practical importance in the field of electric engineering." Two years later he was elected President of the National Association of Corporation Schools. He had conducted classes at General Electric almost from the first day he had reported for work. He also acted as President of the Illuminating Engineering Society, serving during 1915–1916.

Always interested in the inventions of other men, he was one of the first persons to buy an electric automobile, and greatly enjoyed driving it. The service it gave during four years of constant use convinced him that for short hauls, a battery-operated car was far more economical than a gasoline-motored one. But in spite of his delight in proving how well his machine could climb the steep hills on the outskirts of Schenectady, he did not neglect his bicycle, and still rode it back and forth to work. His first warning of the toll taken by years of toil in the laboratory, plus the abuse of his body by not eating the proper foods, came to him one afternoon as he was pedaling home from the plant. Attempting to swing from Wendall Avenue into his driveway, he found it impossible to get his muscles to respond quickly enough, and he failed to negotiate the turn. He was forced to get off and push the bike on to the house where he carefully racked the trusty mechanical steed which had served him for so many years. Then and there he determined never to mount it again.

Other men in his position, realizing that their reactions

were slowing up, would have decided to rest and bask in the fame the years had brought. But not Steinmetz. If he couldn't ride a bicycle to work, he could still drive an automobile, and instead of cutting down on the number of assignments he had marked for investigation, he constantly added to his list of duties. In order to break the habit of late hours at his desk, he fell into the routine of going to the movies frequently and became a rabid fan of Western pictures, rejoicing in the furious chases between the law-abiding ranchers and the "baddies" who tried to rustle cattle. His favorite motion picture star was Douglas Fairbanks, Sr., the dashing hero of silent films, and Steinmetz often expressed a desire to go to Hollywood and meet him—a wish which was fulfilled just before his death.

🜲 🜲 🜲

No sooner had Steinmetz conquered the problem of corona and made it possible to carry electricity efficiently to users great distances away from power stations than he turned his attention to a new field of research. His inspiration for this investigation came to him one evening while he was sitting on the porch of "Camp Mohawk," puffing on a cigar and looking out at the river. He was in a happy frame of mind. The Committee of Sciences and Arts of The Franklin Institute had just awarded him and his employers the organization's 1908 certificate of merit, in recognition of his development of the magnetite arc lamp. His work with the long-distance transmission of electrical power had made him more conscious than ever of the waste that resulted in the conversion of electrical energy to power and light, and although he was sitting quietly, he was mulling this problem over in his mind. As he sat, he noticed the fireflies swooping and looping through the air. For some time he watched them, and then suddenly realized that these insects had a secret no electrical engineer shared—they could give light without heat!

"What are you thinking about, 'Dad'?" asked Roy Hayden from the other end of the porch.

"I have been watching those lightning bugs. What we could learn from them . . . the ideal method of providing light. We should find out how they do it. For when electrical engineers get heat, we waste too much energy in the form of light; and when we get light, we waste energy in the form of heat. Don't misunderstand me, Roy. I don't say that a lightning bug is an efficient power plant, but at least it can do something no human can do."

"What are you planning?" Roy laughed. "Are you going down to the beach and politely tip your hat as a firefly flits by and say, 'I beg your pardon, Mr. Firefly, but how do you manage to avoid generating heat when you turn on your lamp?'"

Steinmetz chuckled at his adopted son's flight of fancy. "Unfortunately," he admitted, "I don't speak the language of lightning bugs. Now if you could find me a well-educated one who knew Latin, Greek, Polish, Hebrew, German, French or English, and introduce me, I'm sure I could get the information I desire. You can't, can you? No, I thought not. I guess the only thing is to undertake a series of experiments dealing with 'cold light.'"

Under ordinary conditions, Steinmetz would have let everything else drop and turned his attention to this new, challenging field of investigation. But the outbreak of World War I in 1914 made it impossible for him to do anything but his required duties arising from his position as chief consulting engineer at the plant. Even though it was to be three years before America entered the conflict, the demands from the combatants for the weapons of war caused an industrial boom. It became necessary to design and manufacture new tools for the factories that were working at top capacity to fill their orders. Steinmetz had no time for research now. He wouldn't have minded, except for the fact that, although the United States was to all intents and purposes still a neutral nation, an ever-increasing wave of anti-German feeling made him feel isolated and actually unwanted. Flag waving patriots baited him in public and after a while he hated to attend meetings of his beloved professional societies for fear he would be singled out as "a Socialist and a German."

Yet if Steinmetz had confined himself to his duties at the plant—work that became ever more important as the General Electric Company geared itself for the production of the tools to defend democracy—he would, in all probability, have been able to overcome the temporary unpleasantness caused by war hysteria. However, when an enterprising reporter interviewed him on the future of Europe if Germany won the war, he foolishly cast aside his normal reticence on political matters and boldly stated that Germany was the natural leader of the Old World. Under her direction, he maintained, a United States of Europe could be organized and it would be the best form of government the countries concerned had ever known. This was too much for Americans who were constantly learning from their newspapers of the brutal acts of German soldiers in Belgium. The man in the street avidly read everything Steinmetz had to say about electricity, and considered him the world's greatest engineer, but refused to tolerate his ideas about Germany's greatness. Unable to understand why public opinion was rising against him, Steinmetz was hurt and bewildered. To add to his difficulties, right in the middle of the heated newspaper discussion of his pro-German views, the *Lusitania*, a British liner with more than a hundred Americans aboard, many of whom were women and children, was torpedoed by a German submarine off the Irish coast, with a tremendous loss of life.

Not since the sinking of the *Maine* in the harbor of Havana, Cuba, on February 12, 1898, had the American people been so aroused against a foreign power. From all sides came loud demands that the United States enter the war on the side of France and England. President Woodrow Wilson tried in vain to make the German government promise not to sink any more unarmed vessels without warning, and without providing for the safety of passengers, but to no avail. At last it was evident that, if this nation wanted freedom of the seas, she was going to have to fight for it. So on April 2, 1917, the President rode along Pennsylvania Avenue in a spring rain to the Capitol, to address a joint meeting of the two houses of the Congress.

Facing the representatives of the people, Woodrow Wilson spoke these historic words: "The world must be made safe for democracy . . . It is a fearful thing to lead this great and peaceful people into war . . . But the right is more precious than peace, and we shall fight for the things which we have always carried nearest our hearts . . . The day has come when America is privileged to spend her blood and her might for the principles that gave her birth and happiness and the peace which she has treasured. God helping her, she can do no other."

Four days later, war on Germany was declared. Steinmetz had no loyalty to the land of his fathers now. All his skill was devoted to the designing of better electrical equipment for the armed forces of America and her allies, and no one who knew of the long hours he put in at the laboratory could accuse him of lack of patriotism. His brilliant achievements for the war effort were recognized when Secretary of the Navy Josephus Daniels announced that he was setting up a Naval Advisory Board consisting of distinguished scientists who would pool their talents to improve the fighting potential of the Navy. The plan was for all the leading technical schools in the United States to nominate candidates, and those who received the most votes would be asked to serve. On making this arrangement public, Mr. Daniels gave the newspapers a list of three men whom he was going to appoint to the Advisory Board, regardless of how many votes anyone else received. The first name was that of Charles Proteus Steinmetz. At this news a howl went up from one end of the country to the other. The Secretary was accused of making it possible for a "German spy" to hide a time bomb in the hold of every ship in the American Navy and thus blow it and the crew to bits. Daniels paid no attention to these charges, but Steinmetz was so deeply hurt at the attitude of his fellow citizens that he suffered greatly. He did not seem to realize that a public statement of his changed viewpoint would have straightened things out quickly and effectively.

As a matter of fact, the Naval Advisory Board accomplished little or nothing—even a "hush-hush" invention of Edison's failed to make the tide of history flow any faster. At last, with the coming of peace, Steinmetz was able to return to his normal way of living, and to all appearances he seemed to forget the heartache and shock experienced during the war years. Yet the suspicion and criticism to which he was subjected left scars which were never completely healed. Perhaps that is why he said, long before a war-weary world banded itself together in the United Nations, "War is always a waster. It must therefore stop. Arbitration is a dream toward which we must go."

ᛒ ᛒ ᛒ

In 1915, two years before the entrance of America into World War I, Steinmetz was asked by a newspaperman if he thought the progress of civilization would be set back by the conflict which was ravaging Europe. The scientist snorted with indignation and said, "Far from it. Let me tell you, sir, that it won't be long before, thanks to electricity, men will only work six hours a day, five days a week. International radio broadcasts will be commonplace and millions will hear the finest orchestras and opera companies giving concerts right in their homes. The motion picture and the talking machine will be perfectly synchronized; while buildings and homes will be heated, cooled, and ventilated by electricity. Much of our cooking will be done on the table, and electric stoves will be equipped with a dial that will automatically start and stop the heating unit, so that housewives will be able to put their dinners in the stove, leave their houses, and come back and find their meals ready to put on the table. The labor of the farmer will be made lighter by electricity, and the power itself will be much cheaper than it is now, as well as available to many thousands who do not as yet enjoy its advantages."

Steinmetz might have been a poor political prognosticator, but his average in the above predictions is almost one hundred per cent. Today most men work only five days a week, although they labor eight instead of the six hours Steinmetz planned; not only is international broadcasting a commonplace, but now we can see as well as hear the world's history-making events as fast as they happen, by means of the miracle of television—a development in electrical engineering that would have delighted Steinmetz. The "talkies" have confirmed his forecast of the combination of motion pictures and the phonograph; many new homes have electrically heated hot water and ventilating systems and completely automatic electric stoves, coffee makers, and toasters; while electric milkers and other devices have made life on the farm much easier. As for the price of electricity, it is far cheaper today than it was forty years ago, when this interview was published.

What would Charles Proteus Steinmetz prophesy were he alive today? What forecast of the uses of electricity would he give for the world of 1956? It probably would read like a page from a science-fiction novel—but if past performance is any criterion of his ability to foretell the future, most of it would come true!

> *"The purification of politics is an iridescent dream"*
> —John James Ingalls

13

𝔉 𝔉 𝔉 𝔉 DESPITE the fact that his youthful enthusiasm for reform had forced Steinmetz to leave Breslau in order to avoid being arrested by Bismarck's secret police, and had also meant the end of his early ambition to be a college professor, he had paid no attention to the activities of the various political parties in America. In the first place, he was far too busy with his calculations and investigations. Over the years the ardent Socialist of 1888 had given way to a practical idealist who found in his engineering skill a more satisfactory method of advancing the lot of the working man than by improving conditions through the ballot box. During his association with Eickenmeyer, he had, to be sure, discussed the ideals of Socialism with his landlord, Edward Muller, who was also a political dreamer; but it is very doubtful that Steinmetz was even conscious of the existence of the American Socialist Party in later years.

The reason for this lack of interest was a simple one. None of the social evils Steinmetz had rebelled against as a student in Germany existed in the United States. In his adopted country, men of every race, creed, color and position had an equal opportunity—and his own experience had shown him that even the severely handicapped had a chance to prove their individual worth in the New World. So there was absolutely no cause for him to agitate for a society in which every man would have the same rights and privileges —it was already in operation in America.

Steinmetz did not think of himself as an exceptional person. He firmly believed that what had happened to him in this country could have happened to thousands of others. He made this clear at a banquet held in Buffalo, New York, where he was the featured speaker: "Any American boy can achieve as much as I have achieved, if he has the right opportunity"—and there was no doubt in the scientist's mind that everyone did have "the right opportunity" in this country. Perhaps that is why he was perfectly content to work for a gigantic corporation, for in a true Socialistic government such an organization would not be allowed. This is another of the paradoxes in Steinmetz' life—while he sincerely believed that society should control the means of production, he was a strong advocate of corporations and worked happily for one of the world's largest for over thirty years.

His feeling that corporations should not be abolished in America was based on his observations at the General Electric plant. As he looked about, he could see no social gap between the foremen and the workmen, and he knew that every employee could, if he wished, save his money and use it to buy shares in the firm. Moreover, as a shareholder, even an unskilled person who held the most unimportant position at the works could, at the annual meeting of the stockholders, vote to discharge the directors and elect others in their places. As the son of a poor man, Steinmetz also appreciated the fact that any worker who bought stock in the concern for which he worked shared in that company's profits through the payment of dividends.

As an engineer, Steinmetz was intensely annoyed by waste of any type, whether in a light bulb, along a production line or of an individual's talents. Therefore he approved of corporations because they avoided unprofitable and unproductive methods of manufacture. He was convinced that the efficiency of Big Business made it a most important factor in the development of a better life for all the people of America. Unlike the family-controlled factories of Europe which did all they could to hinder the emancipation of the working classes, firms in the United States encouraged their employees to improve themselves. To be sure, Steinmetz could see some abuse of wealth by individuals, but on the whole he realized that the American system, including corporations, was as near the ideal democracy as anything ever conceived by starry-eyed dreamers in a secret meeting.

In one of his few non-technical books, *America and the New Epoch*, Steinmetz expresses his attitude toward corporations. It is a fantastically strange work for a one-time editor of a rabid Socialistic paper, for while it presents a sharply drawn blueprint of a more co-operative world, the volume shows how syndicates and combines of various types could help bring about a better standard of living. Perhaps his views on traditional Socialism are best summed up in a story told by Dr. Ernst Berg. "I remember asking him about the year 1900," recalls the genius' close associate at the plant and at Union College, "if he were still a Socialist. I can see the wide grin on his face as he laughingly replied, 'My friend, how can anyone be a Socialist when he makes more than three thousand dollars a year?'"

So Steinmetz continued to spend his days in the laboratory, seeking new methods to make electricity lighten the burdens of mankind, and paid no attention to politics. Then, in 1911, George R. Lunn, who had been a minister in a Schenectady church, became a candidate for election as mayor. A most liberal preacher, Lunn had resigned his pastorate after a heated discussion with the governing board of his congregation about his social views, and he had then announced his intention of running for office. Unable to convince any of the major political parties of his sincerity, and finding that they were not interested in his platform of social reform, Lunn turned to the Socialist Party for support.

Seeing in the former minister an excellent candidate, and knowing that he would be supported by the working men of the city, the Socialist Party endorsed him. Yet as a matter of fact, Lunn was not a true Socialist. He was really a Democrat in the tradition of Thomas Jefferson, and much of his way of thinking would have been heartily approved of by Franklin Delano Roosevelt. On hearing of Lunn's decision to run for mayor, Steinmetz' old interest in politics was revived, and he made an appointment to discuss the matter with him. After talking with the candidate for several hours, the engineer was sincerely convinced that the man would give Schenectady and its citizens an excellent administration, and he offered to assist him in any way he could.

After a heated campaign, Lunn was elected mayor. One of his first official acts was to appoint Steinmetz to the Board of Education. No appointment could have delighted the electrical wizard more than this one, for now he would be able to do something for the children of the entire city— not just those in his neighborhood or in the public institutions. At the organizational meeting of the Board, he was elected president. If the other members had craftily reasoned that by placing him in the position of chairman of meetings and confining his duties to signing routine papers, they would not have to worry about his progressive ideas, they soon found out how mistaken they were. Steinmetz refused to sit idly by as a mere figurehead, while others discussed what should or should not be done in the schools, and he became the most active member of the Board.

It was about time that someone on the Schenectady Board of Education became active. The schools of the city had been shamefully neglected for many years. Moreover, with the growth of the General Electric works and other manufacturing plants, the population of the area had increased four times in twenty years. In the first place, there were not enough schools. It had been four years since the last one was built—and that had been erected in one of the suburbs. Steinmetz decided to tackle this problem first and he went to work with all the vigor he displayed when undertaking a project in his laboratory. He carefully inspected the enrollment records of the school system and found that, in all grades, there were three thousand youngsters without classroom seats. With "Give Every Child a Seat" as his slogan, he forced the passage of orders to build three new schools. Before his term was over, he had succeeded in providing ample classroom space for every child in the schools of the city.

Once he had accomplished his first objective, Steinmetz submitted a lengthy list of further recommendations to his fellow members of the Board of Education. An avid sports fan, he suggested that the number of playgrounds be increased, and that trained play teachers be assigned to supervise the children's recreational activities and to umpire games. He also offered plans for a completely equipped gymnasium in every school, and insisted that specialists be appointed to instruct the classes in physical education. Realizing that many of the working people in Schenectady were like his father, who had been too poor to provide proper dental and medical care for his children, Steinmetz proposed the creation of a Department of School Hygiene, with visiting doctors and full-time nurses in every school district. This was a very advanced way of thinking for that time.

While all of these recommendations were educationally sound and of great value to the school system, Steinmetz soon found that the professional politicians were against them on the grounds that "they were a waste of the taxpayer's money." As President of the Board of Education, it was his duty to attend the meetings of the Schenectady Common Council and submit proposals and present the annual budget requested by the schools. Time after time, the Board of Estimate and Apportionment, which had the final authority on the spending of the city's funds, would refuse to grant the necessary money to carry out his program. With characteristic energy, Steinmetz would set out to battle for "the basic needs of the children of this city," sometimes convincing those in charge of the civic purse that he should be given the appropriation he wanted, but more often failing in the task.

Grimly determined to make Schenectady's schools the best in the country, Steinmetz would never accept the rejection of any of his proposals. He used every possible means to secure the money needed for the expansion and improvements he advocated. His skill at bringing pressure to bear on the right officials won him the reluctant admiration of seasoned politicians. At last, weary of the constant battle for what was so obviously necessary for the school population, Steinmetz decided that the easiest way to achieve his desired goals was to be elected President of the Common Council—for in that post he would automatically become entitled to a place on the Board of Estimate and Apportionment. So he ran twice for that office. In the election of 1913, he was badly defeated, along with Lunn, but two years later the pair were swept into office by a large majority. In both elections Steinmetz conducted a most unusual campaign—he gave no speeches, held no rallies, made no promises, and spent no money. "The people know what I stand for," he explained. "If they elect me, I will give it to them. If they do not vote for me, that will be proof that they do not want better schools."

When the election results were tabulated, it was plain that the people did want better schools. Now in a position to secure the money needed for the reformation of the school system, Steinmetz wasted no time. Once his original recommendations were carried out, he immediately offered another long list of aims and objectives to improve the schools. Among other things, he proposed that classes for retarded children should be established, and suggested that on the roof of every schoolbuilding a glass-enclosed classroom be built so that youngsters suffering from tuberculosis could be exposed to the healthful rays of the sun while studying. Perhaps he was recalling his bread and sausage days in Zurich when he outlined a program for the proper feeding of undernourished pupils, to be directed by nutrition experts. He was certainly thinking of himself when he insisted that a system of special classes for handicapped children be organized.

By degrees all these features were adopted. But Steinmetz still was not satisfied. He set up a system of summer schools to provide special instruction for those pupils who had failed during the regular academic year, and thus enabled them to advance with their classmates. When this was accepted, his fellow members of the Common Council felt that they had heard the last of "Steinmetz' foolishness"— but they were mistaken. He presented a comprehensive plan for classes for immigrants and ungraded groups, on both the adult and juvenile level. This was more than his associates could bear and the politicians serving on the Common Council rebelled and flatly refused to grant his requests.

Their open opposition to his activities did not bother Steinmetz in the least. By devoting long hours to the task of securing the support of parents, teachers and civic-minded groups, he was able to muster enough political strength to force the acceptance of his program. Although deeply engrossed in the problem of utilizing the water power of the nation as a source of electrical energy, he took time out from his investigations to attend every meeting of the Common Council, carefully checking that no funds earmarked for educational purposes be diverted to any other city service, and speaking eloquently in favor of his proposals.

His unselfish devotion to the betterment of the schools earned him the honor of being reappointed as a matter of course to the Board of Education by mayors of all political parties, and he continued to serve the children of Schenectady until his death. Strangely enough, despite his technical training and natural interest in scientific education, an examination of his record as an educator shows that he was a strong advocate of the classical course for high school pupils. The scientist's recollection of the lack of mathematical ability among his students at Union College made him insist that the fundamentals be stressed on all levels of instruction, with particular attention paid to arithmetic.

Unlike most men concerned with the administration of a large school system, Steinmetz did not confine himself to attending meetings, reading reports, and discussing the "cost-per-pupil" aspect of education. From the first day he was appointed to the Board of Education, teachers and pupils alike never knew when the classroom door might open and the gnome-like man would lurch through it, slide quietly into a seat in the back and take an active part in any lesson, challenging the youngsters to prove their answers, or illustrating the topic being taught by some humorous incident. He attended as many extra-curricular activities as his laboratory duties would allow, and his great love for little children is best illustrated by the fact that on Halloween, when it was the custom of the students in the lower grades to masquerade, he would visit every elementary school in the city, shake hands with all the fancy-dressed youngsters, and join happily in their childish games.

᚛᚛᚛

All the time Steinmetz was working to improve the school system of Schenectady, he was constantly engaged in scientific investigations. Most of his experiments were of a highly technical nature, so the average person heard nothing about them. The endeavors of this super-mathematician, electrical genius and exceptionally capable physicist did, however, enable other men to develop tools and machines that made for an easier and richer life for mankind. Then Steinmetz, as the result of a routine assignment as chief consulting engineer of the General Electric Company, did something which captured the attention of the public: he solved the problem of how to make electricity pass through concrete, an accomplishment which made the building of the subway system of New York City possible.

Through the years Steinmetz had been held in high esteem by engineers in all fields; now he was famous as far as the general public was concerned. The newspapers reviewed his earlier work and told of his reorganization of the Schenectady schools. From now on, Charles Proteus Steinmetz was to be considered "good copy." Although he was always modest, he frankly enjoyed the publicity which made his name so well known, and took a more active part in social and civic affairs. His political career reached its climax in 1922, when he agreed to run for State Engineer and Surveyor on the combined Socialist and Farmer-Labor ticket. There was no doubt in anyone's mind that he was the most qualified candidate for the post, but thousands of voters who respected him for his engineering ability had no liking for the party which sponsored him. So from the day of his entry into the contest until the final tabulation of the votes was made, there was little chance of his election. Yet even the conservative *New York Times* highly praised his knowledge, although it did not endorse him when it said editorially on July 4, 1922: "For a great engineer to be a Socialist is not strange. He sees all about him neglected opportunities —work which should be done, but which Capital is too cautious to undertake. His mind naturally turns to the state."

As was to be expected, Steinmetz did not engage in an

active campaign. He did, however, grant numerous interviews to newspapermen, telling them what he would do if he were elected. By this time everything he said was front-page news, and journalists visited him daily at his laboratory, where he greeted them dressed in his usual garb—baggy trousers and undershirt.

When the correspondent for one of the New York City papers asked him in mid-July when he was going to start campaigning, Steinmetz replied: "I am too busy with my work to make a campaign. If, however, the people elect me State Engineer, I shall give to the state all the benefits of my skill and experience as an engineer. I would give a more definite answer to your question, but I cannot. In fact, I know nothing about the campaign. I haven't the time to keep in touch with the details of political movements."

Steinmetz was very busy, but reporters quickly discovered that he was never too engrossed in an experiment to stop, light a fresh cigar, climb up on a laboratory worktable and outline what he would do if he were elected. Since his chief interest during this period of his life was the development of electrical energy from water power, he would explain at length how, as State Engineer, he would harness every fall in New York State, from the smallest drop in a farmer's trout brook to the mighty Niagara. The lack of attention paid by electric light companies to the possibilities of hydroelectric plants was a constant source of irritation to Steinmetz, and he was doing everything he possibly could to make people realize that the water power wasted in this country could provide millions of people with electricity cheaply and efficiently.

As a lover of nature, Steinmetz could appreciate the grandeur of Niagara and enjoy the lovely sight of water spilling over moss-covered rocks in some woodland stream, but as an engineer he deplored the loss it represented. He knew that the coal resources of the nation would not last forever, and in the interest of conservation, water power as a source of electrical energy should not be neglected. This great man admired beauty, but knew that shackling the "white coal" of America to machines would bring the benefits of electricity to regions far from coal deposits and would release humankind from much back-breaking toil. Moreover, as a mathematician he had figured out that by using Niagara to turn generators and selling the current derived from them, the State of New York could add two billion dollars to its treasury.

Steinmetz told one interviewer: "Every steam engine must be scrapped. The time will come, and in a very few years, when electricity will completely take the place of coal. Power for industry, supplied from hydro-electric stations, will flow from one end of the country to another through a network of wires. Why in New England alone, 50,000,000 tons of coal would be saved in a year. Do you realize how much coal that is? If it were loaded on coal cars placed end to end as they are in a train, they would reach from Boston to Cape Horn in South America and there would be several million tons left over!"

As the average citizen scanned the morning paper while he gulped his morning coffee, he read Steinmetz' statement about the coal used yearly in New England, but merely shrugged his shoulders. Then one morning a story appeared which caused many a reader to wonder if his eyes were playing him tricks. Here was no listing of facts and figures but a startling suggestion that Niagara Falls be immediately turned into a gigantic power plant!

Nothing Steinmetz could have said as a candidate for public office could have attracted more attention than this, for to the man in the street there was something utterly fantastic in the suggestion to change one of the world's scenic spots into a commercial enterprise. Readers scanned the story with mingled feelings of respect for the mind that could visualize such a project, and repugnance at the idea. The public excitement about his views reached its height when Steinmetz said in another interview, "To utilize the falls fully would mean to harness the whole stream and dry up the falls."

The reporter was stunned at this remark, as his readers were to be, but managed to ask, "What about the hotel owners who depend on the thousands of people who come from all over the world to see the falls, and how about . . ."

"Ah, that's just the question," interposed Steinmetz. "Should we dry up the falls and ruin them in return for one or two billion dollars which could be used for public improvements and enable New York State to do much for its citizens? However, I think I have a way to keep the tourists and hotel-keepers happy and at the same time use Niagara as a source of power. We could let the falls be purely scenic on Saturdays and Sundays, and generate elsewhere on those days. It would be a simple matter to control the force—you know, just like a faucet."

If any citizen of New York State hadn't heard of Steinmetz' candidacy for election as State Engineer before the publication of this amazing suggestion, he heard of it now. The idea of turning Niagara off and on like a hot or cold water tap on week ends captured everybody's imagination, and while most people thought it an impossible scheme, it did make the public conscious of the possibilities of hydro-electric power. And knowing Steinmetz' sense of humor, this might have been what he had in mind all the time, for his only campaign promise was to survey every source of water power in the state. There were, of course, some voters who thought his plan to use Niagara as a means of providing electrical energy a "typical Socialist scheme," but they were far fewer in number than those who were appalled at his ideas of what should be done with the wasted heat present in the Japanese current.

Explaining his views on this subject, he said: "Naples, Italy, has the same latitude as Labrador—yet look at the difference in temperature. It's the warm Gulf Stream that modifies the climate of all Europe, and makes it a much milder place than America.

"Now there's the Japanese Current that encircles the Pacific. Bering Strait is narrow and comparatively shallow. If that Strait were blown up and widened and deepened, we would be able to divert the whole course of that current to the north of North America. If the current ran north of our country, it would melt all the ice and snow of Canada and Alaska, and there would be no more glaciers in Greenland or icebergs in the Atlantic. It would open up a whole half continent for cultivation and population. It would make all of North America warmer in winter and milder in summer. It would double the available habitable globe. It would remake the world."

Perhaps such a project might "remake the world," but the average New York voter was under the impression that any man who thought such radical things was no individual to elect to office, and Steinmetz was defeated. Yet this scientific dreamer was absolutely correct in his views on hydroelectric power. His program for the conservation of coal and the using of the underdeveloped water power resources of this country had but one flaw—it was presented a generation too soon. It would be years before private firms and Federal agencies would belatedly endorse his theories by damming small mountain streams and launching such tremendous projects as the Tennessee Valley Authority.

Too advanced in his thinking for his times, Steinmetz ruined whatever small chance he had of being elected. For it is possible that, despite his sponsorship by the Socialist and Farmer-Labor groups, he might have been elected if he had not advanced such bizarre ideas. His reputation as a scientist had caused many voters to overlook his political views and he had made it plain that "what can be accomplished under the conditions that exist depends not at all upon the political belief of the engineer in charge, but on his capacity for engineering. We are all interested in pure water, safe bridges, adequate communications and the elimination of waste. If elected, I should try to serve the people of New York at least as faithfully as I have served the General Electric Company."

No citizen of a democracy could ask for more loyalty than that from any public servant—and it is fascinating to speculate what might have happened had Steinmetz been elected to the post he sought. Perhaps instead of the glorious sight of multi-colored searchlights playing down on Niagara Falls at night, turning the spray into swirling rainbows, to the delight of thousands of breathless watchers, something dreadful would happen. The usual tourists gathered on the shores of Whirlpool Rapids late on a Sunday night would see a single state guard flick an insignificant switch. Immediately afterward, the mighty 167-foot cascade would begin to dwindle, until only a trickle was left. Then Niagara would disappear completely until the next visiting hours came around again. This layman's nightmare fortunately, perhaps, has never come true, and in the modern battle between technological progress and age-old beauty, Niagara Falls still thunders magnificently down its rocky course.

> *"The future is a world limited by ourselves"*
> —MAURICE MAETERLINCK

14

⊪ THE widespread publicity given Steinmetz' ideas on how Niagara Falls could best be converted to a state-managed power plant completely changed his life. No longer would he be allowed to conduct experiments in the privacy of his laboratory, enjoy his simple pleasures unnoticed, or "fish" on the waters of the Mohawk River. From now on, everything he did or said was public property. Sunday supplements in every major city in the country were filled with interviews given by the scientist as newspaper editors, looking for circulation-building stories, took advantage of the public's interest in the crippled electrical genius. In addition, average citizens had become vitally interested in the technical developments of industry as a result of World War I, realizing for the first time the important part research experts and inventors played in their lives. Most of these investigators were unknown figures and had little about them to capture a reader's imagination, but the humpback who was chief consulting engineer of the General Electric Company was a journalist's dream—he was "colorful copy" in every respect.

Dubbed "The Wizard of Schenectady" by headline writers, Charles Proteus Steinmetz was always being interviewed on what he thought the world of tomorrow would be like.

At first he resented being constantly bothered by reporters, but as time went on, he began to enjoy his publicity and never refused to answer newsmen's questions. He did, however, dislike being called "The Wizard of Schenectady," as he was afraid his friends and associates would think he took the title seriously and considered himself too important.

Most of the interviews Steinmetz granted to reporters resulted in screaming headlines. To a generation not used to reading science-fiction novels and comic strips dealing with life on other worlds, or watching space cadets on television screens soar from one planet to another, his statements about the future were fantastic, bizarre and even shocking. Yet the scientist was absolutely sincere when he predicted what marvels would be accomplished in the years to come through the magic of electricity. As a result, he could not understand why his statements caused so much excitement. He had been greatly embarrassed when Elbert Hubbard, the author of *A Message to Garcia*, had written a laudatory article about him in *The Fra*, a literary magazine, but he saw no reason for any fuss to be made about his views on scientific progress.

Hubbard had written about Steinmetz after spending a week end with him on a camping trip. There were three other internationally famous scientists in the party: Thomas Alva Edison; Guglielmo Marconi, who had conducted the first successful experiments with wireless telegraphy; and Nikola Tesla, inventor of the apparatus used in the transmission of power from Niagara Falls. Never before had such brilliant engineering minds exchanged views across a blazing campfire. Inspired by the wit of their clever host, whose entire literary career was based on his ability to probe deep into the minds and feelings of celebrities, the men talked freely of their work and future plans. On returning to his desk at East Aurora in upstate New York, where he had established a colony of craftsmen known as "Roycrofters" and had set up one of the most famous publishing houses in America, Hubbard sat down and wrote his impressions of Steinmetz:

᛭ ᛭ ᛭

"Steinmetz, next to Edison, is the world's greatest mechanical prophet. Steinmetz seems possessed of faculties beyond the average man. He has an intuitive sense that is almost uncanny.

"His boys may work on an electric problem for a year or more and fail to make it tangible. Steinmetz will then sit down and look at the machine for about five minutes, light a cigar, blow a cloud of smoke through it, and behold, the thing starts . . .

"Steinmetz resents being called an inventor. He says, 'I am only an engineer. My business is to construct engines that will transport an elemental form of energy into a million factories and homes, dividing this energy into infinitesimal parts so that it can be practically used to run sewing machines, to churn, to wash dishes and to do the dead lift and drudgery that otherwise would have to be done by human hands.

"So let Steinmetz stand as a type of modern engineer, who is not only an engineer, but is an artist, an economist, a teacher and a humanist."

No wonder the modest "Wizard of Schenectady" was embarrassed when he read such praise! Incidentally, Elbert Hubbard, the scientist's great friend and admirer, was one of the Americans who was drowned when the *Lusitania* was sunk in the Irish Sea by a German submarine in 1915.

Very few people read *The Fra*, so not many pictured Steinmetz as Hubbard had painted him. The average man gained his impressions of the scientist from reading interviews in which the electrical genius stated that some day industry would be powered by energy supplied by radio waves, and advocated a method of storing up the heat given off by the summer sun for use during the cold winter months. These newspaper articles continually gave the impression that Steinmetz was "dreaming of the future"—which greatly annoyed him. He was just as upset when asked to prophesy some impossible invention. When one reporter suggested an exceptionally far-fetched use of electricity in years to come, Steinmetz lurched to his feet and waved his cigar under the journalist's nose. Shaking with anger, he thundered, "Foolish dreams! What a waste of time and energy to ponder on them, when there is so much real work to be done! Little by little, our developments in science make the world a better place to live in, and surely that is what we should do—not waste our time dreaming impossible dreams!"

After this outburst he calmed down and said, "We call this the age of electricity, but it isn't. The age of electricity hasn't begun. All that we have yet done is but preparatory to the ushering in of the electrical age.

"When the age of electricity comes—as it will—electricity will do for everybody all that it can do for anybody. It will do this in addition to doing a multitude of things of which we have not yet dreamed.

"I came to America in 1889. It seems a long way back to think where the development of electricity was at that time. It seems a long way ahead to think where it will yet be. For the age of electricity is yet to come. And it will be a great age."

One of the questions Steinmetz was constantly being asked in those days of pioneer broadcasting was to describe the future uses of radio. On April 9, 1923, in a radio talk, he went on record as being convinced that communication with Mars by radio was possible. "Does that mean you feel that some time in the future we will travel from planet to planet?" a reporter asked him when the broadcast was over.

"It certainly does not," came the prompt reply. "Think of shooting a man to Mars in a rocket! That cannot be, the man could not live. Radio is the only practical method of reaching Mars and if we went into the project of developing a means of communication with that planet with the same earnestness and thoroughness as we entered and fought the war, we would most likely succeed in our attempt. But as for the future of radio—how can we tell what will happen with radio in the future? Obviously we are nowhere near the limits of radio development. We may, and doubtless shall, have radio communications between cities as a phase of long distance telephony."

Little did the readers of this interview realize that within three years the first radio network would be established and shortly afterward international broadcasting would be a commonplace.

While Steinmetz gave feature-story editors columns of copy for their special sections, he also provided a great deal of material for the news pages. Firmly convinced that electricity would completely change mankind's pattern of living, he advocated supplying it as cheaply as possible to the user. Customers of utility companies delighted in such headlines as "Steinmetz Favors Lower Electric Rates"—and read every word in the articles. The scientist knew that if the electric companies would stop depending on coal to turn their generators and use water power instead, electricity would cost far less than it did. So he continued his campaign for harnessing the nation's streams, pointing out the saving to both the producer and to the consumer. At one professional society meeting after another he painted a picture of completely automatic hydroelectric stations in such inaccessible places as rugged canyons and river gorges, which would supply never-ending streams of electrical energy. He also urged his fellow scientists to develop a process by which factory smoke, which made big cities so grimy, would be eliminated by the use of electricity for power, instead of coal.

Long before the power companies encouraged the public to buy washing machines, clothes driers, ironers and hot water heaters by offering a special rate for "off hour" current, Steinmetz suggested it in a talk to the New York Electrical Trade School. "If we could find a way to get an even use of power through the twenty-four hours, we might be able to supply power at one or two cents a kilowatt hour," he said. "When we have accomplished that, electric power will be much cheaper than anything else, and then the end will come for gas and kerosene. And that time will come."

In this address, Steinmetz again stressed the fact that the nation's coal could not last forever. "When we reach the end of our resources in coal, in the not very distant future, then the only remaining source of power, the only thing that will keep us from freezing, will be water power, which we will have to utilize to make electricity." Then he went on to advance his theory that the country's streams, both big and little, should be harnessed, and he deplored the waste of energy they represented. Nothing, he told his audience, presented young engineers with a greater challenge than the field of hydro-electric power—although he was quick to admit that there were many other uncharted courses they could follow if they wished to explore.

One of the things he suggested might be worth investigation was the changing of sewer waste into commercial fertilizer by means of electricity. His listeners gasped at this outlandish idea, but today an excellent soil conditioner is made at the municipal garbage plant at Oakland, California, while the sewerage of Milwaukee, Wisconsin, is transformed into an exceptionally high-grade fertilizer that is sold from one end of the United States to the other. Steinmetz pointed out to the students that "In bygone ages, all civilizations started in the Far East, in the big river valleys of Asia, in countries which are deserts today. That soil does not bring forth any crops now, it is exhausted and has been exhausted for a long time." Europe, he explained, was already experiencing difficulty in raising food enough for its population and the day would come when America would be in the same position. Then, hunching over his notes, the scientist ended his talk with these words: "Now all this means that the world needs men who know something about electricity, of the creation and control of electric power. It needs all of us and will need more of us every year. The human race will always need electricians. Its very existence will depend on them."

ᛝ ᛝ ᛝ

For a man who never worried about what he ate, Steinmetz was deeply concerned over the possibility of a world food shortage. On a routine visit to the Pittsfield, Massachusetts, plant of General Electric in October, 1922, he told a reporter that the only way mass hunger could be avoided was to begin experimenting in the development of quick growing edible grasses. He called attention to the Japanese, who consume great quantities of algae, which they gather from small ponds. "A small body of water will yield a tremendous amount of this material," he claimed. "About twenty tons a year can be harvested from a pond an acre in area. Of course, we will have to change our eating habits —but that will be better than starving to death!"

In the same interview he repeated his warnings of the approach of the day when, despite the untouched deposits of coal in America, no more of that mineral would be available. "Water power will take care of our electric needs," he asserted, "but the only way mankind will be able to keep warm, once we have used up all the coal, will be by using the rays of the sun. By covering large areas with glass and collecting the sun's heat, we will be able to store up an immense amount of power."

Once again Steinmetz was ahead of his time—thirty years to be exact—for in 1952 Eugene Ayres and Charles Scarlott announced, as the result of their investigations, that an acre of land in Arizona covered with panes of specially treated glass would furnish the energy equivalent to 150 tons of coal. Meanwhile, at the Massachusetts Institute of Technology a house heated by solar rays is the scene of extensive experimentation to determine the practicality of furnishing domestic heating by means of the sun's rays. Other scientists working on the problem have discovered that in three days the sun gives forth as much energy as could be obtained by burning all the potential reserves of coal, petroleum, natural gas, tar and forests in the world! Experimenters have also used gigantic magnifying glasses to concentrate the rays of the sun on a boiler and successfully generate steam, while in Florida the solar heating of water for household use is a common practice.

It was not only in the newspapers that the ideas of Steinmetz were used to describe the world of the future. Magazine editors often assigned members of their staff to interview him on special topics. In *Hearst's International Magazine* for May, 1923, there is an article in which the scientist is quoted as saying that the railroads of the country should electrify their locomotives. "I believe that the railroads of the United States will soon be operated by electricity," he said. "One of the big systems will start, and the rest will follow." He explained that railroads used 160 million tons of the coal they carry, and if the engines were electrified and the coal was converted into electrical energy at the mines, it would be "equivalent to doubling the freight capacity of our railroads for other kinds of freight; for about half the freight they carry now is coal.

"It should mean a good deal to this country to get rid of the steam locomotive and coal train. They are both wasters. Whatever is wasted is a burden upon the country. It is lost motion to devote approximately half of the freight carrying capacity of our railroads to the transportation of coal that should be burned at the mine whenever possible and converted into electricity.

"No one can limit the use of electricity. Electricity is energy and therefore can do anything energy can do. Electricity is energy and energy is the basis of civilization—and through it unknown horizons lie before us."

Although Steinmetz did nothing in his laboratory to bring about the electrification of America's railroads, he, as much as any man, was responsible for the establishment of electrified train service, for by means of lectures, writings, and personal pleas he showed how much more efficient electricity was than coal as fuel, and eventually saw some lines make the change-over. The idea of powering locomotives by electricity was not new. As early as June 28, 1895, the Nantasket branch of the New York, New Haven and Hartford Railroad was being served by an electric train. However, most major railroads continued to favor steam, until the development of the Diesel-electric locomotive.

One of Steinmetz' strongest arguments for converting locomotives from steam to electricity was the increased speed that would result. "Trains will go two hundred miles an hour," he predicted. "That speed is the absolute maximum, for if they went any faster, the wheels would fly to pieces from centrifugal force. Of course, new road beds will have to be built to support trains traveling at such a rate, but that is a minor matter."

It is interesting to note that no Diesel-electric locomotive, despite modern track-laying methods, has yet approached his prophecy of a two-hundred-mile-an-hour speed. To date the fastest train run ever recorded in this country is that of the *Pennsylvania Special* of the Pennsylvania Railroad, which ran three miles near Ada, Ohio, in eighty-five seconds, or at the rate of 127.06 miles per hour—on June 12, 1905!

All this talk about coal, railroads, and food shortages made interesting reading but none of it was half as appealing to the working man as was Steinmetz' forecast that the man of the future would have to toil only four hours a day, in a spotless city in which refuse would be unknown, thanks to electricity. Once again, he was ahead of his time. Men do, of course, work more than four hours a day, but the ever-increasing use of garbage disposal units and electrically operated oil burners is slowly cutting down the amount of trash that city sanitation departments have to handle.

"Work is a curse," Steinmetz once said. "I do not mean energy or occupation. Doing things we want to do is not work—not the work we impose on the working man. Engineering is not work for me. It is my life, my means of expressing myself. I spend from twelve to eighteen hours a day at engineering. I spend half an hour a day at work."

He made it plain that if men worked only four hours instead of eight, they should not expect as much pay, but pointed out that their living expenses would be less, thanks to electricity. Long before Social Security and Unemployment Insurance, Steinmetz advocated that workers be forced to save for the time when they would no longer be employed. Meanwhile, he recommended that a program of education be set up to train men and women for the time when they would have more leisure, so that they would know what to do with it. This free time, he said, should be "wisely spent in sensible amusements and the kind of recreation that improves the mind and raises the whole standard of life."

Weary men in mines, factories and on farms read his prognostications and sighed. If the four-hour day would only come! But the electrical genius had set the year 2023 as the time when this goal would be reached—and what good would that do them? Meanwhile, they continued to follow his forecasts and shook their heads in admiration when he stated that steam transportation would be a joke in fifty years; and that there would be less gasoline-driven automobiles and more using electricity for power. They were amazed as the scientist went on to describe a world of airplanes, radio, and electricity that would serve a highly organized economic world in which the middle-class merchant had vanished and chain-stores distributed goods of all types to consumers.

While attending a conference of business leaders in Boston, Massachusetts, in April 1923, Steinmetz visualized human civilization somewhere in the latter part of the twentieth century. The strange combination that was Charles Proteus Steinmetz—philosopher, socialist, engineer and scientist—described a world of fantastic change. He told, among other things, how furnaces would be discarded as homes were heated by electricity, and described electrically heated clothing for passengers during flights in the stratosphere. When he had finished, he was cornered by a group of eager reporters who plied him with questions about the future of mankind.

"It seems," he said wryly as he lit a fresh cigar, "that the only thing the world is interested in are those things that may be done in future years. The accomplishment fades almost into insignificance. People are forever demanding predictions. 'Tell us what you are going to do tomorrow,' they cry. And the scientist doesn't know that himself!

"Inventions! Are there really such things? We speak of the telephone as a great invention, but it is only a development. When I say 'only' I do not belittle the achievement. Call it an invention, and the world gasps at the inventor's brilliance. Call it a development and the world is scarcely interested. Developments are not startling and do not satisfy.

"But all things are developments. If such great inventions as you ask me to predict ever come to pass, they will be simply developments of something we already have. In fact, that is all it can be, for nothing is created. We have all the materials with which we may work.

"Every day, let us say, some new development in science is made—perhaps useful, perhaps useless—but if it represents only a slight improvement over the previous development, little attention is paid to it. One day the world notices the streetcar, for example, is far different from the old-time horsecar, and it murmurs: 'Progress!'

"But the world scarcely realizes the great changes that have taken place since the first motor-driven cars rode the rails. The streetcar has stopped being an invention so far as they are concerned. It has been an established fact for years.

"Gradual improvements receive only passing attention, I say, yet it is in these improvements, developments, that the invention consists. To talk of these is dull.

"But if I were to predict that in five or ten years we should be able to do, by the aid of science, something just now inconceivable, the world would gasp and read avidly my prediction. For me to make that prediction would be foolish, for it would be only a dream, and I do not dream."

Perhaps Charles Proteus Steinmetz was not a dreamer. But how many dreamers' dreams did he make come true!

> *"Fill with wild, crackling intermitting light"*
> —WILLIAM ROSE BENÉT

15

᛽᛽᛽᛽ MARCH 3, 1922, began in the usual fashion in thousands of American homes. Men and women sat down to the breakfast table, poured themselves cups of coffee, leaned their newspapers against the sugar bowl, then read with amazement:

"STEINMETZ BREWS THUNDERBOLTS;
HIS STORMS LACK ONLY CLOUDS
Schenectady Wizard Now Able to Make Million-H.P.
Electric Flashes That Crash in Air and Rend
Objects in His Laboratory at Will"

᛽᛽᛽

It all began with Benjamin Franklin, who in addition to inventing the rocking chair, prophesying aerial invasions, suggesting daylight saving, charting the origin of northeast storms which caused so much damage in his native New England, making the first pair of bifocal glasses, and developing a new type of stove, was also the first electrical experimenter in this country. Today we know that the great Revolutionary leader did a most foolhardy thing when he flew a kite in a thunderstorm, in order to prove that lightning and electricity were one and the same. It was a miracle that he was not killed. Strangely enough, the Sage of Philadelphia, because of ignorance, had no fear of being struck by a bolt. He had written to his friend John Lining in 1755, "Too great a charge, might indeed kill a man, but I have not yet seen any hurt done by it." Perhaps if Franklin had a greater knowledge of the power of thunderbolts he would wisely have refrained from engaging in his famous experiment. At any rate, no sensible person would take the same risk today.

In another letter to Peter Collinson, written in 1752, Franklin gave a complete description of the method he used to determine, by means of kite, string, and key, if there was any relationship between lightning and electricity:

"Make a small cross of two light strips of cedar, the arms so long as to reach to the 4 corners of a large, thin silk handkerchief when extended: tie the corners of the handkerchief to the extremities of the cross, so you have the body of a kite; which being properly accommodated with a tail, loop and string, will rise in the air, like those of paper; but this being of silk is fitter to beat the wet and wind of a thundergust without tearing. To the top of the upright stick of the cross is to be fixed a very sharp-pointed wire, rising a foot or more above the wood. To the end of the twine, next the hand, is to be tied a silk ribbon, and where the silk and twine join a key may be fastened. This kite is to be raised when a thunder-gust appears to be coming-on, and a person who holds the string must stand within a door or window or under some cover, so that the silk ribbon may not be wet; and care must be taken that the twine does not touch the frame of the door or window. As soon as any of the thunder-clouds come over the kite, the pointed wire will draw the electric fire from them, and the kite, with all the twine, will be electrified, and the loose filaments of the twine will stand out in every way, and be attracted by an approaching finger. And when the rain has wet the kite and twine, so that it can conduct the electric fire freely, you will find it streams out plentifully from the key on the approach of your knuckle. At this key the phail may be charged: and from the electric fire thus obtained, spirits may be kindled, and all the other electrical experiments be performed, which are usually done by the help of a rubbed glass globe or tube, and thereby the sameness of the electric matter with that of lightning be completely demonstrated."

↶ ↶ ↶

Steinmetz, interest in thunderstorms grew out of his experiments in long-distance transmission of high voltage. As more and more power lines were erected, engineers in charge of maintenance kept sending reports back from the field that one of their greatest problems was to supply a continual flow of current during an electrical disturbance. In rural districts particularly, where the cables cut through forests and across mountains, electric service was constantly being interrupted when a bolt struck, putting the entire system out of control. As a result, utility companies all over the world were anxiously awaiting a more efficient lightning arrester. This is a device whose function is to turn lightning from the service line to the ground, in the same manner in which a lightning-rod protects a house or barn. Many inventors had worked on this problem but had failed to develop anything worth while. Steinmetz, who made a specialty of doing what other men found impossible, decided to devote his full time to the task of creating an effectual arrester, confident that he would succeed. Meanwhile, power companies were sending higher and higher voltages through their cross-country lines to meet the growing electrical needs of industry, so the danger from thunderbolts became greater. The little wizard had never been faced with a more important problem and he accepted the challenge with his usual willingness, patience and skill.

His investigations resulted in a mass of scientific data, and as early as 1919 he published the results of his studies in a volume entitled *Theory and Calculation of Electrical Phenomena and Oscillation,* but he was not satisfied with his work. Every bit of it had been based on long-distance observation of lightning—and as a true scientist he realized that no experiment was valid unless it was completely controlled under laboratory conditions. There was only one thing to do; produce an indoor thunderstorm which contained all the characteristics of one of nature's tempestuous productions. The more Steinmetz pondered on the need of such a test, the more difficult it appeared—how could one create the fury of the elements? Then one day, thanks to a freakish occurrence, he had the solution he had been seeking.

Arriving at "Camp Mohawk" on a spring afternoon in 1921, he found that he had had a visitor—a thunderbolt. The lightning had struck a tree overhanging the camp, tearing off some of the bark. It had then jumped to the building, where it divided. One branch passed to the ground through a post, while the other jumped to the electric wires and made a circuit of the camp, splintering a screen, a mirror, and the bed in which the scientist usually slept.

Steinmetz surveyed the damage with more interest than chagrin. He took dozens of pictures with his camera, measured angles, and filled page after page of his notebook with calculations. Then he carefully inspected the mirror. If he could put it together, he might be able to trace the path of the lightning and see how it had expended its energy. It was a seemingly hopeless task; the mirror had been a large one and it had been smashed to bits. Anyone else would not have thought of piecing together this unusual jigsaw puzzle, or have ventured even to attempt the task, but Steinmetz patiently set to work. At last, every piece was in place and the ruined mirror, placed between two thick slabs of plate glass sealed around the edges, was taken to the laboratory. For weeks the crippled genius examined the mirror, plotting the direction the thunderbolt had taken and figuring what had happened at the instant of impact. As a result of his study, he was ready, with the assistance of Roy Hayden and N. P. Lougee, to attempt to build a lightning generator capable of manufacturing an artificial thunderstorm.

The only purpose behind the proposed creation of man-made lightning bolts was to improve the efficiency of arresters. Steinmetz had absolutely no hope of harnessing the energy dissipated during a thunderstorm and putting it to work. "You see, Roy," he explained to his adopted son, "although there is enough energy in a single flash of lightning to light a five-room house for a month, it only lasts one millionth of a second. So there's no sense in attempting to do anything else but build our generator, create a bolt, and have it strike what we want it to—an accomplishment that will be of tremendous value because it is impossible to tell where real lightning will hit. We'll map out the path of our bolt beforehand, place the object we wish struck in the proper position, turn on our machine and observe the damage that results. This procedure will enable us to check and test any arrester that we develop."

By the fall of 1921 Steinmetz and his two assistants had set up their machine for making lightning. Their task had been made somewhat easier, thanks to the earlier work of F. W. Peck of the General Electric Laboratory at the Pittsfield, Massachusetts, plant, who had conducted a similar investigation, and had freely given his associates his results.

When finished, the lightning generator looked like a football goalpost, with *two* cross-bars, instead of one. On these arms, two hundred condensers, made from large, oblong plates of glass, covered with a magnetic material, were placed and connected to an electrical current which was so controlled that it would flow slowly into the plates, in the same manner that electricity enters a thundercloud by means of rain-drops. At one side of the machine were the "kenotrons," or rectifiers, which looked like over-sized electric light bulbs, while the rest of the contraption was a maze of wires.

Steinmetz and his aides had planned their generator to absorb and store up to 120,000 volts. At this point the device would "break down" and give off the accumulated energy in an artificial flash of lightning. This arrangement was identical with the situation in nature when a thundercloud becomes incapable of holding any longer the stored-up electricity contained in the rain-drops which compose it, and gets rid of the electricity by means of a violent discharge. The scientists had set up their condensers so that they could be connected in various combinations of numbers, which permitted them to create flashes of different voltages. A series of thorough tests ironed out a few difficulties, and at last Steinmetz announced that he was ready to give a demonstration of his new creation to newspapermen.

The "Wizard of Schenectady" could hardly wait for the journalists to arrive. All his life he had been fascinated by thunderstorms and had said, "Lightning has always been the most mysterious and most terrifying of all the phenomena of nature." Now he was going to reproduce this force publicly in his laboratory and he could not wait to display his man-made bolts. It is strange that he showed no signs of nervousness or fear in operating the lightning generator and in the unleashing of its tremendous power, for he had a wholesome respect for high voltage, having received a shock from a "live" wire during his early association with General Electric. Yet he did not have the slightest hesitation in pulling the switch that did succeed in causing a thunderbolt to smash across his laboratory.

On the day of the public demonstration, newspaper reporters, scientists and visiting engineers listened eagerly while Steinmetz explained: "The characteristic of lightning is high voltage backed by a very high power, lasting for a very short time only, and so giving explosive effects. In all other high frequency experiments, the explosive effects characteristic of lightning have been entirely absent.

"In our lightning generator, we get a discharge of 10,000 amperes at over 100,000 volts; that is, a power of over 1,000,000 horsepower lasting for a hundred thousandth of a second. This gives us the explosive, tearing and shattering effects of real lightning. You see, the difference between lightning energy and ordinary electric current is similar to that between a pound of dynamite and a pint of gasoline; the pint of gasoline contains more energy and can do more work than a pound of dynamite, but the pint of gasoline gives off its energy slowly, at a moderate rate of power, while the pound of dynamite gives off its energy explosively, all at once, at a tremendous rate of power; therefore locally tears and destroys. Now if you are ready, gentlemen, we will show you how our generator works. Are there any questions?"

A dozen hands flew into the air and the newspaper cameramen asked, "Dr. Steinmetz, where is the best place for us to stand in order to get the most satisfactory pictures?"

The scientist, who was an ardent amateur photographer, smiled and said, "I expected that question. If you look at the other side of the room, you will see some chalk marks on the floor. Stand there and you will be in an ideal spot to capture the flash with your cameras. Come, line up and let me look at the adjustment of your lenses. I think I can save you time and possibly disappointment, for I've taken dozens of pictures in here and am glad to give you the benefit of my experience. And by the way, don't worry, you'll be perfectly safe in that section of the lab—I can assure you no one has been killed by the generator—so far!"

At last all was ready. Steinmetz waved his hand. A low moan was heard and then, suddenly, the familiar forked tongue of lightning flashed through the laboratory with a deafening crash and a large block of wood which had been placed in the bolt's path splintered into tiny fragments that were hurled into space. Most of the cameramen were so stunned that they stood open-mouthed, forgetting to snap their shutters. They turned sheepishly to Steinmetz and explained what had happened.

The crippled Jove laughed at their embarrassment. "Never mind," he consoled them. "I will explain what is going to happen in the next demonstrations so you'll be prepared. See, the path of our artificial bolt is known to us beforehand, which enables us to leave a gap at a certain point. In this space we place whatever we want our lightning to strike. This allows us to see just what happens to a similar object during a natural thunderstorm. Now Mr. Hayden is going to put this thick piece of wire in the gap. Focus your cameras upon it and you should get an excellent picture of a tremendous flame. Ready, Roy? Cameras all set? Here we go!"

Another discharge, another loud report, and the wire in the gap glowed brilliantly and then disappeared into dust. This time the newspapermen were ready and all were sure they had pictures.

Roy Hayden then placed a limb of a tree in the path of the man-made bolt and returned to his position at the other side of the laboratory. Again Steinmetz waved his arm and a third violent explosion shook the room. When it was over, the reporters looked in vain for the limb, but all they could find were a few chips in the far corners of the workshop.

The demonstration was ended, and the visitors turned to congratulate Steinmetz. To their amazement, he had vanished as quickly as the objects in the path of his thunderbolts. He saw no reason to stay and talk. The lightning generator had proven successful; so it was time to begin a series of tests of electrical products to check their behavior during thunderstorms. There was no time to waste—now a more efficient lightning arrester could be produced.

As his investigations into the influence of "transient electrical currents" or lightning progressed, Steinmetz decided that he needed an even more powerful machine for creating artificial thunderstorms. In 1923 he supervised the building of another generator, which was able to produce a discharge of 500,000 volts, instead of the 120,000 given off by the original one, and the energy in its bolt was equivalent to more than five million horsepower! Once again the newspapers were full of stories about the crippled dwarf, "who, like Jove, hurled thunderbolts." In these interviews, Steinmetz explained that the electric energy of a lightning flash, figured at the power rate of five cents per kilowatt hour, would be worth only seventy cents. Mathematically-inclined readers were fascinated as the scientist stated that he had computed the power of a flash of lightning as 50,000 watts a second—equal in energy to a 900-ton train going fifty miles an hour.

Even those who knew little about science were impressed with these words: "Since Edison's first installation we have increased the voltage in our electric circuits a thousandfold; we have produced and played with over 1,000,000 volts, and the voltage of the thundercloud is only fifty times higher than what man has produced. So, you see, the step from the highest voltage now used to that of lightning is less than was the step which the electrical industry has taken in the last forty years."

All of which would have been engrossing news to the first man to seek a relationship between lightning and electricity —curious but foolhardy Benjamin Franklin.

ᐧᐦ 16 ᐧᐧ

ᔫᔫᔫᔫ THROUGH the action of the white searing flame of artificial lightning which had demolished the objects placed in its path by his assistants, Steinmetz learned how to improve lightning arresters so that they were able to protect the high tension lines that criss-crossed the civilized world. Then, for the first time in his life, he lost all desire to investigate new fields and spent much of his time repeating old experiments, explaining that, "he wanted some fun."

It was wise for him to slow up—the years of nerve-wracking concentration in the laboratory had taken their toll. Yet, with the exception of not engaging in original research, he did not change his routine a great deal. When told he was working too much, he would exclaim, "Nonsense, I have never overworked!" On the other hand, he was always finding fault with his friends, insisting that they were the ones who were driving themselves unnecessarily. The truth of the matter was that work was Steinmetz' life—he lived to work. With a total disregard for his frail body, and paying absolutely no attention to his valvular heart trouble, which he had known about for years, he still spent eighteen hours a day in complicated mathematical calculations.

Those who saw Steinmetz busily engaged in his various activities had no idea he was not well, for he gave no sign that he was completely worn-out in body. His spirit was as gay as it had ever been. He always had time to play a practical joke, write to young Joe Hayden in Morse code, or attend parties given by school children. Yet he was driving himself, punishing his heart, trying to accomplish too much, always offering help to anyone who needed it. But he never let on by word or gesture that he was tired. Cecile A. Rhein, his secretary, once said, "Somewhere, I have read the words 'everlastingly patient' used in relation to Steinmetz. To my mind no words more fittingly describe him. No one ever requested an interview or asked him to deliver a lecture and was refused, if it were considered of importance or for the common good."

Miss Rhein worked with Steinmetz for more than five years, and got to know him better than most people at the General Electric plant. When first assigned to the calculating division, she was quite upset, for she had heard much about the crippled genius who dominated the department. She had never seen the scientist and looked up with alarm whenever someone entered the room, but several weeks passed before she met him. When he appeared, his gentleness and consideration made her feel at ease and all her apprehensions vanished.

The first task she was given was to type the manuscript for one of Steinmetz' textbooks, and to her dismay, she found that the sheets were covered with mathematical equations. It was impossible to discuss the matter with the author, for he had not been in his office for weeks and had sent the penciled script to the plant by Roy Hayden. "I never had occasion," said Miss Rhein in a newspaper interview, "to write equations before, and had not the slightest idea how it was done, but by 'juggling' the carriage of my typewriter, and using a great deal of care, as well as time, I was able to hand in the sheets satisfactory to the Doctor."

Once this chore was out of the way, she decided to learn

her employer's personal system of shorthand. After days of fruitless study, she was ready to give up when Steinmetz made out a list of key signs for her and at length she was able to read the notes he made on the letters he wished answered. At the end of three months of continual study, she was able to read everything the electrical genius wrote in his crabbed hand.

This skill was of great value to her, for the scientist rarely gave verbal dictation. His system was to mark scientific papers in one of three ways, to indicate how he wanted the work done: "As soon as possible," "Immediately," or "As soon as feasible." No matter how anxious he was to have the final typescript, he always gave Miss Rhein sufficient time to finish it. "Don't hurry," he told her the first time they met. "All we want is good work. Do not sacrifice accuracy for speed."

On the days when he came to the plant for conferences he might tell his secretary he was going into the laboratory. If there was nothing to do there, he would remark, "Well, I guess I will go home. So long!"

He never left her without that cheery "so long!"—pausing beside her desk to light a cigar before he left the room. Often he would search in vain for his matches, slapping all his pockets in a vain attempt to find them. Failing, he would look at Miss Rhein and wryly ask, "Do you know who has swiped my matches?" What a strange combination was Charles Proteus Steinmetz, the "modern Jove" who could play with lightning, but had no idea where he had put his matches!

᛫᛫᛫

The public's interest in his man-made thunderbolt amused Steinmetz. He could not understand why his experiment had attracted so much attention, but the reason was simple. Not only did the idea of re-creating nature's fury in the laboratory capture the imagination of newspaper readers, but also the announcement of the experiment was made at the same time as the disclosure that the scientist was earning $100,000 a year—an almost unheard-of salary in those days.

As a matter of fact, the reports of his salary were slightly inaccurate. When he was appointed chief consulting engineer and the question of payment arose, he said, "I do not wish to work for money. Let me draw it as I wish and if I draw too much, tell me. Do not fix an amount. If I think of money, I will not work well."

This arrangement was satisfactory to the General Electric Company and by the time Steinmetz had developed a practical lightning arrester he had been given a drawing account of $100,000 a year, to be used as he saw fit—either for his personal needs or for his private experiments. This strange contract had a most unusual feature—the money was placed at the scientist's disposal each year. If he didn't use the entire amount, what was left was turned back to the firm. If, however, $100,000 was not enough, all he had to do was to ask for an additional allowance and it was given to him without hesitation.

There is, of course, no way of knowing how many times Steinmetz used the full amount his agreement called for, and how many times he asked for more money. Yet it is safe to assume that he rarely spent $100,000 in one year. Beyond his many anonymous gifts to charity, he had little use for money. He could have made millions if he had not assigned his patents to his employers, but it never entered his head to profit personally from his genius. All he wanted was to hasten the day when mankind would live in a world in which electricity would perform all the heavy work.

Weary as he was, Steinmetz became enthusiastic over the possibilities of electrically-driven trucks. Never an astute businessman, he asked no questions when he was approached by a group of promoters and invited to act as the head of a company which intended to manufacture battery-operated vehicles. He was flattered when he was told that the firm was to be called "The Steinmetz Electric Car Company," and accepted the offer. Soon advertisements were appearing in all the leading newspapers and magazines of the country, calling attention to the merits of electric trucks and stressing the fact that the chairman of the board of directors of this firm was Charles Proteus Steinmetz.

All the arguments the electrical genius had advanced back in the days when he had predicted that in time battery-charging stations for electric automobiles would be as common as blacksmith shops were unearthed by the promoters. A Steinmetz electric truck, they told the public, was simply constructed, light in weight, easy to operate, had a great cruising radius, small maintenance and operating cost, while its battery could be charged overnight in any garage. No date was set for the start of production, but anyone interested was invited to contact the main office for additional details. By clever salesmanship, the organizers of the company were able to sell stock in their concern to most of the people who wrote to them.

In a short while, letters began to pile up on Steinmetz' desk. They were all written by worried investors who had bought shares in the corporation, confident that it would succeed because of his association with it. As the weeks passed, they had discovered that the whole thing was a swindle and they had been duped. The scientist, upset and greatly concerned, went to his superiors at the plant and talked over the situation with them. Realizing that their brilliant engineer had been the unsuspecting victim of a carefully planned fraud, General Electric assumed a responsibility that was not legally theirs, and paid back the money to the tricked stockholders. They then made Steinmetz promise not to engage in any other outside activity without first discussing it with his employers.

Meanwhile, he continued to write extensively on electrical and other scientific subjects. He was finding it more difficult to sleep, and many nights he would go downstairs and make his way to the conservatory, while the rest of the family slumbered. Lighting a cigar, he would spend the long hours until daybreak walking among his beloved plants or watching his fish. Sometimes, instead of visiting his greenhouse, he would switch on his bedside lamp and read light fiction until morning.

During this period people first began playing a new game. It consisted in asking what ten books anyone would like to have with him if he were cast away on a desert island. Steinmetz gave his list to a reporter one day, and it read as follows: Homer's *Odyssey*, *The Odes of Horace*, Goethe's *Faust*, Mommsen's *History of Rome*, Kipling's *The Jungle Book*, Twain's *Huckleberry Finn*, Stevenson's *Treasure Island*, Marryat's *Midshipman Easy*, Stanley's *In Darkest Africa* and Sienkiewicz' *The Deluge*.

Although he still spent many hours in his conservatory, Steinmetz did not have many pets to care for during the later years of his life. Yet people always associated him with his zoo, and when Marconi visited Schenectady in 1922, the first thing he asked his host was, "How is your Gila monster?"

The scientist shook his head sadly and replied, "He got too lazy to eat and died."

An engineer in the San Francisco office of the General Electric Company had sent him the Gila monster. When it arrived, Steinmetz let it out of the crate and watched it roam freely around the greenhouse, for despite his great knowledge, the electrical wizard did not know that his new pet was one of the world's most dangerous reptiles, being the only lizard known to be poisonous. About two feet long, usually purplish in color with pink blotches, its poison fangs are in the lower jaw, and a horrible death is usually the lot of any living thing, including man, who is bitten by this native of the desert regions of Arizona and New Mexico. Like an English bulldog, the creature's jaws "lock" when it bites, and it is impossible to break its grip without some type of prying instrument. Blissfully unconscious of the danger, Steinmetz allowed the Gila monster the freedom of the conservatory, pushing him to one side with his foot when he blocked a passageway or tried to get out when the door was opened!

About a week after the reptile arrived, a letter came from California explaining how dangerous the creature was and giving directions how he should be fed. Roy Hayden and "Dad" wasted no time. Armed with wire nooses, they went hunting for the Gila monster and eventually cornered him and placed him in a stout cage. They sighed with relief and then went to the house to get the food recommended for the lizard—raw eggs.

"This is just about as inexpensive a pet to keep as I have ever had," declared Steinmetz, laughing. "According to these directions, one egg a month is all he has to be fed!"

"All I can say is that I hope he eats his egg right away," replied Roy. "Can you imagine how this place will smell if it lays in his cage for two or three weeks before he decides to break it and eat it? Frankly, I'd just as soon not be here —not that I'm not used to the smell of hydrogen sulphide in the laboratory—but I don't think it would go well with orchids and cacti!"

The Gila monster did not devour his rations immediately. In fact, months went by without his eating anything. One time, for an experiment, Steinmetz placed *two* eggs in the reptile's cage and they stayed there for eight months! Worried for fear his pet would die from malnutrition, the scientist decided to provide him with a change of diet. So he secured a pair of rabbits and placed them in the cage. "This is a two-way investigation, Roy," he explained. "Now we'll be able to see just how poisonous this fellow is and find out if he will eat anything else except eggs."

Before eating breakfast the next day, Steinmetz went out to the conservatory to see what had happened to the rabbits. They were hopping about the cage, while the Gila monster slept soundly in one corner. As the kind-hearted engineer watched them, he suddenly changed his mind—he could not bear the thought of these lively bundles of fur being poisoned to death. So he removed the bunnies from their "death cell" and presented them to one of his many friends among the youngsters in the neighborhood.

Now the monster was dead, but Steinmetz did not grieve as he had for John and Mary, his pet crows. With the passing of the years, he had found it more and more difficult to care for pets. His body was tired, although his mind was as active as ever. When Edison came to visit the Schenectady plant, Steinmetz naturally enough was delighted at the opportunity to talk to the man he considered the greatest engineer in the world. He had much to discuss with the magician who had pierced the blackness of night with the rays of the incandescent bulb, but when the two men sat down in the laboratory, the "Wizard of Schenectady" found that the "Sage of Menlo Park" was so deaf that conversation was out of the question. Quickly he found a solution to the problem. Pulling his chair closer to his visitor, he reached forward and tapped Edison's knee. For a moment the great inventor was startled, then he began to smile and in turn started to tap his host's knee. For hours the pair sat lightly touching each other—carrying on an animated conversation in Morse code.

No one knows what was "said" during this conference, but it is safe to assume that fantastic developments were proposed and rejected by the two scientists as they sat "talking." At any rate, we do know that no new investigation was begun by Steinmetz as a result of his meeting with Edison. His activities were limited to writing and lecturing, and while he did spend some time in his laboratory, he did not engage in any important experimentation.

Over the years Steinmetz became an excellent lecturer and teacher. In time he acquired an appreciation of the limitations of his audience and his readers. His great powers of exposition grew greater as he gained experience talking before learned societies, business conventions, members of special groups and classes composed of General Electric employees. No longer was he the professor of Union College days who took for granted that his pupils knew as much as he did, or wrote on the blackboard in a hand so small that it could not be seen beyond the first row. Now he had all the techniques of a good teacher at his command, and he used them to their utmost.

When not engaged in writing or speaking, Steinmetz filled his days with rearranging his collections and labeling his vast accumulation of photographs. He never threw anything away, and if a magazine contained an article which interested him, he would scrawl shorthand notes all over the margins and then, instead of tearing out the pages and filing them, he would add the entire publication to the ever-growing pile of periodicals in one corner of the laboratory. Some of the things Steinmetz kept were most unusual. Once at a convention he offered Edison a cigar, and in refusing it, the latter said, "No, thanks, I don't smoke. I chew tobacco. Here, have a chew." The crippled mathematician broke off a portion of the proffered plug, but he could not chew it, due to the condition of his teeth. So he carefully wrapped the tobacco up in a piece of blue paper, wrote the name of the donor and the date on it, and put the souvenir in a place of honor!

Another activity which filled Steinmetz' time during the latter days of his life was taking part in the affairs of the

All Souls' Unitarian Church in Schenectady. As a younger
man he had paid no attention to church attendance, going
with the Haydens occasionally, only because he didn't want
to hurt their feelings. Then one day Marjorie, Billy and Joe
sat him in their wagon and pulled him from Wendall Avenue to the parish house where they planned to buy some
things at a bazaar being run by the women's auxiliary. While
waiting, legs crossed comfortably, a cigar aglow, with a red-
knit cap perched jauntily on his head, Steinmetz saw Ernest
Caldecott, the new young minister, coming along the sidewalk. The scientist greeted him with a gracious wave of his
hand, and the two men began to talk. In the course of the
conversation, Steinmetz offered Mr. Caldecott a cigar, and
to the engineer's delight, he accepted it and began to smoke.

This was the beginning of a close friendship between the
man of God and the man of science. They would argue for
hours on the seeming conflict between the realm of science
and the field of religious belief. Eventually Steinmetz joined
the church, and from time to time would take over the pul-
pit and deliver a masterly sermon before a crowded congregation. Meanwhile, he fell into the habit of frequently calling the minister on the telephone late at night, when he was
unable to sleep, and asking him to come to Wendall Avenue
and "talk, or take a walk through the conservatory." Mr.
Caldecott always answered these summonses, and in return,
Steinmetz never hesitated to do anything he could for his
clerical friend. Often, when leaving, the minister would find
a check tucked into the band of his hat, and the scientist
would say, "Use it for the church, but don't tell anybody I
gave it to you."

Steinmetz' charitable gestures were always like that—he
gave but wanted no credit. In a newspaper interview Mr.
Caldecott told a reporter: "Few persons realized the extent
of Dr. Steinmetz' charity. As our friendship grew, I was
amazed to know that he continually gave donations to

causes he considered worthy—but always insisted that the gift be anonymous. Once, I remember, I was with him when he opened his mail, and out of a letter a check fell on the table. It had been sent to him as payment for an article he had written for a magazine. Without turning the slip of paper around to see the amount written on its face, he took up a pen and indorsed it over to a relief fund."

Steinmetz' writings were bringing him almost as much fame as had his experiments. Yet he paid no attention to the acclaim of the world. Nor did he bother to explain why he did not take full advantage of the huge drawing account granted him by General Electric. To one newspaperman, anxious to get a Sunday feature story on "The World's Highest Paid Engineer," he said, "My friend, man wants but little here below: but he never knows how little until he finds he can have anything he wants."

Despite his lack of activity in the laboratory, Steinmetz still advocated that young engineers undertake continual investigations in the electrical field. He wrote and lectured on the theme that steam is responsible for the growth of cities, for men have to live near where it is generated, but electricity makes it possible for men to return to the country and enjoy a fuller and richer life. He was so busy he did not have time to go to the tailor's to get his traditional suit of oxford gray, so Roy Hayden arranged for the fittings to be made in the house. As publication followed publication, reporters became as common as cacti on Wendall Avenue, and one of the interviewers led off his account of a conversation with Steinmetz in a manner that reads as if it had been written in this era of atom smashing:

"In this day of daily miracles, it did not seem impertinent to ask Dr. Steinmetz what the scientists are trying to do with the world.

" 'The scientist is not doing anything to the world,' " he replied. 'The scientist investigates the laws of nature. He has no goal. The first man to walk up a hill for the sole purpose of seeing what was on the other side, was a true scientist. When he put his knowledge to practical use, when he used the hill as a vantage to detect the approach of his enemy, he ceased being a scientist and became a practical man. Scientists deal with abstractions. When they make practical use of their investigations, they are no longer scientists; they become engineers.

" 'The study of the laws of electricity is science. The construction of apparatus such as we use in Schenectady to make artificial lightning is not science. People think the scientist is concerned with removing all the inconveniences of life, and that when their goal is attained science will rest. That is not so. We explore the laws of nature. That is all. It is enough.' "

Steinmetz was invited to address a meeting of leading businessmen from all over the world, held on August 8, 1923, at Babson Park, Wellesley, Massachusetts, the headquarters of Roger Babson, the economist and one-time Prohibitionist candidate for President. The little genius gave his listeners an exciting picture of the part electricity was destined to play in the development of American industries. After his talk, he announced that he had a most important experiment to demonstrate, and would appreciate it if all the newspapermen present would gather on the stage at the close of the meeting.

The reporters lost no time in gathering around Steinmetz, who pointed to a table on which there was a glass of water and a large pile of pennies. The water was level with the brim of the glass and the scientist sat down carefully in order not to jar it.

He looked about him inquiringly and asked, "Gentlemen, this is a most important experiment and I must have absolute silence and no movement on your part. You see this glassful of water and the pennies, do you not? Well, how many of the coins do you think I can drop into the water without causing any of it to flow over?"

The journalists looked at one another in amazement. What kind of "important experiment" was this? At last one of them found his voice and said, "Oh, I guess three or four at the most."

"Ah, but you are wrong, my friend," replied Steinmetz. "You can drop in fifty-five without spilling a drop!"

By now the newspapermen realized that the "Wizard of Schenectady" was playing a joke on them and challenged him to prove his statement. He set to work and soon had twenty-eight pennies on the bottom of the glass, when someone shook the table accidentally and the demonstration ended.

Try this yourself. If you can put the whole fifty-five copper pieces in the glass without making the water overflow, you can consider yourself, in one respect at least, as clever as the man who discovered "The Law of Hysteresis," advanced the theory of "The General Number" and created man-made lightning in his laboratory!

> *"Industry, economy, honesty and kindness form a quartette of virtues that will never be improved upon"* —JAMES OLIVER

‖‖ 17 ‖‖

EVER since the days when he had first become an ardent fan of Western and high adventure movies, with their fast, furious action, Steinmetz had expressed a desire to visit Hollywood and see motion pictures being made. The crippled genius had often said that he would rather meet that dashing, athletic hero of screen thrillers, Douglas Fairbanks, Sr., than receive an award from an international scientific organization. At last an opportunity came for him to achieve both these ambitions. Unable to work in the laboratory, constantly weary and in no mood to write technical papers, the invitation from the Pacific Coast division of the American Institute of Electrical Engineers to be their guest of honor at a meeting to be held on October 3 and 5, 1923, at Del Monte, California, could not have reached him at a more propitious time. He did not waste a minute making up his mind: he would accept, take the Haydens with him on a leisurely sightseeing trip across the country—and once in California, ask one of his hosts to wrangle permission for him to see a picture being "shot." Always the optimist, he even dared to hope that he might meet Fairbanks in the motion picture capital of the world.

Planning the proposed trip gave Steinmetz a great deal of pleasure. It would be his longest journey since coming from

Europe, and he spent hours checking train schedules and arranging for stopovers in places where there was anything of historical and scenic interest. All his hopes of a quiet, restful tour of his adopted country vanished, however, once it became known he was leaving Schenectady for California. Every city on his route wanted to entertain and honor him, while engineering societies flooded his mailbox with requests to deliver lectures.

One night he looked up from the piles of letters on his laboratory worktable and complained, "There's no hope for our having a rest, Roy. I am in duty bound to talk to all these people. We'll just have to revamp our ideas about this transcontinental jaunt. Not that we won't see everything there is to see, but we'll have to make more stopovers and spend longer periods of time in some cities. There's one consolation—I won't have to prepare a dozen or so talks—I'll just write two or three and alternate giving them whenever I speak."

"Well, one thing is certain," said Roy. "We won't be able to get away for about three weeks. In the first place, you've promised to attend the Hayden Family Reunion at Haydenville, Massachusetts, with us at the end of May; and, secondly, while you can get away from the plant whenever you want to, I have to get permission to leave. So don't start packing any bags!"

Shortly after the gathering in Haydenville, the scientist and his entire adopted family were on their way. It always seemed as if they had just settled in their seats when it was time to get off the train, meet a group of local dignitaries and be taken to a luncheon or dinner at which Steinmetz would deliver one of the three talks he had prepared. If he were speaking in the evening, The Electric Power Industry would be his topic, while his daytime lectures dealt with Electricity and Civilization and Engineering Problems of the Future. The entire trip to the Grand Canyon, which

Steinmetz had long wanted to see, was a succession of receptions, sightseeing and speeches. After exploring all the beauties of the gorge made by the Colorado River, the party boarded the train on September first for Denver, Colorado, where a two-day stopover was planned.

The Denver reception committee had foolishly thought that only a select group would want to hear a lecture by the chief consulting engineer of the General Electric Company, so they had hired only a small hall. They did not realize that Steinmetz had captured the public imagination with his creation of lightning, and that thousands desired to see and hear him. The result of this oversight was the postponing of the talk until a larger auditorium could be engaged—and five thousand people filled every chair, while several disappointed thousand others were turned away!

From Denver, the Schenectady group went on to Colorado Springs, one of the most exotic places in the entire United States. Steinmetz, the scientist, completely forgot himself as Steinmetz, the nature lover, reveled in the strange formations of the "Garden of the Gods" and wandered through the "Cave of the Winds." After this enjoyable excursion, a direct run to the city by the Golden Gate was made, where Steinmetz addressed a distinguished gathering of scientists and civic leaders.

After this speaking engagement, the party went to visit Nob Hill, made famous in gold rush days; the cable cars; Chinatown; the many parks and museums; and—what Steinmetz enjoyed most of all—the many stands of the flower vendors. It took them a week to see everything, then it was time to go to Del Monte and the meeting of the local group of the American Institute of Electrical Engineers. The scientist's talk on High Voltage Insulation was of extremely great interest and importance to electrical experts in a region that depended on hydroelectric power. His lecture was received with hearty applause, and after it was over Steinmetz had a chance to talk with men whom he had never met, but whose achievements in electrical experimentation were known to him through scientific reports. The Del Monte visit was one of the most exciting events in his life and he was sorry when the gathering was over.

Busy as he was, talking from both the platform and in casual conversation to fellow workers in electrical investigation, Steinmetz found time to take side-trips to any place where there was something worth while to see. For example, he made the trip up Mount Hamilton to look through the great equatorial telescope of the Lick Observatory, maintained by the University of California—for despite the fact that he had done nothing in astronomical investigation since his Breslau days, he still had a great interest in the subject and had not forgotten the excellent teaching of John Galle.

At last it was time to visit Los Angeles, and Steinmetz still naïvely wondered whether he would meet someone who could arrange for him to visit a motion-picture studio in near-by Hollywood. He soon found out that he needed no assistance in getting an invitation to watch actors and actresses perform in front of the camera! He received more requests for the "honor of showing you about" than he could possibly manage. Bewildered at this excess of riches, he thumbed through the letters, wondering which one he should accept. Noticing one from the firm that produced pictures made by his favorite player he naturally enough decided to visit it. To his intense delight, the guide assigned to show him about the studio and explain the mysteries of moviemaking was none other than Douglas Fairbanks, Sr.!

The actor and the scientist were immediately drawn to each other, and made a strange pair as they wandered up and down sets depicting ruined abbeys, Moorish castles, frontier towns and African jungles. Steinmetz had to hobble quickly to keep up with the long strides of the physically powerful Fairbanks—but the latter realized that his guest would be hurt if he slowed his pace or attempted to adjust his stride to the cripple. As they visited every corner of the studio, Steinmetz plied his host with questions dealing with the technical aspects of motion-picture making. Most of the queries were too complicated for the actor, so he turned the engineer over to a group of cameramen and electricians, explaining his problem. Soon the world's greatest electrical experimenter was engaged in a lively discussion with the workmen, and when he left he turned and said, "Thank you, gentlemen. Now I know how you use electricity to make motion pictures."

All too soon Steinmetz had to leave the studio and go back to his hotel. On the way he saw a sign advertising an ostrich farm, and always a nature lover, he expressed the desire to visit it. The next day he went there, and watched with avid curiosity while the owner demonstrated how fully matured plumes were plucked from the birds to supply decorations for ladies' hats. "You see," explained Steinmetz' guide, "there aren't many ostriches left in their native habitat, due to the fact that hunters have killed them off in order to get the plumes. By raising them here, like chickens, we are able to take the feathers that women want so much from the birds without hurting them. Then, of course, after a certain period of time, a new plume is grown and we can pluck it out again. Now, Mr. Steinmetz, you've asked me a great many questions, here's one for you. How would you like to drive an ostrich?"

"Drive an ostrich?" cried Steinmetz. "What in the world are you talking about?"

He soon found out. An ostrich, harnessed to a sulky similar to the ones drawn by pacing and trotting horses, was brought over to him. He was helped into the seat, handed the reins and away the bird went at a terrific clip, with Steinmetz roaring with delighted laughter. After a few turns of the track, he halted his novel steed, clambered down from the sulky and returned to his hotel feeling more carefree and gay than he had in months.

It was rare to have such a pleasant day without being followed by reporters. It did not take him long to learn that newspapermen on the West Coast were no different from their fellow reporters back home in New York State. Practically everywhere the scientist went he was surrounded by journalists and asked countless questions. To one of these reporters, Steinmetz confided: "Do you know that electricity —and I am sorry if what I say sounds trite—is very queer? It is of incomputable value—yet it is worthless.

"What is it worth in itself? Nothing at all. It is useless in itself. But how precious it becomes when wheels turn, and lights"—at this point he jerked the cord of the table lamp—"flash on and off. How much we appreciate it when it makes the automobile self-starter save us labor at the crank. How satisfying it is when we are carried to and from our daily work by it! And isn't it pleasant to just slip a plug into the wall and have a vacuum cleaner sweep our rugs?

"Electricity as electricity can do nothing whatever for us. It is the turning wheel which is of estimable value."

In the first week of October bags were packed and the Steinmetz party boarded the train for the trip back East. As they traveled through the mountains, the scientist gazed at the waterfalls and shook his head sadly. "Look, Roy," he moaned, "all that power going to waste!" Hayden grinned sympathetically, and said, "I know how you feel, 'Dad,' but you mustn't let it upset you. Remember, this is supposed to be a vacation."

The first important stop on the way back to Schenectady was at Salt Lake City. There the party went to the Mormon Tabernacle to hear an organ recital. This low building, with a seating capacity of 10,000, having a turtle-shaped roof which is completely unsupported by pillars or beams of any type, fascinated Steinmetz almost as much as the glorious music which came from the organ with its 5,500 pipes. After delivering a lecture to an appreciative audience, the engineer was sorry to leave the largest city between the Rockies and the Pacific Coast, but he had to fulfill a speaking engagement in Chicago. So, once again, luggage was stowed away and the group went aboard another train.

A fellow passenger this time was William Jennings Bryan, who led the fight for "free-silver" in the 1890's and who became the Democratic nominee for president at the 1896 convention, when he captured the emotions of the delegates by his famous speech on bi-metallism. He was, however, defeated by William McKinley, the Republican nominee, who was later shot to death by an assassin while standing in a receiving line at the Pan-American Exposition in Buffalo, New York, September 6, 1901.

Bryan and Steinmetz talked politics while the train rolled through the countryside. Both men had strong convictions and neither one would give in to the other. Their discussion became heated, but they parted in Chicago the best of friends.

After another round of lecturing and receptions, the last lap of the journey home was begun. On the trip from "the Windy City" to Schenectady, the scientist sat quietly in his seat saying little. The Haydens were worried, for they had noticed that "Dad" had avoided walking as much as possible in the last few weeks; and even at Yosemite National Park, instead of visiting the strange geological formations, the Mariposa Big Tree Grove and Hetch Hetcy valley, source of the hydroelectric power for San Francisco, he had remained quietly on the hotel porch, looking out into space. It was obvious that the strain of travel and the constant lecturing had taken their toll of his vitality. One had only to look at his face to see how his appearance had changed. Then, too, his family knew that he had not been able to sleep in his berth. Often the Hayden boys, waking up in the middle of the night, would peer into their adopted grand-father's compartment, and find him on his knees and elbows, staring out the window at the passing landscape.

Perhaps if he could have been allowed to rest between his speaking engagements, Steinmetz might have been able to stand the strain of his cross-country trip. But everyone wanted to talk to him, shake his hand or discuss some electrical invention or other. As a result, he returned to Wendall Avenue far more weary than he had been before leaving.

The day after returning to Schenectady, Roy Hayden sent for the doctor, who gave Steinmetz a thorough examination. Closing his bag with a determined snap, the physician warned the scientist, "You are completely exhausted. Moreover, your heart is not in good condition. You are to stay in bed. Now, remember, that means you are to remain right where you are. Under no condition are you to walk up and down stairs. If it doesn't bother you too much, you may get up to eat lunch and dinner, but I insist that you have your breakfast in bed. Now get some rest. I'll be in to see you again in a day or two."

Steinmetz obeyed the doctor implicitly. Not only because he wanted to, but because he did not have strength to do anything else. While resting, he recalled the fun he had had on his six weeks' jaunt to the West Coast and decided that he would take it easy, regain his health, and then surprise the Haydens by announcing that the whole family was going on a Mediterranean cruise. So he followed the orders that had been given him, remaining in bed most of the day, reading mystery yarns and the Tarzan tales.

For the first few days he showed a great deal of improvement and began to feel more like himself. Unaccustomed to idleness, he decided that he ought to spend the time in adding to his knowledge, so he sent word to the librarian at the General Electric plant that he wanted a copy of Humphrey's *Physics of the Air*, and read it avidly. On the evening of October 25, 1923, he took up the volume and with his usual disregard for borrowed books, marked several passages that he knew would be of interest to Roy Hayden, as they dealt with devices used for recording atmospheric changes which they had seen at the Lick Observatory during their California trip. At last, about nine-thirty, he put out his light and went to sleep.

Early the next morning, Roy Hayden entered "Dad's" bedroom. "How are you feeling?" he asked. "I know you had a restless night, for I heard you tossing about. Just take it easy and I'll send breakfast up with Billy."

"Oh, I'm O.K.," came the cheery answer. "Don't worry—you won't be bothered with me much longer."

Thinking that Steinmetz meant that he would soon be up and working, Roy replied, "That's right—you'll soon be driving out to camp to spend a week end. I'll see you shortly; lie back and rest."

"That's all I want to do," replied the tired genius and he settled back into the pillows.

Once downstairs, Hayden told the nurse to "Put Dr. Steinmetz' breakfast on a tray, and Billy will take it up to him." The tray was prepared and the boy mounted the stairs, carefully balancing the dishes. He pushed open the door with his foot, and was about to speak to his beloved grandfather, when he noticed something strange. The malformed chest, which always rose and fell noticeably with each breath, was still. Billy set the tray down and bent over the bed. A moment later he was screaming for his father, who saw immediately that the dynamo that was Charles Proteus Steinmetz had completely run down.

☇ ☇ ☇

Steinmetz' death shocked the world. From every country tributes poured into the house on Wendall Avenue and the offices of the General Electric Company. Men on farms and in factories paused in their work to shake their heads in sorrow over the passing of the genius who had done so much to lighten their labors. Important figures in the electrical industry gathered in Schenectady to pay their last respects to the crippled dwarf whose investigations and experiments had made the widespread use of alternating current possible. On the day of the funeral, most businesses and industrial plants in Schenectady were closed out of deference to the man who had brought such honor to the city, while all the schools suspended sessions in tribute to his years of service on the Board of Education. While the cortege wound its way toward Vale Cemetery, five minutes of silence were observed—as if a master electrician had thrown a switch and halted every form of activity.

When the procession reached its destination, the casket, covered with a blanket of orchids, so beloved by Steinmetz, was carried to the grave by Owen D. Young, President of General Electric; C. Pratt, Vice-President of the firm; Lieutenant-Governor George Lunn; Charles A. Richmond, President of Union College; and Dr. Ernst Berg, the dead man's long-time associate. The services were simple enough to please even the plain man they honored, and were soon over.

But Steinmetz continued to be honored in death, even as he had been in life. For weeks his praises were heard on the radio and published in newspapers. One of the most glowing tributes was that of Martin P. Rice, of General Electric, who broadcast the following eulogy of his fellow-worker from the studios of WGY:

"A large part of the world recognized him as an outstanding genius in the realm of electrical engineering and mathematics—a worker of spectacular wonders, a superman of the electrical age. To a few, however, it was given to know him as a friend and companion of winsome charm, intensely human in his fine appreciation of nature—happy in the fellowship of children, loving to animals and trustful of his fellow-man. In the scientific world he was a recognized master of mathematical calculation and theory as well as a genius in the practical application of abstract principles to the design of electric machinery. A creator of complex formulae, he possessed the rare gift of translating them into phrases which could be understood by even young students of electrical engineering."

In addition to praising their former chief consulting engineer with words, the General Electric Company honored him in a more concrete fashion by endowing scholarships in his name at Union College. His fellow-members of the Schenectady section of the American Institute of Electrical Engineers established a trust fund to pay for a series of addresses by outstanding figures, to be called "The Steinmetz Memorial Lectures." Nor did the passing of time dim the brilliance of Steinmetz' name.

On the anniversary of his sixtieth birthday, April 9, 1925, the city of Schnectady threw open the house on Wendall Avenue to visitors as part of a three-day celebration in honor of the scientist's memory. Over three thousand people crowded through the rooms, looking at relics of the great experimenter and examining his collections of butterflies and arrowheads. Highlight of the occasion was the playing of a pallophotophane record over Station WGY, by which Steinmetz's voice was heard—perhaps the first tape recording in history. One of the most unusual features of the inspection of the Wendall Avenue house was the souvenir that each visitor received. Steinmetz, who never threw anything away, had kept every cancelled check sent back to him with his monthly bank statement. Over the years they had accumulated in great quantities. Everyone who went through his old home was presented with a "Steinmetz autograph"—a novel way of cleaning up the house!

Ten years later, in commemoration of the seventieth birthday of Steinmetz, the General Electric Company sponsored a radio broadcast on both long and short wave bands from the Phi Gamma Delta fraternity house on the campus of Union College. There many of the scientist's old students recalled their memories of the electrical genius, while Roy Hayden described life on Wendall Avenue. Meanwhile, a movement to rename the highway between Albany and Schenectady after Steinmetz, and to turn his former home into a city-owned museum sprang up. Neither of these projects was ever accomplished, but Charles Proteus Steinmetz needs no stretch of concrete or building named after him to keep his memory alive in the minds of men. Today the Wendall Avenue house has vanished—in the middle of the lot stands one of the "blue stones" which once held the waters of the Erie Canal in check. According to Neil Reynolds, public relations chief of General Electric, casual visitors to Van Curler's city are apt to think that the tamer of alternating current is buried there—feeling it only fitting that the man should lie where he planned his electrical conquests.

The directors of the World's Fair that was held in New York City in 1940 decided to honor those citizens of foreign birth and of Negro and Indian blood who had made notable contributions to civilization by inscribing their names on a "Wall of Fame." One of the first names to be chosen for this honor was that of Steinmetz. Another tribute to "the cripple with the giant's mind" came from Henry Ford when he established his famous collection of Americana at Dearborn, Michigan. The automobile magnate removed "Camp Mohawk" in its entirety from its location, and set it up again a thousand miles away, exactly as it had been at the junction of Viele's Creek and the river that the electrical genius loved so well.

There are other evidences of the respect and admiration

in which his fellow men held Steinmetz. The next time you are in Schenectady, go to 266 State Street and visit Nicholaus' Restaurant where Steinmetz ate almost daily. If you are fortunate, you may be served by one of the old-time waiters who can recall the days when the engineer so often dined there. Some of the stories he may tell you will, perhaps, consist of more fiction than fact—for the Steinmetz legend has grown with the passing of years. But all around you will be positive proof that the electrical wizard once ate there—perhaps at the very table at which you are sitting— for on the walls hang framed checks signed by Steinmetz for "merchandize purchased" which Miss Claire York, one of the present-day staff who remembers the scientist well, says consisted of "imported beers, goose-liverwurst and cigars."

▨ ▨ ▨

So it can be seen that death has not stopped men from paying homage to the work of this German immigrant who landed in America an unwanted, crippled dwarf and who rose to become a benefactor of all mankind. To be sure, in spite of his large salary, he did not leave money enough to pay his simple bequests. His will shows that he wanted to leave the Wendall Avenue house to the Haydens and intended to give away property worth about $25,000. The public, naturally, was amazed to learn that he died a poor man, although he earned $100,000 a year. Most people could not believe that all he wanted was "a chance to work, to do the things he wanted to do, to investigate, experiment, track down the secrets of nature, uncover some small corner of the mystery of the universe."

All these things Steinmetz did and did them well, and if he failed to amass money, he did achieve fame. To him, work alone mattered, the fame was a by-product. His zest for life and zeal to advance the welfare of mankind make him a far more important figure than many others who have accumulated millions. No one has so well summed up the great value of the "Wizard of Schenectady" as Professor Vladimir Karapetoff, of Cornell University, who shortly after Steinmetz' death said: "It was impossible to make him do anything except what he himself wanted to do. He stayed away from the works for days; he smoked in buildings in which the President himself did not dare smoke; he used the clockwise rotation of vectors when everybody else was using the opposite rotation; he insisted on saying 'ze' for 'the'; he wore a soft shirt and a shabby gray suit at formal functions, and he belonged to a political party which cussed his company and its principal customers for years."

All this was true, but in the process he constantly worked to bring about the day when all humankind might greatly benefit by the magic of electricity and would be relieved of much drudgery and toil. But perhaps, above all, the most important thing in his career is best expressed by Professor Karapetoff in these words: "His life is a glowing tribute to this great broad-minded country of ours which early recognized his genius and took him lovingly into her arms and carried him steadily to the pinnacle of fame."

For although the great scientist's arc lamp was bright and his thunderbolts were brilliant, and the scintillating genius of this modern Jove made possible the control of alternating current, no light means more to millions of people than the one that pours from the torch of the Statue of Liberty. While it shines there will always be a welcome and a place in America for those who wish to give of themselves as did Charles Proteus Steinmetz.

Sigmund
A. Lavine

just missed being cradled in a theatrical trunk. His parents were permanent members of John Craig's famous stock company, and his arrival made it unnecessary for the stage-manager to provide a doll whenever the play called for a baby!

Highly active while in college, he wrote features for the Boston Sunday Post, covered Boston University sports for two wire services, occasionally sold two-line jokes to College Humor, played leads in Shakespeare productions and stage-managed five annual presentations of the Gilbert and Sullivan Association. "This last experience," Sigmund Lavine maintains, "was the beginning of a search for anything by or about Gilbert and Sullivan—with the result that my wife has had to give up our Dorchester, Massachusetts, dining room in order to house my Gilbert and Sullivan collection."

After receiving his M.A., he taught in a United States Government Indian School at Belcourt, North Dakota, for two years, learned to speak both the Sioux and Cree languages, talk in sign language, had long conversations with old-timers who could remember the creak of the axles of covered wagons, and was invited to tribal dances, ceremonies and Indian Court in reservations throughout Canada and the Northwest.

Sigmund Lavine has taught in the Boston Schools for over twenty years and is now an assistant principal. He also lectures and writes literary criticism.

With his wife, their two children (Maxine and Jerrold) and Carrie, their whippet, he lives in a house filled with books, fish-tanks and historical china. His family enjoys cruises to South America, cross-country motor trips and truck gardening on a piece of New Hampshire land "containing all the rocks the glacier had and didn't know what to do with—however, we always have a pumpkin for a jack-o-lantern."